Just Farr Fun

Jamie Farr

with Robert Blair Kaiser

Eubanks/Donizetti Inc.
Clearwater, Florida

1994

Eubanks/Donizetti Inc.
28870 U.S. 19 North
Clearwater, Florida 34621

Book Design by Robert Howard

Grateful acknowledgment is made for permission to re-print lyrics from:

"BUI-DOI"
From the Musicale "MISS SAIGON"
by Alain Boublil and Claude-Michel Schonberg
Lyrics by Richard Maltby Jr. and Alain Boublil
Music by Claude-Michel Schonberg
© Alain Boublil Music Ltd. (ASCAP)

"IF I WERE A BELL"
From "Guys and Dolls"
By Frank Loesser
© 1950 (Renewed) FRANK MUSIC CORP.
All Rights Reserved Used by Permission

Publisher's Cataloging-in-Publication Data
Farr, Jamie. (1934 —)
Just Farr Fun
1. Farr, Jamie. 2. Television Personalities — United States —
Biography. 3. Entertainers — United States — Biography.
4. Comedians — United States — Biography.
I. Title
PN 1992.4 F37 1994   791.45 F
ISBN 0-9640775-0-7

Library of Congress Catalog Card Number: 94-072179

10 9 8 7 6 5 4 3 2 1
First Edition

For Joy, Jonas and Yvonne,
who have made things far more than fun.

Contents

Prologue

When I was working for Armed Forces Radio in Japan in the 1950s, I was having dinner with some old friends of the family, a Lebanese couple who had served in the consular service in China just before World War II, and friends of theirs, a Japanese couple, who had been in their country's consular service with them in China.

The five of us went out to a great, authentic Chinese restaurant, where I was treated to some new things: shark's fin soup, a sweet and sour carp, baked at such high temperatures that even the bones were edible, and bird's nest pudding. Toward the end of dinner, the Japanese lady turned to me and said, "Jamie, what is your greatest treasure?"

I pondered the question. My family? My wife? My children? My good looks? What?

Now, I ask you the question. And at the end of this book, you can compare your answer with mine. (Don't look now. Don't cheat, okay?)

Once I made my big splash on Broadway, there was nothing for Sardi's to do but commission a caricature of me to go up on its hallowed walls. Here's Marilyn Church's rendition, which you can see when you visit Sardi's Restaurant in New York City.

1

Klinger

"You know, Jamie, you are one lucky sonuvabitch."

This was my wife, Joy, talking. We were headed out to a party, just the other day, me in my tux, and Joy in an evening gown. She stopped in front of a full-length mirror to admire herself. Then, teasing, she sighed and said, "Jamie, you are one lucky sonuvabitch."

What could I do except throw back my head and laugh? All I ever have to do is look at her, still a beauty after 30 years with me, and I know. I am one lucky sonuvabitch.

I am not a great actor. But, as an entertainer, I have had 41 good years in show business. I am so famous that I have people like Queen Elizabeth and the Dalai Lama and several American presidents among my fans. I have made a lot of money. I am still making a lot of money. And I have a happy marriage and a great family. How lucky can a guy get?

I didn't always feel this way. Let's go back to a summer's day in 1972. I hadn't worked in months, not even as a day player on a TV sitcom. I was out of unemployment. I had bills to pay. I was even thinking the unthinkable — leaving the entertainment business, taking back the name I was born with, Jameel Farah, and getting a normal job.

Would I go back to Toledo? No. Never in a million years would I consider going back to Toledo. In fact, I'd promised myself that I'd never go back to Toledo unless and until I had earned the key to the city. But I just didn't want to be an actor any more.

I had been in the acting game for almost two decades. Like many another starving thespian, I could tell my bartender (and, this being Hollywood, my psychiatrist) about the times when I had almost made it big. But, right now, I was feeling anything but big. I wasn't working. And it didn't look as if I would be working, not enough to support my family. Joy had worked when we were first married. But then came the children, and the need (we felt) for mommy to be around the house. In order, however, to have a mommy around the house, daddy had to bring home the bacon. This daddy — an actor, a ham — wasn't even bringing home salt pork.

And so, not making it as an actor, I decided to make a lateral move — try to sell an idea for a TV game show. As a kid, I'd listened to all the game shows on the radio. I remember a quiz show called "Take It Or Leave It." Winners could walk off with the magnificent sum of $64. And then I was a fan of TV's version of that show, "The $64,000 Question," a quiz show that fascinated America for months and months before we learned that it was rigged — to make it "more entertaining."

That scandal killed the game shows. But only for a little while. They were going strong again in 1972. And now I wondered if the networks weren't looking for something new. Anyway, that was my thought when I sat down with my buddy, Eddie Carroll, another out-of-work actor, to sketch the outline of a possible game show.

Eddie and I had been talking about something called "Double Take." We thought it had promise. And, naturally, a premise as

2

well: that everyone in the world has a look-alike. Well, we put the premise into a game show format, and then we videotaped one run-through of "Double Take," and it really worked.

We even had ABC interested in "Double Take." They were on the verge of giving us a 13-week deal for daytime — until the head of daytime productions was promoted to nighttime, and his place taken by a young squirt in the business, a little nobody named Eisner. Well, now it was Eisner's call, and he wasn't sure he liked our show. He was leaning toward something that tugged more at people's heart strings, something like "Queen for a Day."

"Queen for a Day" had been a popular radio show and then it became a popular daytime television show. It brought in needy women from all over America to tell heart-rending stories about themselves, and they'd compete on the show, to see who could pull the most sympathy and the most applause from the audience for their stories. Whoever could trigger the most feeling reactions from the studio audience got the nod from the emcee, Jack Bailey. And, then, the winner was Queen for a Day. She got her wish, plus a ride in a limo, and maybe dinner at a swanky restaurant.

So, I tell Eddie, if this Eisner kid wants something like that, then we gotta figure out a way to tug heart strings, too, on our "Double Take." We just needed one neat little twist, something that would make our idea so breathtakingly original, and so damned...poignant, that we'd have Eisner crying his eyes out, while he wrote our checks.

Yes. Checks. Big checks. That got me dreaming. With my first million, I'd buy a big home in Bel Air. With my second million, I'd get some fabulous clothes, and all the toys Joy and I had never had — a Mercedes (one for each of us), a yacht, our own jet, a condo overlooking the third tee at the Mission Hills Country Club in Rancho Mirage....

Or I could go back to work cleaning out the pens on the chinchilla ranch in Burbank It was a Tuesday afternoon. Now Eddie Carroll and I were wondering who we knew who might know Eisner. And then the phone rang. It was my agent, Lew Deuser. I could see him in my mind's eye. He was a distinguished guy, well-groomed, with a handsome white mustache.

"You remember Gene Reynolds?" he said.

I said, "How could I not? He liked me. He liked my work." As director of a series called "F-Troop," Reynolds had given me a week's work once on "F-Troop." I played a stand-up Indian comedian patterned after Mr. One-Liner himself, Henny Youngman. In the segment I appeared in, I was auditioning some comedy material for the Chief of the Hakawis, and I had such memorable lines as, "Take my squaw... please." At the end of my audition, putting a twist on the showbiz cliché, "Don't call us, we'll call you," the somber, unsmiling Chief told me, "Don't smoke signal us. We'll smoke signal you."

My agent said, "Well get over to Twentieth this afternoon. Stage Nine. Ask for Reynolds. He's the executive producer of a new show called M*A*S*H. I don't know anything about it, except that Reynolds wants you to come over and do a bit part."

My heart, which had risen, began to fall. A bit part. That meant maybe one day's work. No more than a couple hundred bucks. But, what the hell. In my position, two hundred bucks was two hundred bucks. It would pay a few bills. And maybe buy me a tune-up on my old car, which was old when I first bought it. The car really hadn't been the same since Joy and I and the car had the encounter in the desert with the UFO on our way back from a short trip to Arizona. It now tended to guzzle an inordinate amount of gas and dribble a little oil. Well, to tell the truth, it dribbled a lot of oil. If you were a wildcatter, you would have called it a gusher.

At Stage 9 on the lot of Twentieth Century-Fox, I found Gene Reynolds right away. He was a handsome, personable guy who'd turned in his SAG card for a membership in the Producer's Guild some years before. A former kid star. He had a big part in "Boys Town" with Mickey Rooney. When he returned to Hollywood after four years in the Navy, he got a few other good roles, but it was a long time between each one. And Reynolds was the kind of guy who wanted to work every day. So then he got in on what is sometimes called "the creative end." Which is to say the money end. In Hollywood "creative" is a code word meaning "dollars." Reynolds became a producer.

4

Reynolds was waiting for me. He was in a hurry. He didn't even bother to show me my lines, much less the script.

"What is M*A*S*H?" I asked. I hadn't seen the movie, which I had heard was a black comedy about some Army surgeons in Korea, starring Elliott Gould and Donald Sutherland. Reynolds explained that it was a black comedy about some Army surgeons in Korea, starring Elliott Gould and Donald Sutherland.

I said, "Oh." I wasn't about to talk myself out of $200.

He seemed pleased to know that I didn't need to know any more. He just took me over to a trailer near Stage 9, where I was to try on my wardrobe for this part. Inside the trailer, all I found was a uniform from the Women's Army Corps, a WAC uniform, hanging on a wardrobe rack. Was I in the wrong trailer? Was I sharing the trailer, maybe, with an actress? No.

Gene said, "Try it on."

"Huh?"

"Yeah." He grinned.

"This dress?"

"Uh huh. You see, you're a corporal, Maxwell Klinger by name. You hafta get out of the Army and the only way you can do it is to get a Section Eight."

"A Section Eight?"

Gene whirled his right index finger in the vicinity of his right temple. "You know? Psycho?"

"I dress in ladies clothes, and that makes me crazy?"

"That's the idea."

I shrugged and thought to myself, "Why that's crazy!" But what the hell! It would pay me $200 for a day's shoot. No. Correction. Gene said this would pay me $250. That's what day players were getting on this show, $50 more than I'd gotten for my day's work on "F-Troop." I looked at the ladies shoes. For some odd reason, they were my size — ladies size 17, with an interesting brand name: El Grande.

Gene said, "Let's go over to the set. Stage Nine."

When I made my precarious way on to the set wearing the WAC blouse, skirt, cap and high heels, everyone started laughing.

And why not? I have the hairiest bow legs this side of Beirut, and my walk is not a mincing one. Like most men in heels, I do not walk, I hobble. What was not to laugh at?

An assistant director came up to me bearing a couple pages of script and a rifle. "You come out of the bushes," he explained, "and you challenge this general.

"That's it?"

The AD nodded. (AD means assistant director. There are a lot of different kinds of ADs. Some are marvels of efficiency. Some are great diplomats. Some are just a pain in the butt. This guy was all three.)

This AD told me, "All you have to do is come out of the bushes here, and deliver your lines." He kind of snickered when he said "lines." I looked at my script pages again. I had 22 words.

I said to the AD, "That's all? I just come out of the bushes and say, heh heh, my lines?" (I wanted to show that I could snicker, too.)

He nodded and said, "Here's the director, E.W. Swackhamer."

I knew Swackhamer. (How could I forget him, with a name like Swackhamer?) He was the director when I had a bit part, once, on a series called, "I Dream of Jeannie." I asked Swackhamer, "How should I play Klinger?"

"Swishy."

"Really?" I said. I thought, "Are you out of your mind? We'll never get away with that on television." But I said nothing more. I needed the work. And the money.

And so — Lights. Camera. Action. With one great big swish, I leaped out of the greenery and did a dreadful, lisping, limp-wristed, high-pitched, "Halt! Friend or foe?"

The general stiffens. "I'm General Barker," he says.

"How do I know you're not one of them?" asks Klinger.

Now the general is relieved when he recognizes Klinger. He says, "Still trying to get out on a psycho, eh, Klinger? Well, I can tell you it'll take a lot more than this."

Klinger says, "Then, I'll just have to keep trying, Mary." And he skips off in his high heels.

Swackhamer yelled, "Okay! Cut! Print!" And that was it.

Oh, no, I forgot. I was to have one more scene, in the epilogue, or "tag" of the show. In the tag, Hawkeye Pierce, played by Alan Alda, is walking along with Trapper John, the CO, Col. Henry Blake, and the visiting general.

So, as they walk along, Klinger jumps out of the bushes again. Only this time Klinger is wearing exactly nothing except a WAC cap on his head. At least he looks naked. Swackhamer is shooting me from the waist up.

Klinger cries, "Halt! Friend or foe?"

The four officers react in shock. Then Hawkeye says that the least Klinger could have done was put on a dress. And that was it.

Swackhamer yelled, "Cut! Print!" He worked fast. And I was on my way home with the $250.

The next day I was back to work on my game show with Eddie Carroll. I'd forgotten all about M*A*S*H. "You know," I said to Carroll, "if 'Double Take' doesn't fly, we have to give 'Fact or Fancy' another try." ("Fact or Fancy" was another one of our great game show ideas, another show that was "close, but no cigar." By close, I mean we even produced a pilot.)

But then, along about two o'clock, I got another call from my agent, Lew Deuser. "They want you back at Twentieth," he said. "They want to re-shoot. Same scenes you did yesterday."

I was sorry to hear I'd disappointed my friend, Gene Reynolds. He'd liked me enough for my work on "F-Troop" to write my name down in his little black book of special people. That's the way it worked in those days. Success in Hollywood depended very much on who knew you and who liked you. And, since Gene Reynolds knew me and liked me, I was happy to get another chance.

I hustled over to Fox, squirmed into the WAC uniform again, and tried to look like I knew how to walk in heels. I approached the set, and got another big laugh from everyone. Now, "everyone" included Producer Reynolds and Writer Larry Gelbart, who proceeded to tell me they'd looked at the dailies, (the raw film they'd shot on the day before), and they weren't happy with what I'd done, but they knew I had just taken my cue from Swackhamer. What did I think? How did I think Klinger should come across?

To save my part, I had to come up with something, and I had to come up with it fast, one chance and only one chance to make this work. I said, "How about if I play Klinger absolutely straight? As if he were not wearing women's clothing? You see, if he wants to look crazy, he wears the dress and pretends it's completely normal!"

Reynolds and Gelbart looked at each other. Had I said the right thing? Gelbart looked at me. I think he could see in me the beginnings of a new character, someone "from the streets," someone who was fast on his feet. I guess that in real life I was doing Klinger before I was Klinger. "Try it," he said.

Later, I found out that the name "Klinger" came from one of Gelbart's playmates in Chicago. But Gelbart had created this Klinger role inspired by a story that had gone around about the great 1960's comedian, Lenny Bruce. Bruce, a natural comic, had served in World War II, but being in the Navy didn't take the comedy out of him. When he saw orders on a bulletin board saying, "REPORT IN DRESS OF THE DAY," he decided to be a smart ass and report for duty wearing a dress. Or, to be more precise, a WAVE uniform. And pretending like there was nothing wrong. Like he was saying, "The orders said, 'Wear the dress of the day.' So, I'm wearing a dress."

In a way, this is just what I was suggesting — that I play Klinger "straight" — albeit wearing a dress. By luck and by intuition, maybe I had it just right. Reynolds agreed with Gelbart. It was worth a try.

And so, I played Klinger straight, using my own booming voice. And it seemed to work, because it added one special piece of broad comedy to the show. And I went home with another $250. At the very least, the extra money would pay the rent. Maybe I'd get some new retreads for the old Lincoln.

I certainly never thought I'd get a call back from M*A*S*H. And, then, when I did, I thought very seriously of turning down the chance. I told Eddie Carroll, "This will ruin my career. Imagine me — wearing dresses all the time! What good things can I possibly expect after that?"

But, because I am one lucky sonuvabitch, I said that, yes, I'd come back for another episode as Klinger, the wacko who wanted out of the Army so bad he'd do anything. And then, a funny thing happened. Gelbart began writing me into more and more of the shows that followed. He later said that "Jamie, as Klinger, provided color to the show that nothing else was doing — just an absolute piece of madness every week. He was a lucky accident for us."

The brilliance of his inventing a nut like Klinger (and my hunch to play him straight, and my dumb luck in taking a chance that might ruin my career) was soon confirmed. We'd shot the series in the summer and fall. But, once the series got on the air in the fall of 1972, the CBS polls of audience reactions around the country started to tell producers that the Klinger part was helping raise M*A*S*H's ratings. And the show, aired at 8 p.m. on Sunday nights, needed ratings. In fact, M*A*S*H's Nielsen ratings went up and down so much during that first year, that CBS thought seriously of cancellation. We ended up number 51.

But the network gave M*A*S*H a break in its second season. Fred Silverman, the head of programming at CBS, stuck M*A*S*H in between two other hits on Saturday nights, "All in the Family," and "The Mary Tyler Moore Show." That helped us a lot. Once America was in its seats, and didn't flip the channel, it began to see what this show was all about. Apparently, America liked what it saw.

And one of the things America liked was Corporal Klinger. The producers decided I had to be a part of M*A*S*H. I appeared in about one-quarter of the shows during M*A*S*H's first season. And in most of the shows the next season. And the next. In fact for many, many seasons.

And so this is my story: I came to visit M*A*S*H for one day and made it my home for eleven years. Since M*A*S*H was also, on several counts, the best network series in the history of television, it was the nicest home an actor could find.

Needless to say, I dropped the idea of pitching Michael Eisner on "Double Take.'" Just as well. He didn't remain in the job very long. He went to work for Walt Disney, and he learned how to become head of the Disney Studios.

I went to work for Twentieth Century-Fox — and learned how to walk in high heels.

2

Beginnings

This is not going to be the story of my life. The average Joe or Jane (and I am an extraordinarily average Joe, though not your average Jane) doesn't exactly shake history. We are born. We die. And things happen in between. This is going to be a book about the things that happened to me "in between."

Most of the things that happened were good things. All in all, I have lived a charmed life. By "charmed," I mean lucky, because I am indeed fortunate to have, in my maturity, a measure of the American Dream. The most important part of that measure: a beautiful, funny, loving wife, and two beautiful, accomplished, healthy children. Everything else, come to think of it, is really secondary.

Let me tell you more about my wife, a gal named Richards, the daughter of a truck driver, the Joy of my life, who never put on airs, and has never been afraid to call a spade a shovel.

One night — this was when M*A*S*H was one of the biggest things on TV — Joy and I were among the invited guests at the Carousel Ball in Denver, a charity affair for the rich and famous given by the man who owned Twentieth Century Fox, Marvin Davis. Joy was wearing a black satin evening gown with a plunging neckline that exposed a nice portion of her nice portions.

Please do not misunderstand. The gown was elegant, and so was Joy. But, when we were introduced to the Secretary of State, Henry Kissinger, he turned quickly from me to focus on Joy. Or, rather, on her cleavage. "Hello, Mrs. Farr," he said, never once taking his eyes from her bosoms. "So pleased to meet you."

Joy said, "Nice meeting you, Henry."

When Secretary Kissinger moved on, I said, "Joy, I call him Mr. Kissinger, or Mr. Secretary. How in the world could you call him Henry?"

She said, "Jamie, if he can look at my tits, I can call him Henry."

With a wife like that, how can a man like me go wrong? Joy is the kind of no-nonsense woman every man needs: someone who can keep him honest — and humble and grateful, too, because we have so much to be thankful for.

Most of the people I have learned to love in my business are the kind of people who never forget to be thankful for their blessings. Doris Von Kappelhoff of Cincinnati, for instance — better known as Doris Day. I had a small role in her last movie, and got to know her quite well. In fact, she was one of my sponsors when I applied for admission to the Academy of Motion Picture Arts and Sciences. Doris Day never put on airs, never forgot who she was — Doris Von Kappelhoff of Cincinnati. And she never forgot to thank all the people around her who made it possible for her to be Doris Day of Beverly Hills.

In this respect, Wayne Gretzky is a lot like Doris Day. Wayne Gretzky, as you may have heard, is one of the greatest hockey players of all time, and, now that he is making $8 million a year for the Los Angeles Kings, easily the most well-paid. I became friends with Gretzky in the early 1970s, when I was doing my first play in Edmonton, Alberta, and found that he and many members of the Edmonton Oilers were staying in the same apartment hotel that I was in, the Edmonton Plaza.

When he moved to Los Angeles and played his first game as a King against the Detroit Red Wings, he had me and my son, Jonas, as guests in his box, along with his wife, Janet Jones, his mom, Phyllis, and his father, Walter. I've always admired the way Wayne keeps reminding people about the debt he owes his father — for giving him the tender, loving tutelage that made him a champion.

With that kind of early education, I think that if Gretzky hadn't ended up as the greatest hockey player in the world, he would have been the greatest stamp collector — or the greatest waiter. I guess that's what I love about Wayne. He's the Doris Von Kappelhoff of the National Hockey League. He hasn't forgotten where he came from. Neither have I. In fact, I still travel with an iron and a mini-ironing board, so that I can press my own things on the road. It's a trick I learned from Red Skelton, who was one of my early mentors. But I am getting ahead of my story.

My story begins at Woodward High School in the north end of Toledo, Ohio, the poorest neighborhood in town. There I was not what they then called a BMOC — Big Man on Campus — but, rather, a BNAT, a Big Nose around Town. That was a measure of my popularity, I guess, because the only people who make fun of my nose are people who like me. And, all my life, a lot of people have made fun of my nose.

At Woodward High, I edited the school paper, played varsity tennis, served as class president, and was voted the outstanding student when I graduated in 1952. With those credentials, I could have won a scholarship to one of Ohio's fine colleges, and become, well, anything but an actor.

But that would have been too simple. And maybe too boring. For one thing, I wouldn't have all these stories to tell. No. I had to pick something really hard. I had to pick show business.

Why? Because I was in love with that particular kind of magic we call "theater." You see, I had led the drama club at

Woodward High, and while I knew I didn't have the looks to understudy Tyrone Power, I knew I could approach the magic because I knew someone with a background exactly like mine who showed me how it all worked. That man was Danny Thomas, one of the greatest comics of our time, who shall always be known as the best press agent St. Jude ever had.

I followed in Danny Thomas' footsteps (or, maybe, his nose-print). We grew up in the same neighborhood. We both had Lebanese parents. Our families were close friends. And we both went to Woodward High. He'd gone through Woodward at least a decade before me, but didn't graduate, then returned for a special convocation in his honor, when Woodward decided to give him his diploma, along with honors as valedictorian and salutatorian in this special graduating class of one. I was there the day he came back, a great event, where he made this wonderful speech and recalled, among other things, a variety show that he produced at Woodward High called "Hits of the Day, An Extravaganza."

That gave me the inspiration I needed to resurrect the idea. I produced a new "Extravaganza," much to the delight of my classmates. And to my own delight. Almost everyone in school had a part in "The Extravaganza" — because almost everyone could do something (sing, dance, tell stories, paint a backdrop) and almost everyone wanted to keep on doing what they'd been doing, naturally, from the time they were little kids: indulging in "make-believe."

To me, nothing was more fun.

At that time, I read Theatre Arts, a monthly that covered the world of the theater. Maybe it was because the magazine was edited by Charles MacArthur, a playwright of some reknown himself. (With Ben Hecht, he co-wrote "The Front Page.") Each issue carried the full text of a then-current Broadway play, which I read line by line, trying to imagine myself in one or another (or all) of the parts. I read "Mister Roberts," by Thomas Heggen and Joshua Logan, then playing on Broadway with Henry Fonda in the title role. I read "The Cocktail Party," by T.S. Eliot, which was making its Broadway debut, starring Alec Guinness. And I read the full text of "Death of a Salesman," by Arthur Miller. I even pored over the ads, including one for a play called "South Pacific," starring Mary Martin and Ezio Pinza. That ad helped me conjure up a vision of myself, not playing the Pinza role, but maybe one of the sailors in the cast, a throaty tenor belting out the rousing song, "There Is Nothing Like A Dame." (Never underestimate the power of a dream. Decades later, I was one of those sailors in a Darien, Connecticut, stage production of "South Pacific.")

But if a young man wants to make a dream come true, he has to do more than dream. I decided to do something about my dream. I started perusing the dozen or so ads from acting schools that appeared in Theatre Arts on a regular basis. Ads like this one from the Pasadena Playhouse:

Prepare
television, stage
radio, screen…
degrees in acting,
directing, design, writing and
theatre administration

TODAY write to
GEN. MANAGER
33 S. EL MOLINO
PASADENA 1, CAL

World Famous
PASADENA
PLAYHOUSE
College of Theatre Arts
$65,000 wardrobe - 4 stages
Our 33d Year

I read that ad, and told myself, "Hey, why not?" Then, in December of 1950, in my junior year at Woodward High, I saw an article in *Theatre Arts* by Jay Bullen, director of public relations at the Pasadena Playhouse, that told me more about the Playhouse. I took the article as a direct invitation from Jay Bullen himself to come and learn, as Raymond Burr, William Holden and Robert Preston were doing when they had been discovered, at the Pasadena Playhouse. That seemed like an offer I couldn't refuse. To think that I could follow in the footsteps of Burr, Holden and Preston!

Younger readers will recognize the name of the late Raymond Burr (better known as "Perry Mason"), because he was working in television right up to the end of his life in 1993. Many of Bill Holden's movies (including "Golden Boy" and "Bridge on the River Kwai" and "Stalag 17") still play on television. Preston was quite the dude as a young man, usually playing good looking second leads in movies like "Northwest Passage" and "This Gun for Hire." And then, he had a great second chance a couple decades later when he helped make Meredith Willson's "Music Man" into a hit on the Broadway stage, and, later, again, in the Hollywood film version.

I did some more research on the Pasadena Playhouse, and found that a number of other Hollywood actors who didn't necessarily get their start at the Playhouse used to show up in certain Playhouse productions. Charles Laughton had a kind of actors' repertory company that used the Playhouse for rehearsals. It was there that he rehearsed his celebrated production of George Bernard Shaw's "Don Juan in Hell," with Agnes Moorehead, Charles Boyer and Sir Cedric Hardwicke.

I won't list all the others who learned acting at the Playhouse, then graduated to the ranks of Hollywood's elite. (But I would be derelict if I did not at least mention the names of Gene Hackman and Lee J. Cobb, James Arness and Dustin Hoffman.)

I thought the Pasadena Playhouse was calling me. And so, by the time I graduated from Woodward High in the summer of 1952, I was singing "California Here I Come," and on the train to Pasadena, with $600 in my pocket, mostly from the U.S. War Bonds I had started buying in grammar school.

Speaking of War Bonds reminds me of all the young men in my neighborhood who went off to fight in World War II. I remember the names of two of them. One of them was Joe Baz, who became a paratrooper. The other was Sonny Skaff, who was in Gen. Patton's Army in Europe. Skaff's family had his picture in their living room window, along with a blue star in a little flag, until that blue star came down one day and a golden one went up, because Sonny had been killed in action fighting with General Patton's army in Germany. Joe Baz was reported missing in action about the same time. When someone in our neighborhood lost a son, it was as if we had lost one of our very own. The whole neighborhood cried. But imagine how we laughed when we saw a sign go up one day in the window of Mr. Baz's grocery store, big letters written on white butcher paper: "Joe is safe and on his way home! Free ice cream bars for all the kids!"

Well, back to me and my trip to Los Angeles in the fall of 1952. That's when I enrolled at the Pasadena Playhouse and College of the Theater, along with 50 or 60 young men and women like myself, who felt themselves among the chosen. As one of my classmates said, "We were covered with stardust." And I figured that, if I could just hang in there, maybe some of that stardust would stick to me.

The Pasadena Playhouse added to our sense of vocation by reason of the Playhouse's dedication — not to film, but to "pure theater." (It was really only an accident of geography, perhaps, that took so many Playhouse alumni off to Hollywood.) In fact, the California Senate and Assembly, by special resolution of March 25, 1937, named the Pasadena Playhouse the state's Official State Theater. And so, we all felt we were there on some kind of mission — that we had stumbled into something that was almost better than an appointment to West Point or Annapolis.

I can remember my first day there in the middle of Old Pasadena. I felt so darned, well, privileged, when I looked around and saw the beautiful young men and women who were checking in alongside me. They all seemed so sophisticated and well-dressed and, well... rich. For a moment or two, I wondered what the hell was I doing there — Jameel Farah, son of a meat cutter and a seamstress from Toledo, Ohio. Was I out of my class?

17

I soon found out that I didn't need to worry about that. If there was an aristocracy here at all, I learned it was to be an aristocracy of talent. And that my worth would be measured not on who I was (or who my family was), but on what I could do — in class or out of class.

Yes, we had classes. They were, mostly, classes in the history of Western theater, but our learning didn't come all, or even mainly, out of a book. We learned about Sophocles and Euripides by doing their plays. And we learned about Plautus, the Roman writer of comedic farce, by doing his plays — and so on, right through Shakespeare and Molière and Goethe and on up to modern times.

While we were doing a particular era, we also studied the manners and morals of that period. We learned how people of that era lived and worked, what gods they worshipped, what they ate, how they dressed, what kind of homes they lived in. So, although we didn't have many courses that were formally labeled as such, we learned, in vivid, interesting ways, a lot of history, and art, and cultural anthropology, and sociology and philosophy (but not much math or science). On the other hand, we had to learn set design and lighting and costumes, as well as acting and voice and dance.

Some of us grumbled about the dance bit. Little did I imagine, then, that the dance training would help me make my Broadway debut, more than 40 years later in "Guys and Dolls." How did it help me? Well, I was a terrible dancer at the Playhouse. I split my pants doing an arpeggio one night and had to back off the stage. And I was terrible, again, at the Martin Beck on Broadway — until dance captain Mark Esposito took me under his tutelage and showed me enough moves to prove that, in fact, you can unklutz a klutz.

So, much as some of us at the Playhouse hated it, we did some dancing, too. And if there weren't enough hours in the day to do all of this, then, well, we'd just have to carry on through the night. But we never never looked upon any of it as work. Work was what you had to do. This is what we wanted to do. And in one of the neatest places in the world, Pasadena, California.

3

Playhouse Days

I'll never forget my first holiday season in Pasadena. I didn't go home for Christmas. Couldn't afford it. But being in Pasadena on New Year's Day almost made up for that. For 50 years, Pasadena's city fathers had been putting on something called the Tournament of Roses, a salute to Southern California in the wintertime, when flowers of every kind were in bloom here, while the rest of the country was freezing its buns off. What better way to celebrate the sunshine than have a parade on New Year's morning, with floats made of the flowers that surrounded us, and then a football game in the afternoon, played in the high seventies?

On New Year's Eve, we had the usual parties, toasting out the old year with a beer called 102, toasting in the new. I'll never forget Brew 102. The Maier Brewing Co. managed to make it, and put it in the market — six-packs of 16-ounce cans — for only 98 cents. That was the nectar of choice for all out-of-work, down-and-out actors. (They had a cheaper brew, Brown Derby, a six pack for 79 cents. We didn't stoop that low. We had more class.)

Then most of us walked over to the streetcar barns and watched hundreds of people putting the finishing touches on their floats. And then, not so hung over that we couldn't walk or find a place where we could watch the parade, we strolled over to Orange Grove Avenue, picked up some heavy cardboard cartons from behind a television store, and hauled them along to an open spot behind the crowds that had already commandeered their places along the curb. There, we would sit and wait, and then, when the parade started, we planned to stand up on the TV cartons, so we could get the best possible view, over the heads of the folks along the curb.

Or so we thought. When the sounds of the first marching band were upon us, we stood up on the boxes, congratulating ourselves on our ingenuity — only to come tumbling down as the boxes collapsed under the weight of just one too many young thespians. We didn't see much of the parade.

What a far cry that was from the day, some 25 years later, in the glory days of M*A*S*H, when I was doing color commentary on the parade for the CBS Television Network. Then, of course, I was perched atop a mighty tower looming over Orange Grove Avenue near Colorado, with a mike in my hand, and everyone in the parade stopped to talk to me, and, through me, to 30 million viewers across the land.

Naturally, I made some good friends at the Playhouse. The kids there, well, many of them came from money, but you'd never find them putting on airs.

Lucy McAleer was typical. Her great uncle, Owen McAleer, had once been mayor of Los Angeles, and her family had a very successful wholesale hardware company in town, and a beach house at Malibu. But she was just as down-to-earth and friendly as anyone from my old neighborhood in Toledo. Lucy was a Debbie Reynolds type. Perfect features, silky brown hair, great legs. She was also a good dancer, and she could sing, too. One night, she

20

entertained the student body with her rendition of "Honey Bun"
from South Pacific. When she was finished, she called me up on
stage. So, I climbed up and joined her, and ad libbed some of my
own lyrics to "Honey Bun." And so did she.

We were a smash hit. The next day, in my mail box at the
Playhouse, I got a love letter from a secret admirer who'd been in
the audience. In the note, she said she'd reveal herself to me, if I
would put a flower in my lapel when I walked into our class on the
history of the theater. That kind of narrowed things down a bit. It
was somebody in my history class.

But, well, I didn't do it. I didn't put the flower in my lapel. I
chickened out. To this day, I do not know who this forthright
young woman was. Maybe if she reads this, she will write me in
care of my publisher and clear up the mystery. Now, I am very
happily married, of course, but it would be fun to know who the
mystery woman was, and fun to talk about old times at the
Playhouse.

Occasionally, I have run into Lucy McAleer over the years.
We talk about our great days at the Playhouse, and about the
parties we used to have in the years that followed, at her parents'
beach house at Malibu. Through Lucy, I met James Dean, one
great Sunday afternoon at the beach. Dean was already somebody,
by reason of his star turns in "East of Eden," "Rebel Without a
Cause" and "Giant." But, of course, he didn't hang around long
enough so we could become friends. (As you know, he soon died
in a car crash, driving all by himself up the coast.)

James Dean was shy, didn't talk a lot. But he was with us,
laughing and enjoying our high jinks. He had what I would call
compelling eyes. And, up close, I began to understand what
writers mean when they say someone has "great charisma." There
was an aura about James Dean. He exuded something special. I
guess if you wanted to take a cynical view, you could say he was
too special to live.

Lucy McAleer? She was discovered by Warner Bros. and she
became Lucy Marlow and achieved some fame in at least two great
movies, with roles in A Star Is Born (with Judy Garland), and The

Queen Bee, (with Joan Crawford) — until she got married and had kids with a star third baseman from the New York Yankees. His name was Andy Carey, and he distinguished himself with some marvelous hitting, and fielding, in a number of World Series games.

I made another good friend at the Playhouse. His name was Bob Furiga, and he later became an executive with ABC Television, and a member of the board of the Pasadena Playhouse Association. Furiga never wanted to be an actor; he wanted to be in production, and so he spent a lot of time in the Playhouse's machine shop.

Which is why I let him help me make a balsa wood model for a set, which I had designed to scale. While Furiga was cutting out some of my pieces on a jig saw in the machine shop, he managed to cut his hand pretty bad on the saw. I felt terrible. On my project! Not only did I feel terrible, I fainted when I saw him all bloody. But, fainting at the sight of blood was nothing new to me. From the time that I was a little kid, I never could see blood without fainting. Once, when my mother cut her finger in the kitchen, she told me to run and get her a Band Aid from the medicine chest in the bathroom. I never showed up with the Band-Aid. When my mother came down the hall to investigate, she saw that I was lying in a dead faint, right in the middle of the hall.

Since Furiga had, in effect, shed his blood for me, he and I became buddies. We were a great pair. He was tall, a light-skinned Italian, and I, of course, was dark. I could pass for any number of ethnic types: Mexican, Spanish, French, Sicilian, Greek, Moroccan, Egyptian, Jewish. One night, we were coming out of a pizza parlor together, and we met some bad-ass characters who thought I was Jewish. At least, I assumed they did, because they called me some of those names that Jews have been called for centuries. And they wanted to fight me.

I found my reaction a curious one. Instead of telling these rednecks that I wasn't Jewish, but Lebanese, I really got into a new feeling. I was scared, all right, but I wasn't going to save my skin by even implying that it was unfair to call me names, but fair enough to do so if I were a Jew. I'd been raised according to certain principles — that it wasn't fair to call anyone names. Furiga was a little nervous. He didn't want to get into a rumble. But he stood by me, not revealing my true identity as Clark Kent, and these guys just faded away.

Life at the Playhouse was not all Rose Parades or rumbles with rednecks. We were in a school that wasn't so much a school as it was a commitment, a total immersion in a way of life called "the theater." Which is why I had to take myself seriously.

I already knew I had certain comedic gifts, and I found a professor there, Jack Lynn, who believed that if an actor could do comedy he was also able to do tragedy — because comedy was harder. So Lynn had me playing the lead right away in a mainstage production of that great Shakespearean comedy called "King Lear." It was a great acting lesson for me. For one thing, I had to learn all of King Lear's lines for only one performance. I was only 17, but with a lot of makeup and a big beard, I did a very presentable Lear — "presentable" meaning that nobody laughed at my effort.

Of course, I did do some comedy, too. I played Ensign Pulver in a Playhouse presentation of "Mister Roberts." This was a pretty funny play. But I thought I could improve on it. I had seen and heard comedians like Jack Benny do ad libs on radio and on television, and so, now, I thought it entirely appropriate for me to insert some lines of my own.

It wasn't appropriate. "What are you doing?" cried our director, Jack Woodford, one of the finest speech teachers I ever met. He was a marvelous teacher. I remember that he had us each record a speech at the beginning of year, and, then, at the end of the year, the same speech. The idea was that he thought we needed some evidence of our progress. From speaking Brooklynese, or Mississippian, or Ozarkian, we learned to speak Broadcast Standard. Not that there was anything wrong with regional speech. It was just that, according to Woodford, we'd be more likely to get work if we didn't show up at an audition talking like we'd just got off a turnip truck.

23

Well, I told Woodford these were my ad libs. He shook his head. "No, not here. You're throwing off the other actors. They don't know what's going on." He paused. Then, reflectively, he said, "Now tell me, Mr. Farah, tell me why the ad libs?"

"This 'Mr. Roberts?' I thought I'd spike it up a little bit."

"Mr. Farah," he said. "This isn't punch. It's a play. It doesn't need spiking."

I shrugged. And I thanked Jack Woodford for this valuable lesson, thinking to myself, but not saying, "Thanks for teaching me the difference between punch and a play."

I had some other good directors at the Playhouse. There were two fine women directors: Leonora Shanewise and Barbara Vajda. And a rotund, bulbous little Egyptian guy named Bobker ben Ali. He was a great director, and something of a legend at the Playhouse. But he was never lucky enough to make it as a director anywhere else, though he wanted to. Like all good teachers, and coaches, he made things simple. And I never forgot his simple formula, one that seemed to work for me throughout my acting career. "You don't act," he told us many times. "You react."

There was a corollary to that axiom. "If you're going to react properly, you have to listen. Listen to the others around you, really listen. And, if you do, you will react — naturally. Then you won't have to 'act.' You just have to be." That made sense to me: Being is easier than acting. Years later, I heard Spencer Tracy giving some advice to young actors. He, too, was the soul of simplicity. "Know your lines," he said, "and don't bump into the furniture." Louis Calhern had it all down in a few words, too. "Before you go on," he said, "always check your fly."

But I think Cary Grant had the best, also simple, advice, and one that all my readers can follow, whether they are actors or not. Somebody once asked Grant, then 82 and still looking marvelous, the secret of his long life. He said, "I learned to just keep breathing in and out."

The Playhouse was, of course, an ivory tower. Most schools are. Kids can grow up in these ivory towers, at a pace that is appropriate to youth, a time to enjoy, even a time to be silly. Inevitably, however, and in various ways, the real world intruded at the Pasadena Playhouse. There were some old actors and actresses who were a part of the Playhouse community. They lived at the Playhouse with us, or in some cottages near campus, and I was disturbed when I found they didn't seem to have any acting jobs at all. I remember one old gent who used to come and hang out with us, and talk about the theater with great affection. But I soon realized that this guy was around a lot because, though he had the diction and the presence of a great actor, he wasn't working. He could have been washing dishes at a restaurant up the street for all I knew. He scared me.

I thought, "He's an actor, and he isn't working. If he's any good, he oughta be working." And then I thought, "Gosh, can this happen to me? No way!" Little did I know how, in "the business," it happens to almost everybody, even to guys like Dustin Hoffman. To a down-and-out actor who can't get work, and to a Dustin Hoffman who can't get the right work, it is all the same: when they are not working, they are sad. The worst thing a real actor, or actress, can say is, "I'm not working."

This is why I tell young people who come to me and ask about an acting career, "It is a calling. You have to have a great love, a passion for it. It is not an affair. It is the romance of your life. More often than not, you will be rejected. Only your passion will carry you through. Furthermore, to make a living at it, you have to be very lucky." I also advise them to find a trade, or a secondary calling, like teaching, so they have something to fall back on. There's no guarantee in this business, except, of course, heartbreak.

I had my first heartbreak when I realized that I could only spend one year at the Playhouse. I started to run out of money. I came to Pasadena with $600 in my pocket, just enough to pay for one year's tuition at the Playhouse, and working Saturdays and Sundays in a surplus store downtown only paid for my room and board at the Playhouse. I saved nothing. And my parents couldn't help.

My mom, who couldn't take the bitter winter cold any more in Toledo, had persuaded my dad to pull up stakes in Toledo the year before, and move to Phoenix, where he had been promised a job managing a supermarket. But the supermarket people reneged on their offer, and my dad had had to take a job bagging groceries. So my folks were now barely making it themselves.

It was time, I told myself, to find work, preferably in my chosen profession — on the stage. In order to get stage work, however, I needed a union card — Actor's Equity — and, in order to get an Equity card, I needed to have a job on the stage. But I lucked out.

"Mister Roberts" was then playing on the main stage at the Pasadena Playhouse, a company of professionals under the supervision of Harry Bernsen, who, as it happens, is the father of Corbin Bernsen, the handsome, womanizing lawyer from "LA Law." I found that this "Mister Roberts" company was going to go from its run at the Pasadena Playhouse to the Las Palmas Theater in Hollywood. So I went to Harry Bernsen and told him of my predicament. "I can get an Equity card," I said, "if I can get something, any little thing, in your show."

He said, "Fifty dollars a week. That's all I can afford. Fifty dollars. You can play the shore patrolman who brings the guys back to the ship, drunk. But you'll have to do some other things. For one thing, you'll have to make soap suds every night for that Ensign Pulver scene in the third act. You'll have to whip em up every night, backstage. You think you can whip up soap suds, Mr. Farah?"

"Mr. Bernsen," I said, "I'll whip up enough soap suds to give a bath to everyone in the cast." He liked the song I sang. I sang in the key of fun. I got the job.

And I guess I sang in that key, because I was full of the confidence of youth. I thought I could do it. So I did it. (If I didn't think I could do it, I never would have done it.) So, on several counts, getting a small part in "Mister Roberts" wasn't a bad start. I was earning fifty bucks a week — in 1953, when fifty bucks was more like five hundred today. And I got to observe some real pros at work. I learned from Craig Stevens, who played Mister Roberts for a time before he went on to win huge fame on a very popular and very stylish TV series called "Peter Gunn." I learned from practically everyone else in the cast.

Here's how professional this acting company was. One night, on stage, there was a scene when the crew was preparing to head off for shore leave. The script called for a general hubbub, to be ad libbed, everyone talking at once. Well, on this particular night, one of the seamen cried out, in a voice that rose up over all the others, "Okay, guys, don't forget your rubbers." For an instant, everyone froze. In that gentler time, there could have been quite a flap over this line, especially in the polite precincts of Pasadena. Quick as a flash, one of the other actors saved the day. "You're right," he said. "It could rain. Let's take our galoshes."

I was learning the craft of the theater (and I had the cleanest hands in town) for a good many weeks, even months. More important, I had an Equity Card. I was a member of the union for stage actors, and, if I was a member of the actors union, then I was an actor, right? I now had admission to the company of the truly blessed of this world; I had "a career on the stage." It was a career that would last as long as I could keep getting work. I didn't know it at the time, but I was never going to have the security of a steady job. If I'd known that at the time, I might have joined the post office.

But, fortunately for the post office, I didn't know how insecure show business was. I soon had another stage role at the Las Palmas Theater, this time in the classic "Stalag 17." I played one of the mostly anonymous soldiers, and understudied Harvey Lembeck in the role of Shapiro, the guy who got the lion's share of mail via the Red Cross. But I don't remember "Stalag 17" so much for the part I played. It was the friendship I made with an Italian kid in the cast who was born Joe Matarano in Brooklyn, and changed his name to Joe Corey when he became an actor. It was Joe Corey who introduced me to my first agent, a lovely man named Bert Marx, who was the brother of the MGM producer Samuel Marx, the man who discovered Elizabeth Taylor.

Bert Marx was the kind of agent who had two kinds of clients: actors on the way down the ladder of success, and actors on the way up the ladder of success. I was a client of the latter ladder. One of his other clients, a man who was on the way down, became a friend of mine. He had been a big star at MGM. But now he had a serious drinking problem. I can remember Bert getting phone calls from him, day and night, begging Bert to bring him some liquor — beer, wine, anything at all.

Well, I was in "Stalag 17" with this man, and I am happy to report that he soon went into Alcoholics Anonymous and he started taking hold of his life again. He never regained his star status, but he remained sober and worked as an actor until his death. If you are a movie fan like I am, you'll remember this fine actor. He played Judy Garland's boyfriend in "Meet Me In St. Louis," and Richard Rodgers (with Mickey Rooney's Lorenz Hart) in the film, "Words and Music." The actor was Tom Drake. (I'll never forget Tom's tales about MGM in the good old days. He told me once, "I played with two of MGM's greatest stars. Lassie and Wallace Beery. Both of 'em had fleas.")

My agent, Bert Marx got me my first TV acting job, just a single shot on a television series called "Dear Phoebe," with the help of my friend, Joe Corey, who was co-starring in the series. I played in a segment directed by Don Weiss, who would later direct many an episode of M*A*S*H. "Dear Phoebe" was a very popular series in the mid-1950s, about a lovelorn columnist named Phoebe Goodheart (like Abigail Van Buren or Ann Landers). Only Phoebe wasn't a woman. Phoebe was a former college professor (played by Peter Lawford) who wanted to be a reporter, but was thrown into the breach as a columnist by his editors at the "Los Angeles Daily Blade." Much of the humor revolved around Lawford's rivalry with another reporter who also happened to be his girlfriend (played by Marcia Henderson). I played a character named Itchy, a young wise-cracking kid, a car usher in a drive-in movie theater.

Then, in October 1954, the Playhouse called me back to do a part on the Center Stage in a play called "Bernadine," with John Lupton. This was the same John Lupton who went on to play the lead in a very successful TV series called "Broken Arrow," with

Michael Ansara, another dear friend of mine, who played the role of Cochise. I played the role of a nerd by the name of Vernon Kinswood. In one of the scenes, I wore a yellow slicker raincoat and rain hat, and my role called for me to carry around one of these little mop terriers, I think it was a Lhasa Apso.

One night, the dog pooped on me, and the poop dribbled out in the form of little sausages that stuck to the front of my slicker. I didn't know what had happened. But practically everyone else in the theater did, and the audience started to crack up with laughter. John Lupton and his leading lady started moving farther and farther up stage (to get away from me, I guess), and I kept backing up with them until I finally realized why everyone (including the stars on stage with me) were laughing. Once I got the poop scooped, the play went on. The play always went on.

4

Richard Brooks

One night, after one of the performances of "Bernadine" at the Playhouse, a pleasant man came back stage to see me, Al Trescony, a talent scout for MGM, who covered the Playhouse. He said he thought there might be a part for me in a movie called "Blackboard Jungle," starring Glenn Ford and Anne Francis. Yeah, an MGM movie.

I wanted to say, "Are you kidding?" You have to understand. It wasn't very long ago that I was a regular moviegoer at the Loew's Valentine in Toledo, the theater where they screened all the first-run pictures from MGM. And now here was a scout telling me I had a chance to be in a movie at MGM! A movie that would run in, among other places, the Loew's Valentine in Toledo. I'd be going from a high school kid in the balcony at the Valentine to being up there on the screen. I was overwhelmed by this. All I could do was nod yes, okay, all right.

"Call your agent," said Trescony. I phoned Bert Marx, and he made the arrangements for me to go out to MGM in Culver City, where I would soon learn about "Blackboard Jungle." It was a tough drama about a revolt in an inner city classroom, and it would be directed by Richard Brooks. I'd heard about Richard Brooks. He'd been a writer, mostly. He wrote "Key Largo" with John Huston. But now he was writing and directing his own pictures. His movie, "Battle Circus," with Humphrey Bogart and June Allyson was one of the first films to deal with a M.A.S.H unit. Another Brooks' movie, "Take the High Ground," an Army movie starring Richard Widmark and Karl Malden, helped establish Brooks' reputation in Hollywood as a godlike character. An angry god.

The story goes that Brooks had set up four cameras to shoot a major battle sequence in "Take the High Ground," big cast of extras, shows of shellfire, jeeps and tanks ready to roll, oodles of action. He also had some planes in the air; they were up there so they could drop some explosives on the scene he was shooting below. Well, he cries, "Action!" That's when everything is supposed to start happening, in sequence. But then Brooks sees something has gone wrong on the ground, so he yells, "Cut!" Well, of course, the guys in the planes start dropping their charges (which were actually flour bombs) because, of course, they can't hear him. As far as Brooks was concerned, they should have heard the voice of this god below.

Now he is really pissed off. He turns his face to the sky. "I said, 'Cut!' Goddamn it. Cut!"

At MGM, on my agent's orders, I went to the casting office. There were about 100 other guys standing around, young hood-types, with packs of cigarettes folded up above their biceps in their T-shirts. They carried switchblades knives, and wore black boots. I was shaken. I was nervous. Out of this crowd, how could anybody pick me?

Then I was in the casting office. The next guy in line. The next hunk of meat. That's show business: always in line, always waiting for the call, "Next!" All of a sudden, I found myself standing before the casting director, and the producer, Pandro Berman, and the director, Richard Brooks. They looked at me, they asked me a few questions and I was out of there. My head was whirling, but I wasn't so disoriented that I had failed to notice the contrast between the producer and the director. While Berman was togged out like something from the pages of *Gentlemen's Quarterly*, Brooks was wearing a seersucker sports shirt and baggy corduroy pants. (He always wore the same sports shirt and the same baggy pants; but he probably had a dozen identical outfits in his closet.) I later learned that Berman had spent most of his life in Hollywood, while Brooks was knocking about the world. He was a bum who rode the rails during the Depression, a sportswriter for the Philadelphia Record, a writer in Hollywood who, in 1940, hacked out five 15-minute radio plays every week.

Days later, somehow, they decided that I, of all the young LA delinquents who had gathered at the casting office, I might be right for a small, but important role — the role of Santini, a mentally retarded kid who smiled a lot and sat in the front of the class, and would ultimately save the life of the teacher of the class — Glenn Ford.

But I didn't know that at the time. I had just gotten a call from my agent, who told me I was up for a screen test. I was to identify myself at the gate, go to wardrobe, and makeup, and then show up on a stage (it might have been Stage 17) where Richard Brooks would be waiting for me.

Now here I was, face to face with Brooks and a cameraman and another actor, a contract player named James Drury. He would later play the lead in the TV series, "The Virginian," but now he was going to read some of Glenn Ford's lines to me, so I could react to them, according to the script. There was no time to study the lines, much less take the script home. Brooks just handed me the script. He said, "Your pages are marked. You're a little retarded. Let's go."

Just like that. I proceeded to read a few lines, on camera. He didn't tell me how retarded I was supposed to be. I just had to wing it. And then, when Santini's lines were over, he had me answer a few of his questions about myself — but the camera was still running, and I had to deliver my responses as this character, Santini, might respond. And then Brooks was saying, "Thank you very much."

I stumbled out, wondering how I'd done. Of course, they weren't going to tell me then and there. They had to watch the film.

Maybe you heard the possibly apocryphal screen test story about John Barrymore and John Carradine? This happened back in the 1930s, when Barrymore was one of the biggest things in Hollywood, and Carradine, a fine Shakespearean actor on Broadway, was seeking work in Hollywood. Somehow, Barrymore, an old friend, was put in charge of Carradine's test at Twentieth Century-Fox. "Not to worry, dear boy," said Barrymore. "I'll take good care of you."

He took care of him all right. He guided Carradine over to a vacant stage, where a cameraman and some lighting guys were waiting, and explained that the entire test would be done in pantomime. "I want you to come out from behind this door," said Barrymore, "and you're to make the audience feel that you've just had the best feast of your life."

Carradine said he could do that. And he did. He put on a helluva mime show, licking his lips, wiping them with his kerchief, patting his stomach, almost burping with contentment, smiling to himself, sighing with the rapture of it all. "How did I do?" said Carradine, when Barrymore cried cut.

"Terrific," said Barrymore.

"When do I get to see it?"

"Tomorrow. Come to the commissary at noon tomorrow. We'll take a look at it after lunch." So, after lunch the next day, Barrymore corralled a half-dozen of the studio executives to take a look at Carradine, who wondered why his friend was making such a big deal out of a simple, little, no-dialogue piece of celluloid. He found out. Up there on the screen, after his marvelous mime, the camera cuts to the same door Carradine had come out of. Now here comes Barrymore, smiling and winking at the camera and zipping up his fly.

P.S. Carradine got his contract at Fox.

Needless to say, I got a contract at MGM. I must have done something right. My first film role! I was excited to be on the lot at MGM, where Louis B. Mayer had made "more stars than there are in the heavens" during the heyday of the entire Hollywood studio system. After our first production meeting, as soon as we were dismissed, the other kid-actors and I (most of them were cast in New York and flown out to LA for the picture) took off exploring the lot.

I'm not sure how the others felt. They didn't share their feelings with me too much. I was the outsider among the kids. Most of them had been trained in the New York theater, and I was a Hollywood actor, and I think they kind of looked down on me. They included Sydney Poitier, Vic Morrow, who would later become a TV star, and Paul Mazursky, who would become an award-winning writer and director. John Erman was in the cast, too. In the whole picture, he had one line: "Not the FBI." I still like to kid him about that one line — and I can kid him because he went on to become such a success as a producer and director. He would later direct "Roots," one of the most watched mini-series in the history of television.

So I didn't have much to do with these young Turks — not even with Sydney Poitier, the hot young black actor from New York City. Nor with the stars of the show like Louis Calhern, the distinguished veteran of the New York stage, most famed for his lead in a very long-running Broadway play called "Life With Father."

I was shocked at first when I learned that Calhern left the studio every day at three in the afternoon. As a young actor, I thought, how disgraceful, that this man gets to go home. Why should he go home, and we all have to stay here? That's how naive I was. I didn't know, then, that actors of his stature had to fight for three p.m.-clauses in their contracts. Otherwise, the studios would have had them all working till midnight. Clark Gable, also at MGM, had a similar provision in his contract. He never worked after five p.m. Later, I learned how, in the movie business, as you gain stature and get older, you go for these things.

But hanging out with these people didn't matter to me. I was just so thrilled to be at MGM. I mean, it wasn't so long before that I had been paying 26 cents to see Doris Day in a movie at the Paramount Theater in Toledo. Now, all of a sudden, I'm on the same lot with Doris Day! I wondered if I would ever see her.

And then, the first day there, I say to myself, "Oh my God, there's Doris Day talking to — who's that? It's James Cagney!" Yes, I actually saw Doris Day and James Cagney nose-to-nose. She was sitting in her convertible, and he was standing there leaning on her car door, and he was so short, their noses were on the same level. And then it's "Oh my God, there's Debbie Reynolds and Eddie Fisher!" And, "Oh my God, there's Dan Dailey, Gene Kelly and Michael Kidd." They were there doing "It's Always Fair Weather," and they looked like — themselves!

Then, at lunch time, it was off to the commissary. "Oh my God, there's Robert Taylor!" Had I arrived? Yes! I really realized that when I was sitting in a barber chair on the MGM lot — getting my hair cut from the same barber who had done Mickey Rooney. And that I was driving to the studio in my own Model A Ford convertible with a rumble seat, the same kind of car that Rooney drove when he was Andy Hardy.

One day, on the set, I even got a glimpse of Elizabeth Taylor. I had heard she was one of Hollywood's classic beauties, and now here she was, perfection at 22. She'd come to our stage with her husband, Michael Wilding, to say hello to Richard Brooks, who had directed her in a project unlikely for him, a love story called "The Last Time I Saw Paris." All I could do was gawk at her. I thought, "You couldn't put a woman together any better than that."

But enough gawking. I was there, after all, to make a movie, my first. And I wanted to focus on that. I wanted to take advantage of working with one of Hollywood's finest, Richard Brooks. Brooks didn't disappoint me. Brooks, the ex-Marine, still looked every inch the Marine. And when we started shooting "Blackboard Jungle," I began to see that the Marine image was for real. He was all discipline, and he had to be that way with us, because we were all full of piss and vinegar, and full of ourselves. In fact, many of the extras on the show had been recruited out of a vocational school in Los Angeles, and the casting director had really recruited according to type. These were tough kids, and they came to the studio prepared to defend themselves. Every morning, our assistant director, Joel Freeman, had to pat everyone down, so he could confiscate their switchblade knives and their brass knuckles.

Then, when Freeman was done with them, they had to face Brooks — Brooks the perfectionist — who knew how to milk a script for everything there was in it, and more. That kind of an M.O., of course, tended to make a film run too long. I can remember Pandro Berman, our producer, coming on to the set one day and asking Freeman how "Blackboard" was doing. "Fine," said Freeman. "We may be running a little long."

"Oh," said Berman with a frown. "Well. Uh. Why don't you just have 'em all talk a little faster?"

Freeman knew better than to relay that suggestion to Brooks, who would have gone ballistic — until Freeman realized that Berman was just kidding. But Brooks was not one to kid around when he was working. Serious was what he wanted from all of us. He was forever urging us to listen to him. If someone got a line, or a scene, wrong, he would shout, "Nobody listens." And if someone really goofed, Brooks would yell, "Cut!" and then cry, "Shoot that man. Does somebody have a gun? Because if they do, I want him to take this man out and shoot him. Dead."

As far as I know, nobody ever had a gun on the set to comply with Brooks's order. Good thing, too. He could be a madman. Fay Kanin, the screenwriter, once described him as "God's angry man, a man who lived at the top of his voice."

This is why the terrible-tempered Richard Brooks scared the bejesus out of me. In the process, however, Brooks taught me things I never knew before about acting on a movie set. What he insisted on most was absolute attention from everyone on the set. If somebody wasn't paying attention, Brooks would scream, tapping his own chest, "Hey, there, Santini, stay with the money."

Brooks was "the money" — that is, the guy who could make us, or break us if we didn't listen to him. There'd be no talking on the sound stage, not even between scenes. And then, something that few directors did at the time: to insure concentration during a shoot, Brooks would always clear "the sight line" behind the camera. Nobody, but nobody, would be allowed to stand behind the camera and, thus, distract an actor's one-hundred percent attention on his lines — and on the camera lens.

I collected all of the Brookisms I could, and would regale some of the extras with Brooks' imitations. Once, I was holding forth in front of the urinals in the men's room, "doing" Brooks. "Stay with the money!" I said, trying to sound like Brooks. "Shoot that man! Nobody listens!" I was brought up short when Brooks himself came out of a stall. He'd been sitting on the john, listening all the time. I wanted to hide. He said nothing, washed his hands, and sauntered out. I watched him carefully. I thought I detected the faintest twist on his face, the beginning, perhaps, of a smile.

I had other close calls with Brooks. Once, I made the mistake of laughing right in the middle of a classroom scene with Glenn Ford.

It happened this way. Ford had his back to the camera, which was featuring me, and though this was supposed to be a serious scene, he grinned at me. That broke me up. I started to laugh.

"Cut!" cried Brooks. "Santini," he said to me (using my name in the picture), "that is very unprofessional." He didn't suggest that Joel Freeman, the AD, shoot me. But he didn't have to. I wanted to go out and shoot myself.

Later, after the re-take, I took Glenn Ford aside and asked him what had made him laugh. He hadn't bothered to take any of the heat off me by telling Brooks it was all his fault. But I let that go. I just wanted to know what had been going on.

Ford said, "Well, Santini, you just reminded me of one of my best friends."

"And who," I said, "is that?"

"Danny Thomas."

All I could do was shake my head. Ford had screwed me up with my most exacting director on account of my looking (to him) like Danny Thomas. I couldn't believe it. So far, Danny Thomas, my own kinsman, from my home town of Toledo, one of the biggest *machers* in town, even as an unwitting presence, was hurting me. Jeez!

A *macher*! I just used this word, rhyming with "knock-her," because, though I am Lebanese, and Danny Thomas was Lebanese, I had learned to refer to him with a word like *macher*, meaning a real operator, somebody who gets things done in a big way, because, if I was going to make it in show business, I had to learn Hollywood's other language, Yiddish. I learned to use the word, *mensch* — a real sweet guy. And to know, of course, that if I wanted to be a *mensch*, I couldn't be a *macher*. I also learned to use *chutzpah* (unmitigated gall), *machaier*, (wonderful), *nebbish* (nerd), *mazeltov* (congratulations), *meshugah* (crazy), *fablunjet* (confused), *farshtinkiner* (stinking), *farpotshket* (messed up), *nudnik* (pest), *shemozzl* (an uproar) and *shmegegge* (idiot). Sophia Loren once used *shmegegge* in an interview with *The New York Times*. According to Leo Rosten, this word, spoken in an Italian accent by a great beauty and tossed off with an eloquent shrug and a tone of derisive dismissal "marked a high point in the life of this colorful epithet."

For its time, "Blackboard Jungle" was a pretty shocking movie — so shocking that MGM thought it best to put a pious disclaimer on the screen at the beginning of the film stating that all schools were not like this — so as not to alienate hundreds of thousands of schoolteachers all over America. In the script, North Manual High School, in an inner city somewhere, was an all-boys school. Or maybe an all-rat school. We were all openly hostile to this new teacher, Mr. Dadier — whom we called Daddy-O — and just to make sure he understood how hostile some of the kids were, he was beaten up, off-camera, in the second reel.

Gradually, however, he won us over, even and especially me, a grinning, kind-of-idiot boy, who, as I said before, was named Santini. In the movie's most dramatic scene, when things could have gone either way for Mr. Dadier — I mean the class could have ganged up on him and killed him right in the classroom — I am a hero when I seize an American flag and stab one of the young villains in the chest with the American eagle on the end of the flag pole before he can use a knife on Mr. Dadier.

I screwed up the first take of that all-important scene, and learned a lesson from Brooks in the process. You see, after I stabbed this guy in the chest — played by Danny Terranova — with the pointed metal eagle, I thought I had hurt him for sure. And so, scared, I stopped. I wasn't supposed to do that. Brooks blew. "Cut!" he shouted.

Then he came over to me. He was livid. "Listen, Santini, nobody, but nobody, stops a scene except the director."

I said, "But I thought I hurt him."

"I don't care what you thought, Santini. Don't you understand? If you really do hurt him, and you don't follow through with the rest of the scene, then I do not get the shot at all. I can't do a re-take. I don't get the scene. And then we are all in trouble."

I nodded, very chastened by his tirade. I couldn't help thinking that this was a very cold-blooded approach.

When Brooks was finished with me, he was very solicitous about Danny Terranova. "Danny Terranova!" he shouted. "You all right?"

Danny said he was.

Then Brooks was all intent on the business at hand. "All right, let's set up again, everybody, for another take."

For all its shocking classroom violence, the movie was pretty upbeat. As Dadier said, toward the end of the film, "Kids are people. And most people are worthwhile." I enjoyed being a part of a good movie like this, a movie that was trying to say something. What it said was that some inner-city schools were very dangerous places. That was not a welcome message to some. Clare Booth Luce, then the ambassador to Italy from the United States, got the film banned from the Venice Film Festival. And some Congressmen launched hearings to investigate the state of our nation's schools.

The movie made quite a splash. LIFE magazine even did one of its famous features on "Blackboard Jungle": LIFE Goes to the

Movies. I saw the magazine in the mail room in my apartment lobby, flipped it open and saw my picture in LIFE. I had to have it. It was the first thing I ever stole in my life. I wonder even today whether grabbing it was a federal offense, and if it was, whether the statute of limitations has passed by now.

Anyway, "Blackboard Jungle" was a real milestone in my life's journey. I will always owe a huge debt to Richard Brooks for teaching me what I like to call "discipline."

Years later, I was pleased to be able to say much of this in a memorial program to Richard Brooks at the Academy of Motion Picture Arts and Sciences. It was the first in a series of Academy retrospectives, and I was chosen to be the master of ceremonies of the affair. I remember a vivid thing Brooks said that night. "Say what you will about Louis B. Mayer, Harry Cohn, Jack L. Warner and Darryl Zanuck. They were all bastards. But they had one thing in common. They all loved movies. The studio executives today? I don't even think they like movies."

In 1990, the Writers Guild and the Directors Guild teamed up to give Brooks a lifetime achievement award. I was also there for that ceremony, and I still have a note from Brooks: "Jamie — who was there near the beginning. Top man. Top talent. Love — Richard Brooks."

Even today in Hollywood, whenever writers gather, they like to tell Brooks' stories. Fay Kanin once said that Brooks was "irreverent about everything, except writers." And until the end, Brooks was always a writer. One day, in 1988, when members of the Writers Guild had gone out on their last big strike, it was Brooks himself who led the picket line, in a wheelchair outside Twentieth Century-Fox.

"Look," he said, surveying the picket line with a smile. "A mile of writers." After a couple of hours on the line, Brooks asked if anyone could get him a telephone. Someone found a cellular phone and handed it to him. He dialed a number. It was Barry Diller's office. Diller, the head of Fox. Diller was out. (Heads of studios are always out. It's in to be out.) So Brooks growled to Diller's secretary. "This is Brooks. Tell Diller I'm out here picketing and send out some coffee."

Not ten minutes passed. A waiter, in uniform, appeared wheeling a large cart, bearing a silver coffee service. "Mr. Brooks?" he said. "Mr. Brooks?"

"That's me," said Brooks. "Over here."

The waiter proceeded to give Mr. Brooks his coffee. And a full lunch, too.

But all that was long after "Blackboard Jungle." I just thought I needed to tell you who Brooks was, so you can understand what it was like for me, working under him — in my first movie.

5

Agents

I had felt that "Blackboard Jungle" would be my big break. But that was one of those self-delusions that actors need to keep going in a very tough business filled with constant rejection. I hadn't had that many great lines in the film. And then, having played an idiot in "Blackboard," all I could reasonably expect from Hollywood's type-casting directors was another part as an idiot. So "Blackboard Jungle" led me into a kind of desert: no more parts.

Lord knows, I tried out for a lot of other parts. I remember being over at Warner Brothers one day, shooting a pilot for television called "Dhondo." I can't even remember what the story was about. I only remember that I played the part of an East Indian wearing leggings and a Nehru jacket. Jack Warner, the head of the studio, who was Jewish and a big supporter of Israel, had been looking at the dailies (film that had been shot the day before) and I guess he was curious about me. He came by one day, and confronted me with suspicion. "Say," he said, "what's your name? What nationality are you?" I wondered if he'd recast the part if he found out I was Lebanese. I was leery of saying the wrong thing. But I thought I'd survive this moment if I could just make him laugh. "Mr. Warner," I said, "I'm anything you want me to be." He laughed.

I knew that Jack Warner fancied himself a comedian of sorts, but the word was that he was never quite as funny as he thought he was. He got up on the dais at a Friars Club banquet one night and did a comedy routine that bored everyone to tears, including the evening's emcee, a man named J.C. Flippen. You never heard of J.C. Flippen? No wonder. He took the mike from Warner and made a flip, negative comment of his own about Warner that Warner did not take lightly. In fact, J.C. Flippen's agent told him on the spot, "J.C., you just ended your career." Well, maybe he did, and maybe he didn't. As the story goes, Warner said of more than one actor who crossed him, "Don't ever hire him again. Until I need him."

I wish I could report now that surviving my close call with Mr. Warner led to a good many parts for me at Warner Bros. — as... anything he wanted me to be. But this is a story of my near-misses, as well as my direct hits: I did not get an unending succession of parts at Warner's.

But I did get two more parts at MGM, two small parts. In the spring of 1955, I worked in "Kismet," a dish cooked up by one of the great producers of musicals at MGM, Arthur Freed. It was directed by Vincente Minelli (who had been married to Judy Garland), and it starred Howard Keel, Ann Blyth, Dolores Gray and Vic Damone. With those ingredients (and a pretty fair sauce in the form of some memorable music), the movie should have been a feast for moviegoers.

But it was more like a snack. No one much noticed the movie. I doubt anyone noticed me at all, except my mother. I played an Arab orange merchant, and whatever lines I had, I had to sneak in, ad lib. Which would have given me ample opportunity to offer maledictions on everyone involved in this production with little chance of getting caught. But you never knew. Someone out there in some movie theater somewhere would probably catch what I said, and get me in trouble.

I remembered one Saturday night back at the Rivoli in Toledo. Everyone in the neighborhood (including most of the Arab-American community in Toledo) had turned out to see "Sirocco" with Humphrey Bogart, set somewhere in North Africa. There was one scene in a crowded bazaar. As Bogart passed through, and the scene began to fade, one Arab voice rang out, *"Ya hallah deen bayak!"* That almost brought the house down. "What?" The non-Arabs in the audience wanted to know: "What is everybody laughing about?" My buddy, Gregory Morris, decided he would translate. He stood up in the middle of the theater, finding a kind of spotlight for himself in the light of the projector, turned his back to the screen and cried out to the whole crowd, "That means, 'Goddamn your father.'" I am translating here. What he said sounded more like, "Goddamn you faddah." That brought the house down.

And so, I knew how I could turn my role in "Kismet" into a big laugh in Toledo. But I resisted the temptation. In "Kismet," I mostly kept my mouth shut and tried to look like — an orange merchant. Whatever an orange merchant looks like.

Movie buffs who look carefully at a videotape version of "Kismet" today can pick out a character who looks very much like Aaron Spelling, the producer. In fact, it is Aaron Spelling. Maybe it was this acting experience that sent Spelling into production — which only improved his fortunes by about a million percent. He and his wife, Candy, now have a home in LA's Holmby Hills, at least 25,000 square feet of the most luxurious home ever built in Southern California — which I think he richly deserves. They don't make producers like Aaron Spelling any more. He is a throwback to a bygone age, before the Harvard MBAs took over Hollywood, when producers couldn't do enough for their stars. I will have more to tell you about Spelling later.

The next movie part I landed was also at MGM. It was called "Diane," an expensive costume movie about some intrigues in the

Renaissance court of Henri II of France. Roger Moore, later to
become James Bond, played the son of Henri II, and Diane's love.
I will never forget the day he was knocked off his horse in a full
suit of armor. He was really banged up — and this forced many day
players into some fine displays of their acting talents, rushing up to
express their dismay over this accident, hoping Mr. Moore was all
right, even getting a little teary-eyed (while secretly rejoicing that
this could only mean several days delay and, hence, several extra
day's pay). This was where the real acting came in.

Extra days' pay. That is always a devout hope on any movie
set. And so, of course, there are a number of stories about
Hollywood actors getting huge financial windfalls for extra work.
The best one I heard was James Gleason, who was hired for a
three-day shoot, a small part as a cab driver in "The Bishop's
Wife." He was an actor of some stature, so his agent only agreed to
let him work at the then-substantial fee of $3,500 for three days'
work. "But if you keep him around for more than three days, you
have to keep paying him at the same rate." The studio agreed:
$3,500 for every additional three days. But, as it happened, during
the making of this picture, Gleason's small role turned into a big
one, and he ended up working so many days that he ended up
making $85,000, just $15,000 short of what Cary Grant earned on
the picture. This was a year, 1947, when $85,000 was a lot of
money.

Many many years after I worked on "Diane," I would do
another movie with Roger Moore, the first "Cannonball Run," an
adventure I will tell you about in due course, except to note now
that everybody on the production all learned to hate Roger
Moore. Why did we hate him? Because, though we were always
sweltering on our location in Decatur, Georgia, in the hottest dog
days of summer, Roger Moore always showed up in a white suit,
impeccable, with not one bead of sweat on his brow. No matter
how hot the day, or how wilted any of us would be, he would
always appear looking like he had just stepped out of a walk-in
freezer, starched, immaculate, and definitely cool. He was a real
movie star, bigger than life.

What happened to "Diane?" It bombed, and needless to say, it was no showcase for Jameel Farah, who played the role of — a mute squire. I was going downhill. In "Kismet," a few lines. In "Diane," no lines at all.

Getting nothing more in the picture business, I continued to act on the stage, playing in any little hole-in-the-wall theater on Melrose that would have me. If an actor wants to act, he can always find a stage... somewhere. But I continued to make the cattle calls, from Fox, to Paramount, to Republic, to Universal, to MGM, to Warner Brothers to Columbia, and then back again.

You may ask: "Didn't I have an agent?"

And my answer would be, "Yes, I did. Several of them." They were often the ones who sent me on these cattle calls. My agents were very nice men, most of them, and when they weren't very nice, they were funny. One of them, George Rosenberg, with a client list topped by Bing Crosby, had one of the foulest mouths in Hollywood. Every other word was "eff this," or "effing that." And in between all the eff words, there was always room for other obscenities. The nicest word he ever had for anybody was "sonuvabitch." I don't know what this says about me, but I was one of the few people Rosie seemed to like (although I couldn't help wondering how he referred to me when I wasn't around).

When I was around (in hopes of getting work), Rosie would often call me into his inner sanctum, so I could watch him make his deals. He would have some movie mogul or network executive with him, and he'd be cursing up a blue cloud, and then, suddenly, he'd turn to me and say, "Hey, kid, whadda you think?"

Hey, I didn't know these moguls. And I didn't know the business side of show business. So, I always agreed with Rosie. To this day, I wonder if those executives knew who I was, or wasn't. No matter. Without my counsel, Rosie couldn't, apparently, do his business properly. So, in retrospect, I guess I was really indispensable to the progress and completion of a lot of Hollywood deals.

I had another agent, Lester Salkow. Lester's clients included Raymond Burr, Peter Lorre, Vincent Price and Sir Cedric

Hardwicke. And me. Lester was a large man. Huge. Too huge. One day, after Lester had struck a particularly good deal, he decided that he needed to purchase what was then considered a perfect symbol of his success — the most expensive Jaguar sports car on the market. Properly attired for this transaction, dressed in his best charcoal-gray suit, tailor-made in London, he took a taxi to the Jag dealer on Wilshire Blvd., paid cash for his car, and squeezed into the front seat, with the assistance of the sales manager and the felicitations of all the other salespeople and employees of this posh Jaguar dealership, as he toddled off to join some business associates at an important luncheon at Scandia on the Sunset Strip — and incidentally show off what is, in LA, the ultimate status symbol, an expensive car.

Trouble was, when he arrived at Scandia, he couldn't get out of the Jag. After a good deal of fluttering instructions from the valet parking boys, however, Lester escaped from the clutches of his leather seat — only to find that, as he popped out of the car, the door handle of the Jag had seized his jacket pocket and ripped off the entire left side of his coat.

Three hours later, Lester sold his Jag. His used Jag. Net loss: some $30,000. It cost him $10,000 an hour — to make a statement about himself. But, that's show business.

Lester (need I add this?) didn't get me much work. Couldn't even get me a job with his brother, Irving Salkow, a producer at MCA. But of course, as he kept telling me, and I had to realize, I was no Tab Hunter. I was "special." Which reminds me of another agent story, this one involving another agent of mine in the early 1950s, Meyer Mishkin.

Unlike Lester Salkow, Meyer Mishkin was short in stature, but a giant in the making of a deal. Meyer had some very big clients, and he got them some very big money. Charles Bronson, Jeff Chandler, Chuck Connors, James Coburn, Lee Marvin. Some of the biggest box-office guys in Hollywood at the time. He had another client, not quite so well known, named Marvin Kaplan. At the present time, Marvin is president of the Los Angeles Chapter of AFTRA, the American Federation of Radio and

Television Artists, an actor who achieved his biggest notoriety as the hard hat worker who stopped into Alice's Restaurant every week in the TV series, "Alice." You may remember Marvin: he was a kind of Woody Allen type, with a Noo-Yawk accent and all, only heavier and with not quite as impressive a vocabulary as Woody Allen.

Anyway, as the story goes, Marvin hadn't yet made it in Hollywood. He was struggling. And so he paid a visit to his agent, Meyer Mishkin. "You know, Meyer," he said in his distinctive Noo-Yawk tones, "I ain't been working much lately, and things are starting to go a little bad."

Meyer Mishkin rose from his chair and walked over to comfort Marvin. Though Marvin was sitting and Meyer was standing, the two of them were almost nose to nose. "Marvin, Marvin," he said, "you'll get work. You'll get work. It's just that you are — special."

Marvin blinked and said, "Meyer, no one should be this special."

Somehow, even though I, too, was special (let's face it, I wasn't your typical kid next door), I managed to get work, here and there, often work far removed from the film business.

The name of the game was survival. I was no different than other struggling actors, and I won't bore you with the details of the so-called demeaning, non-acting jobs I took, if only because I never felt, at the time, that the jobs were demeaning, or beneath me. Delivery boy, postal clerk, I even worked as an animal keeper at a chinchilla farm in Burbank. Chinchillas, as you know, are large South American rodents prized for their soft, pale-gray fur. My job at the farm: to clean out their cages and nesting boxes on a regular basis — even when these little creatures weren't exactly pleased by my intrusions on their privacy, which was most of the time. They'd stand on their hind legs when I made my appearances and pee at me, accurate at a distance of 20 paces. In self-defense, I took to wearing rain gear — coat, hat and rubber shoes, which allowed me to approach more freely. As a result, the chinchillas got used to me, and let me continue with my work, unmolested. With the exception of one mean little guy who kept letting me have it, every time I neared his cage.

I fought back. I bought a water pistol, and we had a shootout. We created quite a watery mess. But he ran out of ammunition before I did. He beat a retreat into his nesting box, and he never bothered me again. We didn't become friends. But we weren't shooting enemies any more. And I found I could put my rain gear aside.

I felt lucky to have these menial jobs. They helped me survive. They allowed me to keep on trying, in a profession that can be one of the most unrewarding and most frustrating professions in the world. There's a saying among young actors, in both New York and Hollywood, that says the same thing in a more colorful way: "Once an actor, always a waiter."

In retrospect, I think there was one thing made my situation not only tolerable, but something close to fun: I knew a lot of other actors who were in the same fix, and together, like prisoners of war, or New York City cops on assignment in the lower Bronx, we devised a form of black humor that sustained us. In this case, misery did not exactly love company. It was more like, misery needed company.

My best company, in those years, came in the form of a short, stocky, tough-talking actor who was born Michael Vincent Gubitosi in Nutley, New Jersey in 1933. He made his stage debut on the Major Bowes Amateur Hour at the age of eight. He did 80 Our Gang comedies, and 32 Red Ryders (playing the part of a Indian lad named Little Beaver). At the age of twelve, he sold a newspaper to Humphrey Bogart in one of the opening scenes of one of the finest movies ever made, "The Treasure of Sierra Madre." At thirteen, he played the part of John Garfield as a boy in the movie, "Humoresque." In fact, for a family made dysfunctional by drink and drugs, he had been the principal breadwinner until he left home at the age of 17 and changed his name to Robert Blake.

"I wasn't a child star," Bobby Blake used to say. "I was a child laborer."

I first met Blake on a movie we did together in Arizona in 1956, a film called "Three Violent People," starring Charlton Heston, Anne Baxter, Gilbert Roland, Forrest Tucker, and Tom Tryon, in his first movie. It was a cowboy flick at Paramount.

This was not exactly my forte, playing in what *Variety* called "oaters." At a casting call, Producer Hugh Brown asked me if I knew how to ride a horse.

"Well," I said, "I'm no Roy Rogers."

That made him laugh. And I got the job. I have learned that, if you're looking for a job, it helps if you can get a chuckle out of the guy (or gal) who's doing the hiring.

I went out and took a riding lesson, and before I knew it, I was on a TWA Constellation, my first time in a plane, headed for Phoenix with Bob Blake. We shot the film in the foothills of the Superstition Mountains, east of Phoenix. I didn't turn out to be a natural horseman. They gave me the tamest horse in the stable, a twelve-year-old gelding named Old Red, but Old Red's horse sense told him I didn't know how to take charge, not at all.

Rudy Maté was the director, a kind old gentleman who had graduated into direction from cinematography. (A Hungarian, directing a Western in the Superstition Mts. But, what the hey! If a Dimitri Tiomkin can write music for a western, like "High Noon," why can't a Rudy Maté direct a western movie?)

Maté had enough sense to put me first in line for all the riding scenes. (The reasoning was that, if you put the worst rider last, you'd probably never see him on camera.) But not even that ploy would work. In our very first take, I led the pack all right. But only for a little while. The script called for us all to ride right. That's when my Old Red decided to go left. Didn't seem to matter what I was telling him what to do, or what the other horses were doing. Old Red had his own notions. If I was no Roy Rogers, then Old Red was no Trigger.

"Oh, well," said Maté, after the scene was over, and I came up puffing on Old Red. "Thank God, there won't be any more horse scenes, Mr. Farr." He didn't blame me, God bless him. He blamed Old Red, who, according to Maté, was "getting too old for this

51

anyway." (If you ever see the movie, don't look for me in any of the chase scenes.)

Years later, I did a movie of the week at Universal for Howard Morris (about whom more later). Howie asked me if I could play an American Indian. I said, "Sure. Okay. As long as I don't have to ride a horse." First day of shooting, what do you think I was doing? Right? Riding a horse. Howie said, "Roll 'em," somebody hit the horse in the behind with a stone, he bolted and I was lucky to finish that scene in one piece. I was still no Roy Rogers. And this steed was no Old Red. I called him El Diablo.

Have I told you that actors are an insecure lot? No? Well, they are. They always seem to need a great deal of reassurance. So, during this shoot, we all became kind of discombobulated by Maté, whose assurance was always ambiguous. "How'd I do?" one or another of us would say to him. Then his head would start to shake from side to side. "Omygod," we'd say. "How did we fail?" Then he would say, "Vonderful. Spectacular." Turned out that his head shake was caused by a kind of nervous affliction. How are we doing, Rudy? Shake shake. Beautiful. Vonderful.

We grew to love the guy, even (and especially) when he became tongue-tied. One time, Forrest Tucker, Bruce Bennett and Charlton Heston put on a helluva fight scene, choreographed mayhem, jaw-breaking punches, crunching kicks, an enchilada of violence. When they were finished, Maté cried, "Action!"

"Huh!" they said. Wasn't that what they were giving him? Action?

"No. No," said Maté "I mean, 'Cut.'" Shake shake. "Vonderful."

We had one of Hollywood's greatest stunt men on this picture, a real pro named David Sharp, who had served as a double for many a leading man. He was a great leaper, jumper, fighter. And he taught me many a thing about making an action movie. He taught me how to fire a movieland pistol (from the hip). He taught me how to fall. You may wonder, "What's to teach?" Well, the main thing was not to hurt yourself. Davie Sharp showed me — showed all of us, in fact — that preparation was everything.

Before a fight scene on a ranch house porch, for example, he'd rake the ground, make sure there were no sharp stones there, or bits of broken glass. He'd also go around the porch with a hammer and an awl, and reset any nails that were sticking up. And he checked every piece of the porch, looking for slivers that could stab us.

I'll never forget one piece of advice he gave me, "If you can avoid doing stunts, avoid it. Never do your own stunts." I usually tried to follow that advice. Who ever would know the difference? Movies are illusion. Cameras — and the men and women who run them — can show anybody doing anything. Which is why I always told my directors, "I never do anything dangerous. I even have a stunt man do my love scenes."

Some of you may recall that I did a stunt once in a TV special called "Circus of the Stars." I lay on a bed of nails with a hunk of concrete on my chest so a muscleman armed with a sledgehammer could shatter the slab. Sensational! Or, at least, an illusion of the sensational — because this is not a dangerous feat. It is just science. One nail might puncture me. Two nails might puncture me. But if my weight is evenly distributed over a bed of nails, nothing happens. Joy was impressed when she saw me do this. Really, it was no big deal. (But I don't encourage any of my readers to try this, unless you're in the hands of a pro.)

Making "Three Violent People," Bobby Blake and I became roommates at the Adams Hotel in Phoenix. He became a kind of friend and mentor to me, and we spent many a dinner hour at The Flame, a Phoenix eatery once-famed for its prime rib. Blake liked his rare. He'd tell the waiter, "Just knock the horns off it and serve it." He was about the same age as I. But he'd done a heap more of living. In his teens, he'd been a thief and a drug pusher, and he was kicked out of five schools. But these were experiences that made him an interesting guy.

The Bobby Blake of that time was most interesting when he was sharing his opinions with me. He had opinions about everything, spoken proudly in the dese-dem-dose accents of his native New Jersey, and often summed up with his favorite Blake-ism: "And dat's da name a dat tune."

What I admired most about Blake was his intensity, and his fierce desire to make it in Hollywood without losing anything of his integrity and his individuality. After "Three Violent People," it would take him a few more years "to make it." But he did it his way ten years later in the Richard Brooks' movie version of Truman Capote's non-fiction novel, *In Cold Blood*, playing a memorable felon, the gimpy, aspirin-popping Perry Smith.

In fact, I was so inspired after I heard that Brooks was going to direct the movie version that I sat down and wrote a letter to Brooks, suggesting that Blake was Perry Smith. I take no credit for Blake's getting the part. I suspect Brooks had Blake in mind even before he got my note. But it was nice to see some good things happen to Bobby Blake. That role in "In Cold Blood?" He took that and, quite literally, put it in the bank.

6

Red Skelton

As I have said more than once already in these pages, good things always seemed to happen to me. How about this chain of events? You remember how I told you that, not long after I left the Pasadena Playhouse, I landed a small stage role at the Las Palmas Theater in Hollywood? In "Mister Roberts," starring Craig Stevens? Well, here's the rest of the story.

After Stevens left "Mister Roberts," he landed the lead in a TV pilot called "The Mighty O" and he noted there was a role in "The Mighty O" for a young man named Snorkel, a sailor with a big nose who could smell things a mile away, someone to play opposite the ship's cook, a simple, incompetent, good-natured fool named Cookie.

"Hey," Craig Stevens told his producer, Cecil Barker, "there's only one guy in the world who has this kind of nose. His name is Jameel Farah. Wait'll you see him! Talk about a Snorkel!" To make a long story short, I got that part. And the reason why I have to make the story short is this: "The Mighty O" never made it beyond the pilot stage. I got a few weeks work on "The Mighty O" (after signing a contract affirming that I was not a member of the Communist Party), and I was soon back on the street — again.

But there's a sequel to that story, too, because meanwhile, over at CBS Television City, the producer of "The Red Skelton Show" — who just happened to be Cecil Barker — found out that the head writer on the show, Sherwood Schwartz, was looking for another character, maybe a Navy character. Barker suggested to Schwartz that this Cookie character could become one more character in a long line of Skelton characters: Willie Lump Lump, Clem Kadiddlehopper, Freddie the Freeloader, Deadeye, Cauliflower McPugg, the Mean Widdle Kid. And Schwartz thought it was worth a try. Skelton had a catalog of maybe 400,000 jokes, and a goodly number of them had to do with the U.S. Navy. Of course, why not a sailor shtick, why couldn't Skelton be a Navy cook?

Barker and Schwartz found agreement from Madison Avenue's man on the spot, Bill Brennan of Young & Rubicam. Not only did Brennan think Cookie was a good idea. He studied the pilot of "The Mighty O" and he liked the Snorkel character, too. So he endorsed the notion of a comedy pair, Cookie and Snorkel, Navy sidekicks.

And that's how I got the call to go over to TV City to meet the great Red Skelton. Gosh, Red Skelton! Skelton was one of my all-time heroes. He was one of the biggest stars in TV. His "Red Skelton Show" had a Nielsen rating of 24.6, and a 39 share. A 39 share means 39 percent of the all the TV households in America. So, considering that there were about 100 million TV households in the U.S. at the time, Skelton had a weekly audience of some 39 million people. Today, no regular show on TV gets those kinds of numbers. Roseanne Barr gets a Nielsen rating of 18 on ABC. "60 Minutes" gets a 21 on CBS.

But Skelton's standing in the TV world wasn't the half of it, for me. In my own pantheon of stars, Red Skelton was right up at the top. At age eight, I used to listen to him on the radio, in bed, under the covers, so my mother couldn't hear, 'cause he came on after my bedtime. And later, when I was old enough to start going to the movies, I never missed a Skelton movie. In the 1930s and 1940s, Red made more than 30 of them.

One night, I even got a spanking because I didn't want to miss a Red Skelton movie. It was "Dubarry Was A Lady," a costume farce starring Skelton and Lucille Ball. It happened this way. The movie had already made a run in the downtown theater in Toledo, and now (as *Variety* would say) it was in "the nabes." In other words, it was at my local, neighborhood cinema, The Mystic, over near the fire station.

Those were the pre-videotape days, when we all had neighborhood theaters. The Mystics and the Rivolis and the Orpheums and the Rialtos and the Pantheons, which, if they were anything like my Mystic, were pretty run-down places, complete with rats running up and down the aisles, or, if we were lucky, cats chasing the rats. My Mystic welcomed the men from the firehouse, which was right next door, let 'em in free, which was why we had a fire bell in the back of the theater.

For ten cents, plus the price of popcorn, five cents, we could have a fantastic Saturday afternoon at our neighborhood theater. Some would save the popcorn nickel — and bring in a bag full of goodies from home: feta cheese, olives, tabouleh salad (made with onions and garlic), pita bread. Those in the theater who were not Arabs soon learned to live with the aroma of onions and garlic. After all, the nabe offered a heckuva bargain. A quarter for adults, a dime for kids, we could see a newsreel, the latest installment of a Captain Marvel serial, a double feature, a short and three cartoons. When World War II came along, the government slapped on a ten percent entertainment tax. Then the whole package went up to 26 cents. Or, for children, eleven cents.

This particular night, this Wednesday night, was "Dubarry's" last night in town. I knew that, if I ever wanted to see "Dubarry," tonight was the night. I had to pay a visit to the Mystic.

So, after dinner, I jimmied open my piggy bank, drew out enough pennies for the price of my admission and some popcorn, and hustled down to The Mystic — without telling my mom. As luck would have it, the first screening of "Dubarry," at 6 p.m., was almost over when I found my seat, so I had to sit through the second feature at eight before I could see "Dubarry," showing again at ten.

I guess it was close to midnight when I got home.

There was absolutely no chance of sneaking in. My mother was hovering near the front door when I got home. I got the usual questions: "Where have you been? I was gonna call the police. I was gonna check the hospitals." But, once she found out I was perfectly all right, then she gave me the kind of treatment she'd feared I might have suffered at the hands of others. I got a spanking. For Red Skelton.

You may ask what my father thought of this. My father didn't think anything of it. My father, whose name was Sam, was a meat cutter. (That's why they called him Butch.) He worked hard, seven days a week, and he had to be up at five a.m. because he had to take two buses to get to work. He'd open the grocery in the morning and close it at night and get home for an eleven p.m. supper. He should have owned that store, and wanted to, but the people who owned it sold it out from under him to a young nephew.

On this midnight, he was already abed, and anyway, he regarded my mother as the boss of the household. He only gave me one spanking in my entire life — and this was at the request of my mom.

I was thinking about all this history when I parked my jalopy in the capacious lot at CBS Television City and trotted up to the big white building dominated by the CBS television eye. I was told to ask for Producer Cecil Barker, and did, and he came out with a twinkle in his eye and said that Red was home, sick that day, and would I mind if we went up to his home on Bellagio Road in Bel Air?

Would I mind? Was Dwight David Eisenhower president of the United States? No, of course I wouldn't mind. So Barker drove me up to Red's 27-room mansion on Bellagio Road, and announced himself at the black box on the gate, and told the cook who we were and the cook said Mr. Skelton was expecting us in the den.

Our footsteps echoed on the parquet oak floor, and my eyes widened at the works of art everywhere, and I goggled at the floor-to-ceiling books everywhere.

In the den, Red met us with a big unsmoked Perfecto Garcia jammed in his mouth. He was dressed in a fancy Japanese kimono. And despite the cigar and the kimono, he — looked — just — like — himself — Red Skelton! Wispy red hair, florid complexion, dimples, just like his pictures! For a while, he pretended he wasn't really that interested in talking to me so much as to a big tropical bird sitting in a huge wrought-iron cage. He asked us to sit. And then we waited, respectfully, while he spent maybe a half-hour trying to get his pet South American macaw to eat some sunflower seeds.

Finally, Skelton finished with the macaw, and turned to me. He said, with a little wrinkle of his nose, "So you think you can be Snorkel?"

Barker said, "He is Snorkel."

I wanted to say, "Mr. Skelton, I got a spanking once because of you." But I didn't. I tried to steer the conversation to the shtick — Cookie and Snorkel. I understood the premise here. I had a big nose. Mind you, I didn't grow up thinking I had a big nose. It was the other people with little noses we thought strange. In my neighborhood, you were either Italian, Greek, Jewish or Lebanese: everybody had a big nose. And so, now, with Skelton, I made it clear that I wasn't sensitive about my nose. I joked about it.

And so, then, did he. He made a few jokes about big noses. He asked, "Was your mother frightened by an anteater?" He suggested that I could "hitch that thing up to a horse and plow a field with it." And guessed that I'd "just have to take one big breath in the morning, and that's it for the rest of the day."

That's about all there was to our first meeting. Skelton wanted to see what kind of chemistry there was between us. And I think he could see, right away, that the chemistry was there. I was a performer. He was a performer. We had something in common right there. I didn't know it at the time, but we had other things in common. We were both born in July. We were Cancers. We both came into this world without much of its goods. He had come up the hard way, through hard work, and though I was just beginning my show business career, I was prepared to work hard, too.

Barker could see that Skelton and I were getting along just fine. And that was the whole point of this meeting. Skelton liked me. It was that simple. I got the job. It was worth the spanking I got from my mom.

For at least two glorious seasons, I was a regular on "The Red Skelton Show." Let me tell you, ladies and gentlemen, this was a very big deal in America in 1955 and 1956. Red had TV audiences of 20 million, 30 million.

Of course, to CBS, there was a big ratings difference between 20 million and 30 million. In the early 1960s, his ratings began to go down a little, and then quite a lot, all because his writers didn't really understand who they were writing for. Skelton's producer Cece Barker, had the good sense to call in another head writer, Sherwood Schwartz, a gentle soul but a man who was supremely confident in his own abilities and good judgment. Schwartz had been one of Bob Hope's top writers for years, and he would go on to create one of the most widely syndicated TV show of all time, "Gilligan's Island." And another successful show called "The Brady Bunch."

Barker told Schwartz CBS would give him a pot full of money if he could save the Red Skelton Show. "Not on your life," said Schwartz. "I know Skelton. He hates writers. Nobody can work with him."

"Just look at his last few shows, won't you?" said Barker. "Then see what you think."

Well, Schwartz screened those shows as recorded on what was then known as "a kinescope" — nothing more than a crude 16mm film taken off the TV screen, hardly broadcast quality. And he immediately saw what was wrong. It was Skelton's writers. They were writing stuff for him that was far too verbal — long monologues that might have been okay in the mouth of a Bob Hope, but were totally inappropriate for Skelton.

Skelton was not verbal but visual. He was a mime, a clown, who made people laugh, not at what he said but at what he did. Schwartz told Barker he knew what was wrong, and furthermore, that he knew how to fix it. But he wouldn't sign on with CBS if had to take story meetings with Skelton.

Not meet with the talent? Barker shook his head. He didn't think the network would go for it. But when he told the top people at CBS what Schwartz wanted, they said, "All right, all right." Schwartz was that good. And CBS knew it.

"No story meetings?" Barker said to the CBS executives. "We have to put that in Schwartz's contract."

"Okay. No story meetings."

So that's how Schwartz came to write for Red Skelton. Of course, he had to revamp the entire show, so that the show would play to Skelton's strong suit: pantomime. Now came a new prescription according to Dr. Schwartz: Action, not words. In the monologue at the beginning of a show before Thanksgiving, for example, Skelton might wonder how turkeys were feeling this week, then play the role (without words, naturally) of a turkey trying to avoid the inevitable ax. To save his neck, why, he'd just pretend he was a sick turkey. Who would want to kill (and eat) a sick turkey? And then, for a wildly wacky minute or three, he'd be a sick turkey, lurching all over the stage, limping, going cross-eyed, and letting his wings droop dejectedly.

And then, after the first commercial break, instead of having Skelton do bits and pieces of all of his characters in one show, Schwartz would take just one of them — say, Freddie the Freeloader — and build a story around Freddie's efforts this Thanksgiving to find a good meal. That story, with a beginning, a middle and an end, would fill the rest of the show. No one would see the Mean Widdle Kid that night. And no TV viewer would see Freddie the Freeloader again for at least a month. That way, Schwartz reasoned, audiences wouldn't get tired of Freddie, and be more than happy to see him again when he did make another appearance.

Dr. Schwartz had the right remedy. Skelton ended up that season number one in the ratings. And Schwartz won an Emmy.

From then on, Skelton insisted on having himself credited as one of the show's writers — so he could get an Emmy, too. He did, but Schwartz didn't care. Just as long as he didn't have to take a meeting with Skelton. In fact, in seven years on the Red Skelton Show, Schwartz never had a meeting with Skelton. Anything he had to say to Skelton, he said in the script — or through Cece Barker, the show's producer.

All this is somewhat reminiscent of the comedy writer in the movie, "My Favorite Year" — the writer who only spoke to other writers on the show through an interpreter. In fact, Schwartz saw that movie in shock, because he felt that Norman Steinberg and Dennis Palumbo, the screenwriters of "My Favorite Year," had modeled the Mark Linn-Baker character on none other than Sherwood Schwartz. (Neil Simon, the Broadway playwright, believes that he was the model for that character. In fact, Simon has a current Broadway play, "Laughter on the 23d Floor," that serves as a kind of fond memory of Simon's days as a comedy writer, along with Mel Brooks, and the others on "Your Show of Shows" and "The Sid Caesar Hour" on NBC in the 1950s.)

I will let Schwartz and Simon fight over this themselves. I should point out, however, that in "My Favorite Year," Mark Linn-Baker was the apprentice writer on the show. As such, he was given the unenviable task of trying to keep the guest star (played by Peter O'Toole) sober for a week. The O'Toole character was a former star who could have copyrighted the term "swashbuckling" — but according to the story line, he had now gone the way of all drunks, and was totally dedicated to the task of downing three bottles of vodka a day. As you know, the O'Toole character was modeled on the once-great Errol Flynn.

Schwartz points out that he was the head writer on the Red Skelton Show when Errol Flynn came on that show as one in a long line of stars that included Vincent Price, George Raft, Bobby Rydell, Fabian, Boris Karloff, Jayne Mansfield and Peter Lorre. He says he was the one who had to go meet Flynn himself. He found

Flynn at his Beverly Hills hotel, poolside, where Flynn was sipping on a glass of water with a comely young woman, a very young woman named Beverly Aadland, lying next to him on a chaise lounge. The water, it soon became clear to Schwartz, was really straight vodka.

"This is terrible," Schwartz reported to Cece Barker. "Flynn starts drinking in the morning. He is sloshed all the time. How can he possibly do this show with Red?"

Barker said he wasn't sure. He'd think of something. But Barker came up blank. And, for his part, Schwartz hadn't been able to do a thing with Flynn. He just seemed to float through each day and each night on a sea of vodka. By Tuesday morning, Schwartz was in despair. He knew Flynn would ruin the show that night. But when Schwartz got to the Skelton stage at CBS's Television City, he found that Barker had a gift for Flynn: three bottles of Russian vodka, Stolichnaya, all nicely wrapped in cellophane, tied with a red ribbon.

"What, Cece, are you crazy?" demanded Schwartz.

"Shhh," said Barker. "I watered the vodka. It's only half strength. With luck, Flynn will only be half-sloshed by five p.m."

Wrong. When Flynn arrived — with his vacuous 17-year-old blonde in tow — he was absolutely delighted with Barker's gift, but then proceeded to open one of the bottles forthwith, pour himself a glassful of the stuff, offer a toast to the success of the show, then, after a sip, turn to Barker, and say, "Oh, no, my dear boy. I think you've been sold a bill of goods here. This stuff's been watered down. You'd better go get your money back."

"Gee, Mr. Flynn," said Barker, at a loss for words.

"Never fear, dear boy," said Flynn, opening his briefcase, which wasn't really a briefcase, but a portable bar, containing not one, but three, bottles of his own brand of English vodka. "I just happen to have my own supply here."

Well, somehow, Schwartz got a very hammered Flynn onto the stage — not for the four o'clock rehearsal, but at least for the five p.m. show, to be televised live for an eight p.m. start on the East Coast. The script called for Skelton and Flynn to do a dialogue of sorts, with everything up on cue cards. Only trouble was, that Flynn started reading Skelton's lines.

Now, remember, this is live television, with a live studio audience to boot. But right there in front of God and man and everybody, Skelton and Flynn have a discussion about the cue cards.

"No," says Skelton, "you're reading my lines. Your cue card is over there, in front of you. Mine is here, in front of me."

"Right, dear boy," says Flynn.

So Skelton starts again, gives Flynn his line, and Flynn comes back with Skelton's next line. By now, the studio audience is beginning to break up. The audience thinks this is an extremely funny routine. And you know what? It is funny. Only it's not the routine written by Schwartz and his two writers, Dave O'Brien and Jesse Goldstein.

But, what the heck? What difference did it make? Skelton had just sized up the situation, and, with the skill of a great comedian, did what he could to salvage a show. He did more than salvage it. It was, by all accounts, one of the highlights of the year on the Red Skelton Show. And everyone gave credit to the writers for a very funny skit, for their absolute genius in recognizing that there was only one thing you could do with a lovable old drunk: let him be a lovable old drunk.

Schwartz would go on to become one of the most successful of the Hollywood comedy writers. And, after a five-year-long lawsuit, he was even allowed to share some of the profits from the re-runs. (As television watchers, you all know what re-runs represent — for you. Later, I will tell you what re-runs represent — for actors.)

I liked Schwartz. When he wasn't writing comedy, he was a pretty pleasant guy. Now let me explain that crack. Comedy writers are a dour bunch. I don't know why they, as a group, have to be such sourpusses. I have met few of them who laugh, or who really look like they're only being polite when they do laugh.

Maybe it's because the comedy writers I have known were always under such pressure to produce. It was not uncommon for guys like Bob Hope in his glory days to have a whole stable of writers working more than full time every week in a mostly vain effort to please him. The same was true for all the others: Jack Benny, Fred Allen, Jackie Gleason, Sid Caesar, Milton Berle. You name 'em, they all had stables of writers, and most of those writers were a frustrated lot, because they could never please the star, not completely.

And if lightning should strike, if these writers could please the star they were working for, often enough something else, or someone else, intervened to make the gag unacceptable. The story is told how one of these comics, who shall be nameless here, took a meeting one sunny afternoon with two of his writers — in his New York hotel bedroom suite. The writers were stunned to discover that their man wanted to take this particular meeting during a hiatus in some heavy lovemaking with a young, would-be actress. The meeting took place, let us say, informally, with the two writers perched in chairs at the star's bedside, while the star and the starlet sat up, buck-naked, with a sheet over their loins.

"Uh," said one of the writers. He shifted his buns on the chair. "We have the monologue ready for tonight's broadcast."

"Fine," said the star. "Let's have a look."

They gave him the script, he glanced at it, then handed it over to his well-stacked collaborator.

She read the first page, then seemed to lose interest. She flipped quickly through the rest of the script, then gave it back to her lover. "I don't think it's very well written," she said. "Isn't very funny, either. They can do better than that."

"Okay, guys," said the star. "You heard her. Go back and make it funny."

The writers slipped out of the suite as quickly as they could, and in silence. One of them punched for the down elevator. Neither of them spoke. Finally, as the elevator arrived on their floor, one of them said, "Gee, I don't tell her how to make whoopee."

7

More Skelton

They were a great combination, those three writers: Sherwood Schwartz, cool, kind and professorial. Jesse Goldstein, a former English teacher, a brilliant, literate guy who knew everything about everything. And Dave O'Brien, who was almost illiterate — so illiterate, in fact, that he had turned Schwartz down when Schwartz asked him to come on the show, as a writer.

"I can't even spell," he said.

"Hey," said Schwartz, "we got secretaries who can spell."

"Then why do you want me?"

The reason why Schwartz wanted him was that O'Brien was a comic genius who was very much like Skelton. He even looked like Skelton — big and beefy, but now going bald. O'Brien had been (and still was) an actor. He'd played in cowboy movies in the 1930s and 1940s. He played in many of the cowboy serials I used to watch at The Mystic, which is why he was one of my boyhood

idols, and he was a principal in a long-running series of movie
shorts called "Pete Smith's Specialties." But at this time in his
life, O'Brien reveled in comedy, off-camera as much as on-camera.

Getting on an elevator, he'd tuck in his two middle fingers,
and deliberately get his fingers "caught" in the door. "Owwww,
ooooh," he'd cry — for the benefit of his frightened fellow
passengers in the elevator. Then, when the car stopped and the
door opened, O'Brien would just walk right out as if nothing
happened, leaving the others with their mouths wide open,
astonished.

Other times, right of the blue, O'Brien would crumple and
fall all the way down a flight of stairs at a fancy restaurant,
terrifying the patrons and the management alike. Or he'd pretend
that he was choking on a piece of steak. Or drowning with his face
down in his soup. Anything, just anything for a laugh.

O'Brien was so good, in fact, that Cece Barker often cast him
in some of the Skelton skits. I'll never forget the night that
Skelton, who was supposed to be a patient on a hospital gurney,
went right to sleep on live television. Davey O'Brien was there, at
his side, ad libbing like crazy, and trying his best to rouse the star,
his boss.

When he finally succeeded in awakening Skelton, O'Brien
was startled to hear Skelton asking, "Where am I? Where am I?"

"You're on the Red Skelton Show," said O'Brien. "And —
you're — Red Skelton!"

You'd think that, with the success of the show on CBS,
Skelton would be satisfied. But no. He was a guy who liked to
work at a killing pace, 12 months a year. When summer came,
Skelton was off to do the club circuit: Tahoe, Vegas, Miami
Beach. Schwartz told me Skelton did this, "so he'd have less time
to brood."

Like me, Skelton was a Cancer, a crab who'd often retreat
and feel sorry for himself. Maybe that's why Red and I got along so
well. I think he thought I needed cheering up from time to time
(just as I am sure he did), so he'd often say, "Don't take life so
seriously. You're never going to get out of it alive."

In fact, Red had everything anyone could ever want: fame, fortune, respect from his peers in the business. But he still brooded. Maybe he was brooding about his mother, who'd worked as a char-woman in a vaudeville house when his dad died two months after Skelton was born. Or maybe he was brooding over his son, Richard, who had died at the age of 14. I can remember visiting Red's home and his taking me up to show me Richard's room. It was like a museum, everything left just as it was when Richard was 14, including the boy's model train. Red would stand there, eyes welling up with tears, and take it all in for a moment or two with me at his side. Then we'd move on.

He had one compulsion and one compulsion only, and that was to be the kind of clown that would make people laugh, even people who didn't want to laugh. There's a story told about Red when he was doing vaudeville in Washington, D.C., four shows a day at the Majestic Theater. He was at the top of his game. But in this one particular performance, he spied a guy in the front row who was just sitting there with a straight face. Everybody else was in hysterics. But this guy wouldn't crack a smile. Now that was a challenge to Red. So Red began to play to this guy, almost as if he was the only one in the audience.

But Red didn't have any luck at all. Nothing Red did could make this guy grin. Much less laugh.

After the show was over, Red issued a standard invitation. He said he'd like to thank every member of the audience for their support — personally. That's right. He wanted to come down in front of the stage and shake hands with anyone willing to wait.

So a big line formed, and Red went into his grateful mode, and after he'd chatted with a couple hundred people, he noticed that the guy in the front row who wasn't laughing, old sourpuss, was hanging at the edge of the crowd. Finally, curious, Red beckoned to him, and the guy came over.

"Mr. Skelton," he said, "first of all I want you to know I've never enjoyed anything so much in my life."

Red could only stare at him, wanting to say, "Well, then, why weren't you laughing?"

And then the guy said, "I drove three hundred and fifty miles to see you tonight."

Red raised an eyebrow.

The guy tried to explain. "You see. My little boy. He was very very sick. And we were listening to you on the radio. And my little boy turned to me and said, 'I'll bet Red Skelton is a nice man.' And those were his last words on earth. He died then and there. And this is the first time I've been out since then. So that's why I wanted to come and see you. And maybe talk to you."

Red melted. After that, he could never assume that even the sourpusses in his audience weren't appreciating Red's efforts to make them laugh. "They must like me," he wanted to tell himself, "or they wouldn't have bought a ticket."

But, most of the time, according to Sherwood Schwartz, Red was a classic case of the insecure comic. He was only as good as his last performance. So he always ran scared. They liked him yesterday. But who could say whether they'd like him tomorrow?

To handle this, Red played a little, light psychological game with himself, taking on an alter ego named "Victor Van Bernhard" in his own mind, so that whenever he performed, he would not be Red Skelton, but Victor Van Bernhard. He shared this with me, a little self-mocking strategy he employed, in a kind of self-defense. If the jokes and the pantomimes weren't going well, then it wasn't his fault. It was Victor Van Bernhard's. If they went well, then Red Skelton took all the credit. I wonder how many people got the joke, years later, when they saw the credits roll on a TV show called "Lost In Space." That show was really done by Red's production company. But the credits said it was "A Van Bernhard Production."

Television, of course, was not vaudeville. In vaudeville, Red (usually) knew when he had the audience in his pocket. A few hundred people in a vaudeville audience would be reacting, or not reacting, right in front of him. Once, in San Francisco, however, Red did a whole show without getting one laugh. He was working in front of a big spotlight, so he couldn't see the audience. It was only after the house lights went up that he realized he was working before a house full of Chinese tourists, who were bowing to him and smiling, but not clapping. These folks thought it bad form, apparently, to laugh or clap. But they loved Red's pantomime, which transcended language.

But a TV audience, that was not like vaudeville. A TV audience gave as much instant feedback as that theater full of Chinese tourists in San Francisco. Which is to say, no feedback at all. Red had to take it on faith that 40 million people were watching him, and enjoying his brand of comedy. And I am not sure that he was always enjoying television as much as his audience was, even when those audiences were watching him. Television was a big maw, that not only gobbled up a comedian's material, but could (and in fact did) destroy a comedian's entire shtick.

Red told me about a vaudeville couple that only had one act. He was dressed in tails, she in an evening gown. The curtain would go up and reveal the couple standing toward the back of the stage, at the top of a stairway. They take one elegant step down, then a second step. But it isn't a step at all. It's a chute that carries the couple right down into the orchestra pit. Whoosh! That is their act. Period. They make a living at it, touring the country with it, and then, when they finish the circuit, they start all over again.

Red also told me about the guy whose sole act was to toss a cannonball into the air and catch it. Easy huh? Not quite. He caught the cannonball in the nape of his neck, no hands. And that was all he did. One night, after the first show, and after the applause, he told the stage manager, "I think I'll go down to my dressing room, and die." And he did.

For those of you who never saw Skelton at work, I find it hard to reproduce his comedy, here on the page of a book. They say there are two kinds of comedians: 1) one who opens a funny door, and 2) the other who opens a door funny. Red Skelton was the second kind of comic. Jack Benny's writers could give Benny's material to Skelton and it would bomb. Ditto if they gave Skelton's material to Benny. Comedy's a gift. It belongs to the individual. You can learn as many jokes as you want. But you may not be funny. The twinkle and the tickle is inside.

You may ask how it was for me, playing alongside Skelton. Well, it was great, but I always had to remember that I was the foil and he was the star. I would never never upstage him. I would play along with him, have fun with him, laugh with him, make him feel comfortable. I had no cue cards. Only Skelton had the cue cards. And if we were running too long, I'd get the word from Willy Dahl, the stage manager, who got the word from our director, Seymour Berns, who would tell me something in code — like, "Skip to the ducks." From that, I was supposed to figure out instantly, that Red had skipped ahead, from page 21 in the script, to page 23. And that I was supposed to get right in synch with him.

No question, Skelton was the star. He was making star dollars, and I was a day player, making $350 a week. In this business, day players quickly learn the difference between day players and stars. Which reminds me of my first and only fatal run in with Johnny Carson.

It happened on an early Carson summer stint as a replacement for Jack Benny. In those days, a star like Jack Benny did 39 weeks for the network, and retained ownership of the other 13 weeks, which he could fill in almost any way he pleased. On this particular summer, Benny filled in his summer 13 with Johnny Carson, whom he had liked when he saw him subbing very successfully one night for Red Skelton.

Well, not only did Mr. Benny call in Carson, Benny's writers called me in, too. They said they'd liked me on the Skelton Show. I had worked well with Skelton; they assumed that I'd work well with Carson, too. They wanted to build a kind of TV family around Johnny Carson, much as they'd done for Jack Benny. Jack Benny, you may recall (or maybe you don't recall) had a broadcast family: his wife, Mary Livingstone; his announcer, Don Wilson; his black chauffeur, Rochester; his singer, the boyish Dennis Day; Kitzel, the hot dog man; Monsieur LeBlanc, his violin coach. And so now, Benny's writers wondered how they could fit me into a

Carson family. I suggested that maybe I could play a kind of Oscar Levant character, a sour squelch artist, who sat at a piano, but never played the piano. What he did was deliver funny lines — often poking fun at Carson, as some of the Benny characters poked fun at Jack Benny.

They liked that idea, and wrote me into the first show of the summer season. Some pretty good stuff, good enough to get me some big laughs during the rehearsals. But those laughs were a kiss of death. I'd get a big laugh, then during the break, Johnny Carson would go down to the producer, Ben Brady, and whisper to him. And I'd find that my lines were cut. Further into the rehearsal, I'd get another laugh. Then, during another break, Carson would go down to Brady again and whisper to him, and my lines would be cut again. By the time we went on the air, I was left with one line. I appeared on the first summer show. With one line. I learned that Carson was no Skelton. Skelton was a guy who gave you things. Carson was a guy who took things away.

I wasn't called back then, or ever, by Johnny Carson. I never even got a call from the Tonight Show, even when I might have expected an invite, years later when I was a household face in America. It wasn't as if I was beneath recognition. During my M*A*S*H years, Carson was featuring something called "The Jamie Farr Juicer" on his show. He'd put an orange into the top of a model of my head and squeeze, and orange juice would come out the effigy's nostrils. He was quite willing to do jokes on me, but not with me. Why? I do not know. Maybe he saw my squelch character as something of a threat to his budding career, when no one knew what a Johnny Carson was. But later? He had nothing to fear from me.

8

In the Army

In 1957, I got another chance to appear on the big screen. This time, the fates were working for me. The movie was a winner, a comedy called "No Time for Sergeants," directed for Warner Brothers by Mervyn LeRoy, co-starring Andy Griffith and Nick Adams.

I'd been in Jack Kosslyn's acting class with Nick Adams and a few others who would become famous, like Clint Eastwood, and Irish McCalla, who played Sheena of the Jungle, and Tommy Rall, a dancer who dazzled audiences in "Kiss Me, Kate" and "Seven Brides for Seven Brothers. And now that I was in a feature movie with Nick Adams, one in which I got some good notices, I honestly expected that this picture would launch me into a whole spate of feature parts in feature movies.

In "Sergeants," I had more than a bit part, and I wasn't an idiot, or a mute. I was a real, live, by God second lieutenant in the

U.S. Army Air Corps, Lt. Gardella by name, who was the co-pilot to a character played by Will Hutchins, later to become "Sugarfoot" on ABC Television.

But, just about the time we stopped shooting "Sergeants," wouldn't you know it, a real draft board had the audacity to call me up. Demoted, from a screen lieutenant, to a private in the real Army.

Me, Jameel Farah, budding actor. Yes, they were still drafting young men in 1957. The firefight had stopped in the Korean War, but Uncle Sam needed the cream of America's youth to monitor the uneasy peace, there in Korea, and in Europe, too. The Army was drafting those of us, at least, who didn't find deferment by reason of enrollment in college or regular treatments by a shrink. And so it was that I boxed the stuff in my apartment, stored it with my sister, sold my sole means of transportation, a little Vespa motor scooter, and prepared to enter the U.S. Army.

I went to say goodbye to Red Skelton, backstage at CBS Television City. He had been expecting me. He told me that he'd found a pretty good little actor to take my place. He wouldn't be called Snorkel, 'cause he didn't have my nose. But he had had quite a little bit of experience. His name was Mickey Rooney.

And Red was thoughtful enough to present me with a St. Christopher's medal, solid gold, something I still wear, with the inscription, "God Bless You, Jameel. Your friend, Red Skelton." And then, all of a sudden, I was in the Army — where I really needed (and got) God's blessings.

I took basic training at Ft. Ord in northern California, and there, by chance, I ran into my first steady girlfriend, Janice Falce, who had thrown me over for the drummer in the Woodward High School band. For me! I had given the girl my class ring, I was the student body president, I was in the honor society, and the editor of the paper and the varsity football and basketball manager, and she throws me over for the drummer!

But now, here she was again. We started dating. She sometimes took me to her Italian grandmother's house in Redwood City for dinner, and I felt honored by her grandmother's usual friendly greeting, "Hey, here comes *Grande Naso* and *Grande Culo*." Until I discovered she was saying, "Here comes 'Big Nose' and 'Big Bottom.'" During the six weeks that we palled around, Janice seemed to have one favorite song. It was "If I Were A Bell," from "Guys and Dolls," which had just finished a long run on Broadway. She'd sing:

> *Ask me how do I feel,*
> *Little me with my quiet unbringing.*
> *Well, sir, all I can say is*
> *If I were a gate I'd be swinging.*
> *And if I were a watch I'd start popping my spring*
> *Or if I were a bell, I'd go*
> *Ding, dong, ding, dong, ding.*

When basic was over, the Army — naturally — sent me thousands of miles away from Janice — to a far-off foreign post, the U.S. Army Pictorial Center in Long Island City, Astoria, Queens County, New York, where I helped the Signal Corps make training films. I didn't appear in them or write them or film them or produce them, exactly. What I did, as something called a script supervisor, was hold a clipboard and a pencil while others applied their particular skills. So why was I given this assignment? Hey, this was the Army, a place where nothing ever quite made any sense. All I could ever figure was this: I was an actor. So where else would the Army send an actor? Someplace where they made movies, right?

I am not complaining now, as I did not complain then. One of my friends from the Pasadena Playhouse, Bob Furiga, was called up at the same time I was, and he got assigned to Queens along with me. If I had to be in the Army, it wasn't bad duty. We were close to Broadway — close enough to motor in from Queens in official Army vehicles on a given night, and park right in front of the theaters without being tagged by the New York police. And we could enjoy the New York stage. No more reading the scripts in *Theater Arts*. We could see them performed, live, at the Mark Hellinger or the Martin Beck.

Naturally enough, though my main job was to help make training films, I had to suffer all the indignities of Army life. Like everyone else in the Army, we rose at dawn for reveille and lined up for roll call, even though we had to do so in a parking lot outside our ersatz Army base (actually the old Paramount movie studio, where the first Marx Brothers movies were made back in the 1930s), which now happened to sit right in the middle of some apartment buildings. I imagined that these natives of Queens, the people living in those apartments, didn't much appreciate the bugles at 5:30 in the morning, and my suspicions were confirmed when we turned out one morning to find someone had painted big white letters on a wall overlooking the parking lot: YANKEE GO HOME.

Oh yes. I also had to take my turn at KP. You know, scullery work, pot scrubbing, peeling potatoes, mopping the kitchen. I couldn't help telling Skelton in a note one day: "Dear Red. I like it just fine here in Queens, which I think must be better than standing guard on the 38th Parallel. If I just didn't have so much KP...."

Couple weeks later, I was called in to the commanding officer's headquarters, where the man in charge seemed miffed. "I got this telegram here," said Maj. Cohen. "It says I should take you off KP and it's supposedly signed by Red Skelton." He was miffed, because whoever composed the telegram was attempting to make a joke about the then-current Suez Canal blockade, and the fact that Jameel Farah, an Arab, might be tempted to divert the Army's dishwater to the Arabs.

"Yes, sir?" All I could do was remain noncommittal and polite. I always try to be polite, and when it comes to Army majors, I always try to be extra polite. (Once, on temporary duty at Fort Huachuca, Arizona, I was sitting in a parked jeep, when a major strode by and started screaming at me because I wasn't saluting him. It wasn't that I was ignoring him. I was daydreaming, and I just didn't see him. "Private!" he cried. "Why don't you salute me?" I promptly saluted him. He wheeled on me and stalked off — right into a telephone pole. Knocked himself out. God forgive me, but I couldn't help laughing.

I laughed again, in somewhat similar circumstances, when another major (what is it about majors?) pulled his jeep up right in the midst of a scene we were shooting at Fort Knox, Kentucky. He was quite officious. Just parked his jeep without a word to anyone, stalked over and asked us what we were doing there. Before we had a chance to tell him that we were shooting a training film showing how a tank could crush anything in its path, he soon discovered that for himself. He turned just in time to see a tank rumbling down this little hill, in front of our cameras, squashing his jeep flat, like something in a Road Runner cartoon.)

Anyway, back to Maj. Cohen and the telegram from Skelton. "Well," said Maj. Cohen, waving the telegram. "What's the meaning of this?"

"I don't quite understand, sir?"

"Private," he said, "is this your idea of a joke?" He was still waving the telegram.

I moved closer and asked if I could see the telegram. After I had scanned it, I said, "Well, sir, as you can plainly see, this was sent yesterday from Hollywood, California. I could hardly have sent it myself."

"You want me to believe it was sent by Red Skelton?"

"Well," I said, "Yes."

"You know Red Skelton? How do you know Red Skelton?" I had never told anyone here that I was the one who had done the Cookie and Snorkel shtick on TV. And nobody had ever bothered to ask. But now, since the major was asking....

I showed him my St. Christopher's medal, which I wore right next to my dog tags. I told him I had done some work with Red Skelton. I mentioned Cookie and Snorkel.

"You mean you're Snorkel?" He peered at me. He got up from his desk and leaned over, so he could get a closer look. "Yes," he said." "Yes, by God, you are!" With that, his sternness broke into a big smile.

I smiled back and waited.

"Well, whaddya know about that?" he said leaning back in his chair, and putting the telegram in his upper shirt pocket. "You know, Red Skelton is one of my favorites. Always has been. Good to meet you, Private Snorkel, uh." He looked back at a paper on his desk. "Private Farah." He reached over to shake my hand, then pulled it back.

I alleviated his embarrassment by saluting, which gave him something official to do. He saluted back. He had an afterthought: "Private Farah?"

"Yes, Major?"

"If you ever write a book, don't put me in it."

I laughed. My laugh could have meant, "Okay, Major, I won't." Or, "Major Cohen, you just wait." Well, now you see, Maj. Cohen, wherever you are, I did write a book. And you are in it. But please don't feel bad if I take this opportunity to even things up a bit. After all, you never took me off KP.

Even though I am in the Signal Corps and have a soft job in Queens making training films, I realize that I cannot hope to stay in this assignment forever. So what happens? A huge stroke of luck. After doing some training films at Fort Knox, Kentucky and Fort Huachuca, Arizona, my buddies and I are told that now we should expect an assignment overseas — probably Europe. I promptly bought a book of French phrases, and went around practicing. "*Je m'appelle Jameel*," I'd tell the mess sergeant.

But most of us got sent to the Far East. Most of my buddies — including Bob Furiga — go to Korea. Because I am one lucky sonuvabitch, I draw Japan. Furiga called me lucky, and a few other profane things besides, and demanded to know how come I, Jameel Farah, was so goddam lucky? Who knows? I am just telling stories here. Can I help it if my stories almost always end up with me telling you how lucky I am?

In Japan, I didn't get assigned to Tokyo, which I thought would be the best post I could get, and I was pretty glum about that, until I realized that my assignment was better than anything I could have hoped for in Toyko. I drew Camp Drake at Asakamachi, the Far East headquarters for the Armed Forces Radio Service, an assignment I'd requested — in vain — and only got because I just happened to be standing in the right place in line. As far as I can tell, it was an utter accident that I ended up in

Asaka-machi with Armed Forces Radio. But, at this point, I wasn't asking questions, I was just having fun. Hey, I was still in show business! I was happy.

My first bunk mate in Asaka-machi didn't seem to share my enthusiasm. He growled at me the moment I entered the place where we were to work together. "What? You say you're from Hollywood? You say you're an actor? What credits do you have? I never saw you. I never heard of you."

I sat down across from him. We had adjoining desks. And I sighed. I said, "Look, I don't know who you are or where you're from. But, if our roles were reversed and I told you I'd just gotten off a troop ship where I spent 15 days in steerage to arrive in a country where I cannot even read the street signs and know absolutely nobody — the first thing I'd say would be this: 'Lissen, ya big-nosed sonuvabitch, lemme buy ya a drink.'"

Silence. My bunk mate, who turned out to be Paul Raush, a handsome young man of privilege from Manhattan — New York City, not Manhattan, Kansas — Paul Raush was processing what he'd just heard. Finally, he looked at me and said, "Lissen, ya big-nosed sonuvabitch, lemme buy ya a drink."

Paul Raush and I became best friends. And Camp Drake turned out to be a very nice place, a place to which men and women from the Army, the Navy and the Airforce all drew assignments. As members of Armed Forces Radio, we were treated like very special people. Again, I was one lucky sonuvabitch. We didn't have beds, we had bunks. We didn't do KP. We had house boys. We had dressers for our clothes — and kept dummy footlockers at the foot of our beds that we never used. They were packed with our stuff, according to regulations, so that when we had an inspection, our foot lockers would pass muster. But we never touched the things inside. And since this was the headquarters of Armed Forces Radio in Asia, we had a great sound library, original dramas, classic documentaries, the sounds of the great bands, everything. We even had our own golf course.

I thought I'd probably fight the rest of the Korean War from the comfort of my post at Camp Drake. I only had one close call.

It was on a trip that we made to Seoul, to open up the Armed Forces Television Network in Korea. On our return flight, on a little old two-engine job called a DC-3, we waited at Kimpo Air Base all night to take off. It was literally too cold to take off. Finally, at dawn, they got the engines started and we did become airborne, but it was still freezing — so cold we couldn't even put our feet down on the metal floor of the plane for fear of freezing our toes. Then, over the Sea of Japan, at the point of no return, our motors started sputtering, and they began handing out the parachutes.

"I don't know why we got parachutes," I said to myself. "If we have to bail out, we'd freeze to death in that water." The plane was losing altitude, and one of the flight crew was desperately trying to pump alcohol into the wings. The starters were whining. But the engines wouldn't turn over. It looked like we were going to have to ditch. But we wouldn't think of ditching. We'd rather ride this ship down. Usually, when I tell this story, I pause here. "Well," people demand to know, "what happened?"

I say, "We died."

But seriously, folks, I have to report that, finally, when our plane was almost skimming the waves, the engines both caught hold, and they stayed that way until we were home free.

I determined to make the most of my stay by learning Japanese. You could never tell when Japanese would come in handy. I learned that it would come in handy a lot sooner than I thought.

A Japanese performer named Miki Ayuro used to come out to Asaka-machi to play golf. I made his acquaintance, and I soon learned that he hosted a Japanese quiz show — it might have been called "The Sixty Million Yen," built along the lines of the American quiz show, "The $64,000 Question" — and he urged me to apply as a contestant on the show. "Why not?" he said. "You can use the extra money, and you speak enough Japanese to get along." So I got on the show, an American GI with a big nose who could speak Japanese.

I'll never forget my big night. I had to come into Tokyo all the way from Asaka-machi, an hour's train ride, in the middle of a hurricane that had disrupted transportation and communications all over Japan. I was very lucky to even make it, lucky to get into Tokyo to pick up my date, a young lady from a high-class Japanese family who didn't speak much English. I had just met her a few days before, but I thought taking her with me to a TV quiz show was a nice way to get to know her. By the time I arrived, however, I was a bedraggled mess, totally wet when I knocked at her door, looking like I had come through — well, a hurricane. She was tapping her foot, steaming mad at me. "Why?" she said. "Why you late?" (No more late. First and last date.)

Somehow, we made it to the TV studio in time. I was still somewhat wet and bedraggled, with my pants legs rolled up against the streets that were running like rivers. But I was pleased to learn that I had drawn a subject I liked — classic movies. I figured I had a good chance to win sixty million yen. Indeed, after I sailed through half a dozen preliminary questions, I thought I was in the money. They'd flashed scenes on the screen from a number of famous movies; I'd identified every one of them. This was as easy as collecting unemployment, only a lot more lucrative. I was stoked for the final question.

And then they flashed a scene on the screen that really made me feel stupid. I couldn't identify any of the people up there on the screen. I couldn't figure out what they were doing. I couldn't tell where they were. I didn't have a clue.

"Oh, I'm very sorry," said Miki Ayuro (in Japanese, of course). And since he was my friend, he really was sorry. The studio audience, which was also on my side, cooed their regrets, too. They really wanted this nice big-nosed American who spoke their language to come up with the right answer, which was Eisenstein's "Battleship Potemkin." "Potemkin" is, of course, a classic movie. But it is not the kind of movie I might have seen at the Mystic in Toledo. It is the kind of movie you see if you go to film school, or study film-as-a-science in some avant-garde college course in the humanities. Never having been to film school, much less college, I was flummoxed and *fablunjet*. And, needless to say, yen-less.

I've forgotten what my consolation prize was. Maybe a voucher for dinner-for-two at a nice restaurant in Tokyo. (An unexpected prize turned out to be a lasting friendship with Miki Ayuro, who in later years had occasion to visit us in the U.S. Joy and I have gotten to know him and his wife, Chie, and their son, Goro, and I am still holding a small bank account for them, for their pin money when they are in the U.S.)

But my real consolation prize was connected in no way to the TV show. It came in the form of a cable to my commanding officer at Camp Drake, USAF Maj. Peter O.E. Becker, who called me into his office, waving a telegram in his hand. Another telegram. This time, it was not from Red Skelton, but, it was pretty close to a telegram from Red. It was from the Defense Department. And it informed my CO that Red Skelton, who was going to be touring all the Army bases in Korea, had requested me, Private Jameel Farah, to join him on the tour.

Well, whatever Mr. Skelton wanted, Mr. Skelton was going to get. My superiors quickly detached me from my duties at Camp Drake and sent me off to an airport near Tokyo to greet the great Mr. Skelton — along with a band, and a lot of the brass to help me salute him when he climbed down out of a U.S. Army Air Corps plane, wearing a homburg and sporting a big Perfecto Garcia cigar. (Red never smoked his cigars. He always chewed them. He had a big clipper. After he had sufficiently masticated the end of a Perfecto Garcia, he'd clip off the mangled end and put it in his pocket for later.)

After a night in Tokyo, we were soon off to Korea, on a United Nations plane, just Red Skelton and I, no dancing girls, no orchestra, not even any props. There was a large U.S. Army contingent there to greet us when got off the U.N. plane — including my old friend, Bob Furiga, who by now was absolutely furious with me — again for being so lucky. "Why you...." he said in a stage whisper, as I marched past him with Skelton. "I don't believe this."

You may wonder why Hollywood comedians like Bob Hope and Red Skelton ever wanted to tour U.S. battlefields. I think the

simple answer is that Red Skelton, at least, was a man of great
feeling, the kind of man who had no trouble putting himself in the
other guy's shoes. In this case, he remembered what his own days
in the service had been like, during World War II: It was a dirty,
depressing life, and one that was filled with danger.

Red told me of his own return to Metro-Goldwyn-Mayer,
during World War II, and going in to say hello again to Louis B.
Mayer, the head of the studio, still holding forth in his white
office, the one with the white carpeting that seemed almost a foot
deep.

"Red, Red!" said Mr. Mayer. "Nice to see you. How is Army
life?"

"Mr. Mayer," said Skelton, "I don't like it at all."

"Don't you get fed well?"

"Oh, yes, Mr. Mayer. Three square meals a day."

"You have a roof over your head?"

"Oh, yes, Mr. Mayer. We always have a roof over our head.
Barracks. Tents. Whatever. It never rains on us when we are
sleeping."

"Clothing?"

"Oh, yes, Mr. Mayer. Wool clothing in the winter. Nice
cottons in the summer. We have nice uniforms."

"Well," said the head of MGM, with a cocky flick of his cigar,
"what is it about the Army that you don't like?"

Skelton paused for a moment, and said, "Bullets, Mr. Mayer.
Bullets."

In any event, there we were in Korea (a place where I would
spend eleven years, in fancy, if not in fact, during the M*A*S*H
years). And Red Skelton was, indeed, humble. The only
introduction he would ever let me make was simply this: "Ladies
and gentlemen, one of America's clowns, Red Skelton."

We had the Special Services people radio ahead during each
of our Korean stops, to make sure they had the few props we
needed for our act, which was basically Red doing all of his most
familiar bits: Gertrude and Heathcliffe, Clem Kadiddlehopper, the
Mean Widdle Kid. These acts didn't demand much in the way of

props. But everyone complied with our few needs, and very cheerfully at that. Of all the things our boys missed, comedy (live comedy, from a Red Skelton at that) was right up at the top of the list. Anything anyone in the Army could do for Red Skelton....

No matter where we landed, we had VIP receptions. In Seoul, they met us at the airport with a motorcade, with one staff car for Red and another one for me! Through the city, on the way to our billet, U.S. Army people stopped as we passed by and saluted smartly at this very official-looking line of cars, festooned with little U.S. flags. They weren't sure whom or what they were saluting. But they saluted nonetheless. After some bootlicking months in the military, I couldn't resist rolling down the back window of my car when I saw a group of officers standing at attention and saluting the cars ahead. When my turn came, they saluted me. And I stuck my head out of the limo and showed them my unadorned sleeve. "Private!" I shouted, pointing at my sleeve. I was wondering — and hoping — that maybe that major from Fort Huachuca was among those standing at attention — and saluting me.

The one puzzling thing about our receptions, as we made our way from base to base in Korea: No matter where we landed, they always had a shaker of iced martinis waiting for us. We'd get off a plane and into a command car, and some colonel's aide would be stirring us a martini. And in our billet, we always found a bottle or two of gin.

"Hey, what is this with the booze?" Skelton and I asked ourselves. We weren't teetotalers, but we weren't notable drinkers, either, much less gin drinkers. What was going on? Was the U.S. Army going drunk on us? Only later did we figure it out.

In one of Skelton's skits, he did a pretty good imitation of a drunken liquor salesman who got progressively drunker as he proceeded through his pitch, knocking back shots of gin as he went, and commenting as he did so: "Smoooooth!" The liquor of choice was gin. Brand name: Guzzler's Gin. And the prop we requested was "a gin bottle" — which we intended filling with water for the act. Instead of getting a gin bottle from our Army hosts, we got, instead, a bottle of gin. They had entirely misunderstood. They thought we were knocking off a bottle of gin at every stop. Hence the bottles of gin.

Smooooth!

For our final show in Korea, we appeared in a roaring, makeshift amphitheater not far from the battle zone. The men had been under a great deal of strain, and it was clear to me and Red that everyone in the audience seemed really plowed, so plowed that they gave a big Bronx cheer for the CO, a Maj. Gen. Bush, when he appeared down front before the show. They didn't want to see him, they wanted to see Skelton, and they said so as obscenely as they could. Much to our surprise, he waved amiably at them and sat down.

When Red got the microphone, he acknowledged all the cheers and smiled at all the raucous remarks that sailed forth from the crowd. Hey, these guys were having a good time! Finally, Red told them, "This is the first time I've ever been given a testimonial drunk."

After the show, Red turned to me and gave me his own testimonial. "Look," he said. "This business is tough, Jamie. If you need any help when you get out of the Army, come see me."

I thanked him, but I never thought he really meant it, or that I'd need his help.

This was my dad, Sam, and my mother, Jamelia, in the living room of our home on Michigan Avenue in Toledo. It must have been taken on a Sunday, because my father worked from dawn to late six days a week as a meatcutter.

And this was the firstborn son, me, Jameel Farah. I think that's a teddy bear I'm holding.

I played in "Electra" in my first year at the Pasadena Playhouse — which was also my last year, because I didn't have the $600 I needed for my second year's tuition.

On the set of "Blackboard Jungle" at MGM in a publicity still with Sidney Poitier, Anne Francis, Glenn Ford, Vic Morow and Rafael Campos.

As far as the Loew's Theater in Toledo was concerned, Jameel Farah was the star of "Blackboard Jungle."

(Photo left) This was "Three Violent People" with Charlton Heston and the late Gilbert Roland, a handsome man who did his own stunt scenes. Not me. Too dangerous. If I had my druthers, stunt men would do my love scenes.   (Photo right) Here I am, playing Snorkel to Red's Cookie, with Larry Buster Crabbe on "The Red Skelton Show" on CBS.

When I went in the Army and was sent to Korea, Red Skelton came over to entertain the troops and he asked for me. So I did all the bases with Red, introducing him as "one of America's clowns." Here we are at Kimpo Air Base.

In "The Grearest Story Ever Told," I played one of Jesus' apostles and Max Von Sydow, the great Swedish actor, played Christ. Here we were, dining in the production mess tent on some loaves and fishes.

This is a portrait of me, playing Jude Thaddeus in "The Greatest Story." It was done by another member of the cast, Roddy McDowall, a great actor who also happened to be a great photographer, too.

My bride, Joy Richards, wore white. And the groom wore a beard, because we were still in the middle of shooting "The Greatest Story." Max Von Sydow was among many members of the cast at the wedding, but he made the priest nervous because he said he'd never worked in front of the boss before."

We did a lot of satires on "The Danny Kaye Show" on CBS. Here I am with, from left, Bernie Kopell, Danny Kaye and Dino Natali, doing a takeoff on a then-current movie called "Viva Zapata."

When our firstborn, Jonas, made his entrance into this world, I was on location on the sands of Yuma, doing a Coca Cola commercial with a camel named Clyde.

The M*A*S*H troupe — including costume and makeup people, cameramen, lighting crew, grips, writers, producers, directors and cast members. It was more than a troupe. It was a family — and one of the happiest families in the history of television.

(Photo left) Two special friends, Executive Producer Burt Metcalfe and Harry Morgan, my smokin' buddy. Here we're smoking cigars cadged from an executive dining room at the Fox commissary.   (Photo right) One of the highlights on any week at M*A*S*H: picking out my wardrobe. Loretta Swit said she was jealous because I got to wear all the pretty clothes, while all she wore was her nurse's gown or her olive drabs.

Here's Henry Kissinger, flanked by me and Joy on one side and Sherry Lansing and Barbara Davis on the other. Barbara was the co-host of Denver's annual Carousel Ball, put on to benefit research and treatment of diabetes.

At the Carousel Ball with my boss at Twentieth Century-Fox, Marvin Davis. Not long after he took charge at Fox, Mr. Davis gave big bonuses to all the members of the M*A*S*H cast.

9

Family

I got out of the Army in 1959 and found that Hollywood was pretty much the same Hollywood I had known before, except that everyone was two years older — and many of the actors who had been my friends a few years before were now in the money. Dan Blocker was a fixture on the very popular TV series called "Bonanza." Craig Stevens had his own fine detective series, "Peter Gunn." Clint Eastwood was a big big star on a TV series called "Rawhide." Dennis Weaver won fame in "Gunsmoke." Others had given up and gone back to Iowa, or New York. Many of my actress friends had gotten married to producers.

Years before, I had been madly in love with a gal in one of Jack Kosslyn's acting classes. Her name was Dixie Dixon, if I remember correctly. She changed her name to Tracy Morgan, and she proceeded to get work in the picture business. She was with Kay Kendall in "Les Girls," and she had a part in "Jailhouse Rock" with Elvis Presley. As I said, I was crazy about her. But she had no romantic interest in me. I mean she liked me, and we had a lot of laughs together. But that was all. I wondered whether it was maybe because of the way I looked. I thought of having my nose fixed, and even went so far as to make an appointment with a plastic surgeon in Long Beach.

But when I told Tracy Morgan about it, she took me aside and said with a frown, "You know, Jamie, there are a lot of pretty faces out there. But there are some special people who aren't exactly, uh, pretty, according to Hollywood's standards." I nodded. And I had a little shiver run up my spine. You know how it is, when someone is about to tell you what you know is the truth? In a world — Hollywood — where you get used to a lot of b.s. from practically everyone up and down the line, you find the simple truth is an exciting thing.

"Jamie," she said, "if you get your nose fixed, you'll be like everybody else. If you don't, you'll always be remembered for who you are."

I knew she was right. I would either make it in Hollywood as myself, or I wouldn't make it all. The class soon confirmed that for me. Jack Kosslyn and some of his students at the time, Clint Eastwood, Nick Adams, Tommy Rall, and Irish McCalla moaned when they saw the artistic renderings of my new nose. "Oh, no!" they said, "you can't do that!"

As you know, obviously, I didn't get my nose fixed. My nose was — well it was me, much more than the name I was born with, Jameel Farah. In the first place, Farah wasn't really my family name. My father Sam's real last name was Aboud. Only trouble is that when he landed at Ellis Island and the authorities asked him what his father's name was, he said, "Farah."

"Okay," they said quickly, before he had a chance to tell them Farah was his father's first name, but the immigration people didn't have time, or the inclination, to listen, and our family name has been Farah ever since.

My mother, Jamelia Abodeely, was born in Cedar Rapids, Iowa, then returned with her folks to Lebanon for a visit when she was just a child. On their return trip, she and her mother and father were headed for Southhampton, England's major port, but they stopped in Marseilles to visit a cousin — a cousin I never met, but whom I should thank now, for saving my life before I was born. This cousin insisted my mother and her family stay a little longer in Marseilles, so they canceled their voyage out of Southhampton and made other reservations. Oh yes, the name of the ship they'd been booked on was the Titanic, and this was the Titanic's first — and only — voyage. Which was lucky for them, and needless to say, lucky for me. Thank you, cousin.

Fresh out of the Army, I got the news that my father had died in Phoenix. I wanted to fly to Phoenix, but I was never more broke. And so, though I didn't want to, I went to my old boyhood friend, Andy Fenady, then an executive at Bing Crosby Productions.

"Andy," I said, "My dad died, and I need to borrow —" He cut me off, got out his check book, signed his name, and said, "Fill it in for whatever amount you need." I did not take undue advantage. I filled it in for $50. That was enough to buy me a round trip air ticket to Phoenix.

In Phoenix, my sister, Yvonne, and I consoled each other about dad. The poor man, he died of a stroke, which didn't surprise us. He was only 61, but he had worked too hard, and as long as we could remember, he had smoked two or three packs of Pall Malls a day. He'd light up in the morning, and never use another match. Neither of us could recall that he'd ever taken a vacation. What pleasures he had were few, and not all of those were good for him. He was a pinball addict; whatever free time he did have, he plied his pinball skills at a neighborhood bar, Leo's Grill, where he also played "the numbers" on a regular basis. As far as I know, he never hit a winning number.

The times I remember most with my dad were the occasional Sunday afternoons, when I would take a bus across town to his grocery, then ride back with him and see a movie with him.

My father's death prompted me to think a lot about my childhood. By most standards, I guess you could say I grew up in a poor, mostly immigrant neighborhood, where the Greeks owned the restaurants and the Jews and the Arabs owned the corner grocery stores, and where some of my friends came from families that lived on the fringes of the law. One of my friends, Mike Prephan, used to come to school wearing a brown serge, pinstriped suit — gangster garb, and the kid was still in elementary school! — because he'd been out gambling until after dawn. (Toledo was then an open city, with open gambling.) Like Skelton, Mike had an alter ego named Nick Duquesne. A losing night at the tables wasn't his loss; it was Nick Duquesne's. But the winning sessions were all his. And he had a brother who owned a bar called The Band Box; that brother killed an unruly patron there one night with his fists.

Another friend of mine, Gregory Morris, had a brother, Johnny, who owned a place called Hot Dog Johnny's. One morning, on his way to open up the shop, Johnny encountered his cousin and a companion wheeling a safe down the alley. They made small talk for a few minutes, then Johnny moved on and unlocked his place — only to find that his safe was missing. It was the same safe that he had just watched his own cousin wheeling down the alley.

We had a beer joint in the neighborhood called the J&J Sweet Shoppe, owned by a cousin of Danny Thomas, where they had a continual poker game going in the back, and a resident alcoholic named Dirty Aggie, who was there when they opened the place in the morning, and there when they closed it at night. I don't know. Maybe it had been a speak-easy during Prohibition. I think they had a brawl there every Saturday night. We had to walk by it every Monday morning, and there were usually new blood stains on the sidewalk out in front of the J&J.

In the midst of this sometimes disorderly neighborhood, I was given a stern upbringing by my parents. When I was little, I got my spankings. I never thought of suing my parents for child abuse. They taught me what was right and what was wrong — no gray areas — and they taught me that whatever I wanted out of life, I would have to work for it. They taught me self-reliance.

Nobody ever locked their doors in our neighborhood. And nobody ever stole anything either. Why not? Because we were taught that: 1) it was dishonorable, 2) it was sinful and 3) we'd get the stuffing kicked out of us if we did. The whole neighborhood was "family." We were all human beings, and we all had concern, one for the other.

Those were simple times. And we had simple pleasures. I remember the Sunday dinners at our home, with all the relatives flocking in to enjoy my mom's great Lebanese food. I remember trips to Toledo's big movie houses, the Paramount, Loew's Valentine, the Rivoli, with Mom and my sister, Yvonne.

In 1943, when I was a third-grader, my mother and I took a trip to Mexico City. We had relatives there, and my mom felt she had to get away from the terrible winter we were having in Toledo. So we set off on a long, rough bus trip, in the middle of the war. There were a lot of servicemen on the move, and we ran the risk of getting bumped off our bus at any time.

That actually happened to us in St. Louis, a move that stranded us overnight. With no place to stay and little money, my mom looked in the phone book for a Lebanese name, found one, and called a man who said he could help find us a place to stay overnight. It turned out to be a house of prostitution, but we had a bed and I slept in it, along with some cockroaches, while my mom stood watch through the night. Then we continued on by bus to Mexico.

We were staying at a small hotel room in Mexico City when a volcano was born not far away, at Parícutin. The birth came in the middle of the night, and, although many of the buildings in Mexico City shook and rattled for hours, I slept through the whole thing.

We were there when Mexico entered World War II, and we looked down from our hotel balcony as the flower and the oak of the Mexican army marched past in a parade, led by a lone trumpet and one man with a drum. The men were togged out in World War I uniforms, baggy knickers and leg wrappings wound round and round their calves and they carried old Sgt. York, bolt-action rifles. A burro flanked by two men was pulling an old, two-wheeled cannon and two more soldiers brought up the rear.

A cousin was there with us, looking at the parade from the balcony, and he seemed pretty proud of "*Mexico par la guerra.*" Mexico, he said, was ready to help win the war. Teasing, my mother said, "Boy, is Hitler gonna run when he finds out. It'll be an unconditional surrender." This cousin said the Mexican soldiers were every bit as good as American soldiers. My mom smiled, took a beat, and said, joshingly, "I think one fart from an American soldier could wipe out the entire Mexican army."

My mom's retort was simply a joke, hardly intended to reflect on the Mexican military. But every one in my family knows my mother as a formidable woman. Her brother, Bob Abodeely, tells of the time during World War II when he was in the medical corps at Anzio, pinned down by Nazi fire. He and his buddy (who just happened to be a cousin named Mike Risk) finally decide to high-tail it away from the enemy barrage, and they are running low when Bob drops the sleeveless wool sweater my mom, Jamelia, has knitted for him. He stops and turns back.

"Are you crazy?" says Risk. "If you go back for that sweater, the Nazis will kill you."

"If I don't go back for that sweater," he said, "my sister will kill me." He went back and got the sweater.

Tales of family are still among my strongest and fondest memories. I remember great neighborhood parties at John Haddad's house in Toledo. I remember how we made a game out of Saturday housecleaning, the whole family, together, dividing up the chores — that was a kind of pleasure I look back on with great fondness. It wasn't that I enjoyed the work so much — dusting the table legs when I was very small, or later, cleansing Toledo's soot off our wallpaper with a kind of green, doughy stuff from Sears that soon became black with all the dirt.

I recall the time I held a Halloween jack-o'-lantern too close to my face one night. Before I knew it, my hair was on fire and I streaked through the house like a human torch, yelling my head off and scaring my Aunt Jenny into a faint, and my mother screaming at me to stop running, and my sister Yvonne lassoing me in the kitchen with a dish towel and putting me out. I thank God she did the right thing.

When I got back from Phoenix after my father's death, I Americanized my name to Jamie Farr. It wasn't so difficult. My few movie credits, as Jameel Farah, would open no doors. Career-wise, I was starting all over anyway. But it was a far less radical move than it would have been to change my nose.

Some may have thought that I changed my name from Farah, which emphasized my Arab-Lebanese background, because I was working in a town where most of the casting directors, and producers, were Jews. Not true.

In fact, if it weren't for the Jewish people who have helped me, I never would have worked in Hollywood. Pandro Berman, who hired me on my first picture, was Jewish. Howard Morris, whom you will soon meet in these pages, was Jewish. He gave me work on two pictures, and was always looking to feed me more. Gene Reynolds and Larry Gelbart and Burt Metcalfe, to whom I owe so much for hiring me, and keeping me, on M*A*S*H, are Jewish. Aaron Spelling, who brought me on to "The Love Boat" in 1982, is Jewish. All my agents were Jewish. Jews have been grand to me.

Jews? They keep begetting. They beget one another. They beget talent. They nurture it; they profit from it. They get stronger. I find American Jews to be one of the most fascinating people in the world. They're so much into the arts. And they never stop giving to the community. At Hillcrest Country Club in West LA, a largely Jewish club, they don't look at a potential member's wealth. It doesn't matter to the membership committee how much he has; it's how much he gives to the community. That's what counts. They look at someone's benefactions. Then they decide to let him in the club. Or not let him in, as the case may be.

So, nose and all, and with a new name, I was back in Hollywood, a veteran with some previous film and TV experience, hoping I could get work. I wasn't at all sure what I wanted to do.

Act? Yes. Comedy? Yes, if I could get work in comedy. Movies? That was my medium of choice. TV? TV would be okay, too. I wasn't fussy. I'd take what I could get.

I tried everything. But I got very little. I remember doing a play called "The Last Mile" for Jack Kosslyn at a little theater on Cole Street in Hollywood called The Mercury Stage. It was a good play, written by John Wexley, good enough to showcase the talent years earlier of a New Yorker named Spencer Tracy, and bring him to Hollywood. But you knew Spencer Tracy, and you know I was no Spencer Tracy. "The Last Mile" was almost my last mile in Hollywood. It didn't bring me any work, and I was close to despair.

10

Skelton Again

I turned to Skelton again, telling him I was ready to give up. With my dad gone, I had to support my mom. He said, "I told you in Korea to come to me if you need help. Well, now you need help. So let me help."

I hesitated. I didn't feel very comfortable asking him for help. He said, "Look we're doctors of comedy." Nice of him to say "we." He persisted. "You can't give up. You're too good."

He told me he was going to sign me up to a personal contract. Lord knows why he wanted to do this. Sure, he liked me. But I think there was something more behind his move. Maybe he was thinking of how people tended to help people in this business.

He told me a story. It was about a young man of 10 or 11, who was selling newspapers on a corner in Vincennes, Indiana, when a nicely dressed gentleman came up to him to buy a paper. He said, "Whaddya going to do with all the money you earn today, Sonny?"

The paperboy replied, "When I sell all these papers, I'm going down to the Roxy and get a ticket to see Ed Wynn, the perfect fool, who's playing here in Vincennes just this one night."

"Well, Sonny," said the well-dressed stranger, "I'm just gonna buy all your papers, so you can go see Ed Wynn. And, after the show, you give this card to the manager of the Roxy, Charlie Greenburg."

Which the boy did. He saw Ed Wynn on stage, in his perfect fool makeup and costume. And then he went to see the manager of the Roxy, who looked at the card, then proceeded to take him backstage to meet Ed Wynn. Well, when the boy gets into the dressing room, Wynn is still removing his makeup in front of the mirror. Wynn sees him and nods, and motions for the boy to sit down, which he does. And then, as the makeup comes off, the little boy's eyes get wider and wider. Is it? Yes it is. Ed Wynn is none other than the nice man who bought all of his papers that day.

Now Ed Wynn was, indeed, one of the greatest comics of his day, a giant who was already on radio, on KRKD, Pittsburgh, almost before there was a radio business. And the paper boy in Vincennes? That was Red Skelton.

Red told me that was a fateful meeting. He told Wynn he wanted to go on the stage, and Wynn encouraged him, but advised him to "stick to comedy." Soon, Red joined a medicine show. Then he was playing one-nighters with a stock company, working minstrel shows and third-rate carnivals in tank towns, and breaking in as an apprentice clown with the Hagenbeck and Wallace circus. The rest was history.

He may have started out in life as a poor newsboy in Vincennes, Indiana, but at age 14, he was already earning what would amount to $200 a week in today's dollars, singing blackface in all the tank towns of the Midwest. During the Great Depression of the early 1930s, when you could buy a steak dinner with all the trimmings for one dollar, he was making $750 a week in Chicago vaudeville. By the mid-1930s, he was a star on network radio. And by 1938, he had already appeared in some 40 movies. He had what you might call "a sufficiency of this world's goods." He owned a 27-room mansion in Bel Air, a home in Palm Springs, two Rolls Royces, 22,000 first editions, a priceless collection of ivory and porcelain miniatures, Cruikshank prints, a hundred toy cannons, ten television sets, a thousand funny hats, dozens of music boxes, and countless antique, carved walking sticks. A writer for *The Saturday Evening Post* reported in 1962 that Skelton was "a multi-billionnaire."

Now Red was telling me he wanted me to appear on his TV show, again. He also wanted me to travel with him on his national club circuit. He had bookings at the Chez Paree in Chicago, the Hotel Fontainebleau in Miami Beach, at Harrah's Tahoe, at the Sands Hotel in Las Vegas.

Red Skelton reached into his pocket, and dug out two $100 bills. "Here," he said. "Take this until we can work out the details. Go ahead. Take it. You need it."

I needed it. I took the two bills.

For more than a year, I stayed close to Red Skelton. I remember going into the Chez Paree, which was owned by a couple of characters named Don Joe and Dingy, who were reputedly part of "the mob." Their club was probably an old speak-easy because they took us in an elevator, and stopped halfway between floors to show us where machine guns had been stashed in little vaults between the floors.

In their leisure hours, the owners of this club used to watch "The Untouchables" on TV. "Naw," they'd say, "that ain't the way it happened." But they were fascinated by, well, by themselves, as reflected and filtered and romanticized by Hollywood.

They called me "Mr. Lucky," because, although I had dates while I was there, I never scored. The girl would always get sick, get drunk, pass out, or all of a sudden, have to go visit her sick grandmother. "Hey," they'd say, "here's Mr. Lucky."

One night, I am sitting at the Chez having dinner, and this gorgeous girl walks up to me and says, "Are you Mr. Lucky?"

I was startled, but not too startled to say, "Umm, as a matter of fact, I am."

She says, "Well, I'm Miss Lucky. We ought to get together." And we did.

Later, before I could take her out again, I found out she was the girlfriend of one of the big mobsters in Chicago. He is now deceased. Otherwise, I would not be telling this story. Needless to say, that was the one and only time I went out with her. Which is why I remained Mr. Lucky.

These characters, Don Joe and Dingy, had a kind of worldly wisdom. Once, I asked Dingy, "What is a great nightclub act?"

So Dingy takes me by the arm. "C'mere, kid," he says, and he opens a window looking out on to the parking lot. "Whaddya see out there?"

I say, "A parking lot."

He says, "Whaddya see in the parking lot?"

"A lot of cars."

"That," he says, "is a great nightclub act."

At the Fontainebleau in Miami Beach, where Red Skelton was booked for several weeks doing two shows a night in their main room, I will never forget the chill I felt when I saw Joe Fischetti, also a mobster, tear into Louis Prima. Prima was a jazz trumpeter, with his own band. Keely Smith, his consort, was one of America's great singers. No one called him Joe Fischetti. He was Joe Fish and he ran the Fontainebleau.

Mr. Fish had a demure wife, and a little boy he doted on. When we went to dinner together, Red and I and Mr. and Mrs. Joe Fish and their little Fish, he'd tell his boy, "Eat your artichoke. It'll make you nice and healthy."

Now Joe Fish was having union problems when we were there. One night, someone had thrown stink bombs into the Fontainebleau, and so we got an invitation to meet Joe Fish for a little drink. I don't know why we're going to have a drink with Joe Fish. You didn't need to have a reason. If Joe Fish said, "Let's have a little drink," you had a drink with Joe Fish.

So, there being quite a stink in the lobby of the Fontainbleu, we meet Joe Fish at the Deauville Hotel, across the street from the Fontainebleau — Tony Bennett, Georgia and Red Skelton, and I, and Louis Prima, and Keely Smith.

Now we're sitting there, talking, and Louis Prima gets out of line. I don't know what he says, but it is something Joe Fish doesn't like in a big way. Joe tells him, in a very threatening manner, "Shut up!" But Louis Prima doesn't shut up. He keeps interrupting Joe Fish. And then, I cannot believe this, right in public, in front of everybody, Joe Fish slaps Louis Prima right across the face, and glares at him with eyes that are — well, I'll tell you how his eyes are. If he looks at you like that and you have a gun and he doesn't, you lay your gun down and you put your hands up. You know you are in serious trouble. Then Joe Fish takes his thumb and he runs it across Louis Prima's throat, from ear to ear, and he says, "Remember what happened to Joe E."

And then everybody shut up, while Joe Fish continued to talk and we all continued to listen — because we all knew what happened to Joe E.

Joe E. Lewis, you must understand, had been a saloon singer, and a pretty good one. Until he had his throat cut from ear to ear by persons unknown, only everybody knows it was the mob. He didn't die. But he had a sore throat for the rest of his life. After that, raspy Joe E. Lewis made his living as a nightclub comic. The whole story was retold in a movie called "The Joker Is Wild" — with Frank Sinatra playing the part of Joe E. Lewis.

There was another character down there in Florida who hung out with Joe Fish. His name was Johnny Formosa, and he was a bald, huggable, little Italian grandfather-type. Once, when we were in the Chicago area, he sent a car for Mr. and Mrs. Skelton and me, to come visit his waterside home in Gary, Indiana, where he was reputed to have some influence over the steel mills. The home was rather grand, as I recall, and the living room was scattered with pictures of Frank Sinatra and Dean Martin and Tony Bennett. Johnny Formosa was a delightful host, and he took a liking to me. When we were leaving, he gave me his card and said, "Look, kid, any time you ever need anything, you just let me know."

I took his card with great appreciation. But I burned it. I never wanted to be in that much need.

Knowing I was a little nervous around him, Formosa liked to tease me. One night, we were headed out for dinner, Johnny said, "Hey, kid, come on, you're riding with me and Vito. We'll put ya in the St. Louis seat." I didn't know what the St. Louis seat was supposed to mean, but it scared the hell out of me.

Traveling with Skelton naturally gave me the kind of education I couldn't get at the Pasadena Playhouse. It also gave me a closer, more personal look at "one of America's clowns." That's what Skelton always called himself — not a comedian, but a clown. In that identity as a clown, I think, lay whatever security he enjoyed. His mentor, Ed Wynn, would later flee from that security — turn in his perfect fool suit to do serious drama. In the 1950s, for instance, Wynn did "Requiem for a Heavyweight" on "Playhouse 90." But the experience darn near killed him. The pressure of the part — which Skelton had encouraged him to undertake — drove him to drink, and he had a long battle with John Barleycorn for the rest of his life.

Red himself never left comedy. Comedy was his warm blanket. And, Lord knows, not even comedy was secure. Though he was on prime time with almost half the nation tuning him in every Tuesday night for 17 years, Skelton always ran scared, always dreading that, in his next show, he would absolutely bomb out, get fired and never be seen anywhere again. Every show was like his first. Often enough, he would throw up out of nervousness just before we went on live national TV. Then he would come out and charm everyone.

Furthermore, like a guy who is not quite sure he has arrived, Red Skelton watched his nickels, dimes and quarters. The Sands Hotel won his everlasting regard when officials there set up a dollar slot machine in his suite and rigged it so it would pay off far more often than the machines in the casino. He hardly needed the extra silver dollars. One day, at his home in Bel Air, he brought out a suitcase full of money, $100 bills. We counted them out on his bed, and the amount came to exactly $100,000. Then he put the money back in the case and asked me to deposit the $100,000 for him in his local bank. I took the keys to one of his Rolls

Royces, and the suitcase, and headed for the door and waved. "This isn't so long, Red, it's good-bye." He knew I was only kidding.

Skelton was a set of walking contradictions. He never even came close to a vulgarity on his TV show or in his club acts. But every Tuesday afternoon, during the rehearsal of his network show, he'd pile on heaps of the dirtiest, raunchiest, jokes you ever heard. Secretaries and staff from all over Television City would flock into this rehearsal, which got to be known as "The Dirty Hour." Skelton had another puzzling quirk. When we were traveling, he'd borrow a movie projector from the hotel management, set it up in his hotel suite and open a window, then treat the citizens of downtown Pittsburgh, for example, to projections of pornographic movies on the brick wall of an adjacent building, cackling with delight as he did so.

But that was just one side of Skelton. On the other, more serious, hand, Red would end up painting poignant oil portraits of clowns — generally sad clowns — that demonstrated a dignity and a depth quite at odds with the mischievous little kid manning the projector in Pittsburgh.

When we played the Fontainebleau Hotel in Miami, Red soon lost his desire to play tricks like this. I think he was as scared by the Joe Fishes of this world as much as I was. Maybe that's why he always carried $10,000 worth of traveler's checks. He was always ready, he said, to get out of the country.

Finally, after a year with Red, I realized that I would have to go out and try to make it on my own — again. I'd spent two years in the Army, and then a year with Red. Three years with no credits, I knew I had to get out and bust out. Red understood that. When he said goodbye, he gave me a mustard seed, encased in a plastic bubble with a clip on it, so it could be worn on a silver chain, a trinket that he told me had been blessed by the pope. Perhaps you know Jesus' Parable of the Mustard Seed. The seed is small, one of the smallest of the seeds, but it grows into one of the world's largest bushes. As I understand the parable, if you have the faith, even if it is as small as a mustard seed, it will grow, and nothing is impossible unto you. I still have the mustard seed that Red gave me. My faith keeps growing. And nothing is impossible for me.

As I was leaving Red — it would be for the last time — I said, "How can I ever thank you?"

He avoided sentimentality. He said, "Jamie, if you're walking down one side of the street, and I'm walking down the other side of the street, cross the street — and say hello."

Rather than go see Danny Thomas (formerly Amos Jacobs, but born Muzyad Yakhoob, from my old Lebanese neighborhood in Toledo) I paid a call on his nephew, Ron Jacobs, a producer for Danny Thomas Enterprises, working out of the Desilu-Cahuenga Studios, where they shot "I Love Lucy," "The Dick Van Dyke Show," "The Andy Griffith Show."

Ronny Jacobs and I were friends in Toledo. He had gone to Waite High School, I to Woodward. He played basketball. I was the manager of our basketball team. I can remember one spring night in our senior year, sitting on a swing with Ronny in Riverside Park, talking to each other about our dreams. He was going off to UCLA, I to the Pasadena Playhouse. He was hoping to get a job in production with his uncle. I was hoping to launch an acting career. And both our hopes became a reality.

At the moment, he told me he had nothing for me. But he'd talk to Carl Reiner. Carl was executive producer of the Dick Van Dyke Show. Maybe he'd have something.

Not a very satisfying meeting with Ron Jacobs. But it was lunchtime. I decided to stop by the commissary. I didn't have two nickels in my pocket, so I wasn't going there to have lunch. But maybe I'd run into someone, pick up something from somebody. Maybe a writer or a producer would see me, and cast me in something.

I stopped at the table of a comedy producer who knew me, kidding around, having fun. For some now-unremembered reason, I did "a take." "A take" is one of the standard tricks in any actor's repertoire. A single take is a kind of look, a look of surprise. A double take is, first, no surprise, then a look of surprise. A triple take is a little more of the same.

Well, Joey Bishop, the comedian who was then a member of Frank Sinatra's Rat Pack and riding high, is sitting at a nearby table with a group of his staff from "The Joey Bishop Show" and a night club comic named Lenny Kent. They gang up on me. Out of the blue, and for no reason at all, Bishop says to me, "You call that a take? This is a take! You got that? This is not a take. This is a take." Lenny Kent chimes in with his own instruction on how to do a take. Both of these characters add to this lesson a good many necessary and unnecessary gestures, and sidelong looks at the people sitting at my friend's table to see how they are coming across.

I knew how they were coming across to me. They were coming across as jerks. But I said nothing. I wasn't going to get into an argument with Joey Bishop. He had friends in high places.

I had come there hoping to make a good impression. Instead, I struck out with Ron Jacobs and I was humiliated in front of everyone in the cafeteria. I stumbled out of there, tears welling up within me. What now?

But surprise! Carl Reiner did have something for me. He gave me an ongoing role in a very popular sitcom called "The Dick Van Dyke Show." I played the part of a delivery boy named Snappy Service, and though I wasn't under contract, I made $350 a week, and I got to work for five weeks. It wasn't much, but what there was of it was good for me. And I was grateful for the credit because this show was widely considered to be the best sitcom of the 1960s. *TV Guide* called it "Carl Reiner's masterwork of the sitcom art...perhaps the first great sitcom ensemble. Everybody in the cast got laughs."

11

George Stevens

In the fall of 1960, the word was out around town. One of Hollywood's most fabled and ambitious directors, George Stevens, an Academy Award-winning director, was going to produce and direct the most expensive movie of all time — the life of Christ as related in a recent best-selling book by Fulton Oursler called, *The Greatest Story Ever Told.*

The movie was budgeted at $12 million, a new Hollywood record at the time. Getting cast in this picture, therefore, was the ultimate status symbol in Hollywood.

There were 117 speaking roles. It was only fitting that John Wayne, the biggest box office draw of the day, was the first to sign on. After Wayne's move, the rush was on. Every actor and actress in Hollywood was willing to kill for a role in it, no matter how small, because that would mean that they were a part of Hollywood's elite.

In addition to John Wayne, who played the Roman centurion presiding over Christ's crucifixion, Stevens signed on Charlton Heston as John the Baptist, Claude Raines as King Herod, and Jose Ferrer as Herod Antipas (the son of Herod). Dorothy McGuire played the Blessed Virgin Mary, Robert Loggia was her husband, Joseph. Michael Tolan played Lazarus, Ina Balin was Martha of Bethany, and Janet Margolin her sister, the other Mary. Joanna Dunham played Mary Magdalene. I wanted a part in this movie for two reasons. One, because if my Semitic face wasn't right for this movie, what movie was I ever going to be right for? And two, because if I was part of this prestigious cast, it would mean that no casting director could ever say, "Jamie Who?"

But, at this point in my story, I was exactly that: "Jamie Who?"

I had never hit a lower point in my career — something I was reminded of every time I stepped into my dank basement apartment, or into my moldy shower stall. I had no work, and the benefits had run out on my unemployment insurance. What to do? I considered praying to St. Jude.

Once, when he needed a big favor, Danny Thomas had prayed to St. Jude, the patron saint of hopeless causes, and one of Jesus' apostles. When the favor was granted, Danny was grateful enough to found a hospital in his honor, and to keep raising funds for it until his dying day. Well, I said, if St. Jude could help Danny, he could help me.

By this time in my life, I had met and fallen in love with Joy Richards, a beautiful, salty gal from Danville, Illinois. In fact, it was my friend, Mitch DeWood, who had introduced me to Joy, then trying to break in as a model in LA. I was immediately attracted to her, but she, in turn, introduced me to her roommate — whom I dated a couple of times, but only so that I could stay in touch with Joy. She ended up feeling some of the chemistry I felt, and soon she and I were dating. After that, I never dated anyone else.

Now I was living in a small apartment across the street from her apartment, and I had taken to driving her to work every day in midtown LA, where she was working as a bookkeeper for Fairchild Camera. Near her office, there was a Catholic church that just happened to have a side altar dedicated to St. Jude — with a statue of the saint above and some votive candles below. I noted that a little old lady was praying there, on her knees. When she was finished, she lit another candle, and dropped a coin in a little box (as I found out later) to pay for the cost of the candle.

So I started doing likewise. I'd drop Joy off in the morning, stop by the church, say a prayer to St. Jude, light a candle, drop a quarter in the box, and be on my way. Before I picked Joy up at 5 p.m., I made another call on St. Jude. What did I pray for? A part in "The Greatest Story Ever Told" — any speaking part. I did so very faithfully — every weekday for a couple of weeks.

Of course, I didn't just pray. I also tried to make something happen myself. I took a meeting with Stevens' casting director. And I got some film from "The Rebel" on TV, produced by my old friend from Toledo, Andy Fenady, and starring my old friend, Nick Adams, who played the lead, Johnny Yuma. Nick had a print of a segment I'd appeared in, a serious role, a guy named Pooch. (I never got roles for Tom, Dick or Harry; always guys named Itchy and Pooch.) And Nick let me borrow this film, so I could deliver it to George Stevens over at the Selznick Studios in Culver City. Then I went back and lit my afternoon candle to St. Jude.

Not many days later, I got a call from my agent, Meyer Mishkin, who said, "Jamie, you better go pick up your film. They saw it. But they're going to pass on you at 'The Greatest Story.'"

Well, I went and retrieved the film, but I was crushed, and that afternoon, before it was time to pick up Joy, I paid another call on St. Jude. Now I'm steaming. I'm not lighting a candle, I'm not leaving any money. I'm telling him off. "Hey, Jude," I said. "What am I supposed to do? If I can't be in this movie, and I can't — what am I supposed to do? Be a shoe salesman? A dishwasher? What am I supposed to do with my life? Here's a movie I am absolutely right for. I'm praying to you. It's not like I'm asking for something that's totally impossible." I stomped out of the church, picked up Joy and took her home.

But when I get into my musty apartment the phone is ringing. It's Meyer Mishkin, my agent. He said, "I don't know what happened. You're in the movie. You're playing one of the apostles."

"You're kidding."

Mishkin said, "I knew I didn't have to check with you. I took the deal. It's four hundred and fifty a week. With a twenty-six week guarantee. Go on down there and get your wardrobe test. You're playing the apostle Nathaniel Bartholomew."

"All right!" I shouted. And I couldn't wait to tell Joy. "I'm in 'The Greatest Story Ever Told.' A twenty-six week guarantee." I knew others would be getting more money. I didn't care.

The next morning, after dropping Joy off to work, I drove out to the studio. I took a makeup test and a wardrobe test, and I was thrilled to see Charlton Heston and Roddy McDowall (who would play the apostle, Matthew), talking about how they had just got back from Rome. I kept my mouth shut. I had just got back from the poorhouse.

That afternoon, I stopped in again to speak with St. Jude, to say I was sorry for blowing up at him the day before, and to thank him for this big boost to my career. But that evening, I got another call from Meyer Mishkin. "Jamie, I heard back from George Stevens' office. They've changed their minds again."

I couldn't speak. My heart dropped. What kind of miracle of prayer was this? A one day miracle?

"No. No," he said. "They still want you. Same deal. Four fifty a week, twenty-six guarantee. Only they don't want you to play Nathaniel. They want you for another one of the apostles, St. Thaddeus."

This time, I had to phone Mitch DeWood, my friend from Toledo who had introduced me to Joy. When I told him what had happened, he was stunned. "Jamie," he said, "Do you know who you're playing?"

I said, "Thaddeus."

"Did you know," he said, "that Thaddeus's full name is Jude Thaddeus? You're playing the saint you were praying to."

Of course, Stevens needed 12 apostles. David McCallum got the best of those roles — as Judas. But Robert Blake would play Simon the Zealot. So I'd be with Bobby Blake again. Shelley Winters was the woman who was cured when she touched the robe of Jesus, and Ed Wynn won the role of the man who was born blind. Van Heflin played a character named Bar Amand. Telly Savalas played Pontius Pilate, and Pilate's wife, Claudia, was none other than Angela Lansbury.

Stevens gave a lot of thought to the part of Jesus. He wanted someone with stature. But he didn't want an actor whose previous work had already given him a fixed identity in the minds of moviegoers. He solved his problem by going to Sweden and hiring Max Von Sydow, a terrific actor who had won international critical acclaim for work done under the direction of the distinguished director, Ingmar Bergman — movies such as "The Virgin Spring," "The Magician," and "The Seventh Seal."

You didn't see those pictures? Well, if you didn't, it's because they were "art films," not big box office in the U.S. That's just what Stevens wanted — a great actor who, up to now, hadn't been seen by most American moviegoers, someone to play the perfect Jesus, because this would be a movie for the ages, something that would be valid "fifty years from now," a movie that exhibitors would want to show, proudly, on the 2,000th anniversary of Christmas in the year 2000.

It was only fitting, then, for Stevens to think big. He hired one of Hollywood's best writers, James Lee Barrett, to turn the Oursler book into a screenplay, and he hired one of America's greatest contemporary poets, Carl Sandburg, as a story consultant. He would assemble 30 Academy Award winners — behind and in front of the camera — to work on the picture. Stevens even sent prop people out to search for 22 camels — and four white donkeys, one for Jesus to ride on, and three backups, in case anything happened to donkey number one. The search for the white donkeys took six months.

The Hollywood trade papers were impressed. So, in fact, was another Hollywood mogul, Samuel Bronston of MGM, who decided to flatter Stevens with the sincerest flattery of all: imitation. All of a sudden one day, he decided to compete with a biblical epic of his own. On September 1, 1961, Bronston and MGM announced MGM was already launched on something called "King of Kings."

Over at Twentieth Century-Fox, Spyros Skouras was shocked. And Twentieth's board of directors became apoplectic. They quickly voted to dump Stevens, even though they were already a million dollars out of pocket, and they canceled his epic, "The Greatest Story Ever Told."

But that wasn't the end. Stevens fought back and got his own financing from United Artists. Even better news to those of us in the industry: Stevens wouldn't go to the Holy Land, or anywhere else abroad, to film the picture. Too many producers had run off to make movies in Europe; the unions were complaining they were losing thousands of jobs; the industry was dying. To save the industry. Stevens announced he would build a replica of the Temple of Jerusalem on a sound stage in Culver City, and take most of the cast on location to southern Utah.

Stevens had another, special reason for going to Utah. He thought the real, historic locations in what is now the State of Israel were too old and too worn. Stevens wanted to re-create the land of Israel as he imagined it was 2,000 years ago. Its mountains, as they existed in 1962, weren't tall enough for Stevens' imagination, its deserts not grand enough, its sky not blue enough. If Stevens was going to film "The Greatest Story Ever Told," then he had to find the Greatest Scenery Ever Seen.

That just happened to be the spectacular, rose-colored cliffs of the Glen Canyon Basin, just above what is now Glen Canyon Dam, sites that are now mostly covered by the waters of Lake Powell. "Yes," said Stevens, "I know these locations are bigger than life. But this is a big story." Hollywood likes to redo history, but only if it can improve on history. Furthermore, Stevens wanted to go to Utah in the wintertime. In that part of Utah, it would have been more comfortable to shoot in the summer or the spring. But Stevens liked the winter's light. At this latitude, the sun's winter rays come in at a slant. This makes for the kind of dramatic lighting that makes the cliffs more dramatic, and the actors' jaws more jutting.

And so, that's where this big cast and crew were finally headed in the late fall of 1962 — to Utah. I still remember the day we met at the airport in LA for our charter flight to Utah. Keenan Wynn was there to give a send-off to his dad, old Ed Wynn, still a trouper at 76. One of Keenan's close childhood friends, Van Heflin, was there, and Keenan presented Ed with a portable radio, as a kind of going away present. I thought, "How nice! We're going off on location. There may be no TV there, so at least Ed can listen to the radio."

The radio was really a portable bar, equipped with two bottles of Jim Beam and four silver shot glasses, something I learned the afternoon that Ed Wynn and Van Heflin invited me to join them on location. It was time, Ed said, looking at his watch, "for a meeting." Turned out they were the sole members of an exclusive club, with no officers and no dues, dedicated to one purpose: making sure that the ancient institution of the cocktail hour did not go the way of the dodo bird.

"Promise," Wynn whispered to me as he poured himself a shot. He was only half-kidding when he added, "Please don't tell anyone. It's liable to hurt my career."

Fat chance. You may remember Ed Wynn most for his clownish role in "Mary Poppins," floating up to any ceiling that was available every time he started laughing. But at the peak of his career, about a thousand years before, when he was the toast of vaudeville, he lived in a mansion in Connecticut that was so large that the U.S. government later took it over as the original site of the Coast Guard Academy. Ed had called it Wynngate. (And there are those in the U.S. Coast Guard who still call it that.)

The trouble with Wynngate, it was too big, plenty of room for Ed's many relatives, who would always seem to show up whenever they expected Ed Wynn to have a big payday. The relatives would actually line up and so they could get a handout from their rich benefactor, Ed Wynn.

On location, we weren't living in any mansions. We lived in Quonset huts on a windy mesa, two actors to a hut, and we had a big circus tent for our meals. But I kept getting invited to exclusive "meetings" in the hut of Ed Wynn and Van Heflin, and Ed became a kind of mentor for me. The most important piece of advice he ever game me was this: Save your money. "Every one in this business," he said, "ought to have go to hell money."

What kind of money was that? "The kind of money," he said, "that allows you to turn down the lousy parts that producers are going to force on you when they know you're starving. You need some savings — so you can turn down those lousy parts. I call it 'go to hell money.'" Ed had another rule: "Never live in a house where you can't visit every room in it every day."

I have tried to follow Ed Wynn's advice. I have tried to save my money. Now, I am not rich. But I am very well off. I have made some good investments. We have a very fine home with a big swimming pool in a posh suburb northwest of Los Angeles. But it is not a Wynngate, not so big that I cannot visit (and enjoy) every room in it, every day.

Naturally enough, Ed Wynn told some stories. One of the best involved Thomas Alva Edison, the inventor of the electric light bulb, and motion pictures and a thousand other marvelous things. He was probably the greatest inventor of all time. Well, Ed Wynn was doing his vaudeville act one night at a theater in New Jersey, not far from Edison's headquarters, in a performance that was highlighted by Ed's driving all over the stage on a bicycle that was also a piano. After the show, the stage manager comes to his dressing room and tells him that Thomas Edison has asked to come backstage.

"He wants to see me?" said Ed Wynn. "My, my. What an honor. Thomas Edison."

So Edison is ushered back, and he greets Wynn, and they chat for awhile. Finally, Edison says, "Mr. Wynn, do you mind if I ask you a personal question?"

"No. No. Of course not. Anything at all."

"Well, tell me, Mr. Wynn, about that bicycle-piano of yours."

"Yes. Yes."

"Mr. Wynn," said Edison. "Where in the world do you come up with all these crazy inventions?"

Then there was the time that Ed Wynn played a dramatic role in "The Diary of Anne Frank," the part of the weak, frightened uncle. Our own George Stevens was the director. Now, one scene called for Wynn to do a piece of business in the attic hideaway, then cross and disappear into the bathroom and wait, while the cameras continued to roll in the main room.

Which Wynn did. After a few moments, however, Stevens thought he heard Wynn laughing in the john. Yes, as the laughter increased in volume, he realized that that's exactly what it was: Wynn roaring with laughter in the adjacent bathroom. Stevens cried, "Cut!" and stalked over to investigate. "Ed, Ed! Are you all right?"

Wiping the tears from his eyes, Wynn explained. "I'm sorry, Mr. Stevens. As I was sitting here in the john, I suddenly remembered something my father once said to me long ago, when I told him I wanted to go into show business. He warned me, 'If you go into show business, some day you'll end up in the toilet.' And so I did. Here I am. I ended up in the toilet."

But, of course, he was only kidding. In "Anne Frank," Ed Wynn was at the top of his game. He even won an Oscar nomination for that role. And that was not the end of Ed Wynn. He died in 1966, at the age of 80, with a long, distinguished string of credits, working till the very end of his life. I should be so lucky. (And the way things have been going for me, recently, it looks like I will be. Lucky. And working.)

Our first day's shooting on "The Greatest Story" began shortly before dawn on October 29, right on the banks of the Colorado, at a spot where Mormon wagons had forded the river a hundred years before. The Mormons called it "Crossing of the Fathers." For us, it would serve as the River Jordan, site of Jesus's baptism by Charlton Heston — uh, I mean by John the Baptist. And practically everyone in the cast was there, including members of the watchful Roman legion, under the leadership of my friend,

Michael Ansara. We had an immense crowd — a cast of some 2,500 including the extras, some of whom were locals from northern Arizona — including 600 members of the Navajo Tribe.

The script also called for a certain number of the lame, the halt and the blind; they were on hand, too; casting directors imported them from Flagstaff, Arizona, with the help of that city's welfare department. And so were members of the entire Inbal Dance Company, 30 exotically beautiful young Yemenites imported from Israel. Stevens said they would help give his picture "a certain look, not Arab, not quite Oriental, not at all like European Jews or Christians." He was right. They appeared as extras in a number of scenes — intense, awesome, dark, delicate-featured young women who had the look of ancients.

Only trouble was, after we'd all assembled at dawn, Stevens decided he couldn't shoot. He was the kind of director who likes to capture tableaus with his camera. Now, the composition of the picture he wanted was fine, but the light was just a little off. So we didn't shoot anything that first morning on the river. Instead, Stevens had Van Sydow lead the cast in a recital of the Lord's Prayer — while he poured a jar of water, a gift from the State of Israel, from the River Jordan into the Colorado. Then we were driven back to our little Quonset city, finished for the day. We would try again at dawn tomorrow.

Next day, we are all up again at three a.m., getting on our costumes and our makeup (many of us needed to don fake beards) and then making the motor-trek to the Colorado, a one-hour trip in the pre-dawn darkness.

Second day, same story. The light isn't right for Stevens. Too many clouds.

Third day, same story.

Finally, on the fourth day, things are looking good. I check the clouds and I say to Bobby Blake, "I think we're going to do it, today."

"Jamie," he says, "we'd better. I am gettin' tired a this."

So now, we're all ready, waiting for the moment of truth, for the rising of the sun. Things are looking good. Everyone's in place

124

and poised. Stevens is way up on a nearby hill, ready to give the cry for action. Just then, however, Michael Ansara, playing a Roman centurion, in full armor, is overcome by a call of nature. Somehow, he has come down with a bad case of diarrhea, on this morning, of all mornings, and he has to go.

Like a shot, Ansara's off his horse, and headed for some nearby tules near the river, shedding his armor along the way. Blake and I, and a few others who are aware of Ansara's problem this morning, watch, fascinated by his progress. Eventually, we assume, he does his number in the tules, then starts hopping back toward his horse, picking up his clothes and his armor as fast as he can, and getting back into costume along the trail from the tules to his horse. It is like a movie run in reverse. Miraculously, he makes it back to his horse, just as Stevens is calling, "Action!"

All I could say was, "Good thing Michael made it. Otherwise, Stevens — or Blake — might have killed him."

In "Greatest Story," Telly Savalas played Pontius Pilate, and for that role, he shaved his head — for the first time. That gave Telly a certain look, one that he thought would set him apart from a hundred other tough guys from New York vying in Hollywood for the same kind of parts. It did set him apart, and he kept the shaved head to his dying day, and as Kojak fans all know, didn't do that badly as a baldy.

If there was one human emotion that Stevens wanted to portray in this film, it was awe. And so, Stevens tried to do whatever he could to impress the members of this movie company with the seriousness and the majesty of the project. One way he did that: He overshot every scene. He shot every scene from every angle. (That strategy had saved one of his movies, "Shane." Harold Kress, Stevens' film editor, found the movie didn't cut — until he presented the whole story from the point of view of the little boy, which was only possible because Stevens had shot the kind of camera angles that lent themselves to this kind of editing. Thanks to Kress' artistry, the audience becomes the little boy, which was one reason why that little boy, played by Brandon de Wilde, won an Oscar nomination for the role.)

We spent three whole weeks shooting the baptism of Jesus. At this rate, someone said we'd be there for three years. That didn't seem to bother Stevens. He took another three weeks to shoot the raising of Lazarus. (They had to heat the freezing rocks we walked on with blowtorches.) And a whole week to re-create the first Palm Sunday, Jesus's triumphal ride into Jerusalem.

Many members of the cast caught colds, or the flu. In the frigid November waters of the Colorado, Charlton Heston almost had a heart attack, and so did many of the multitudes who waded in with him for their baptism-by-immersion. On film, the expressions on their faces may have come across as ecstasy. In fact, it was sheer, unadulterated fear — fear that they'd die of hypothermia. As it was, many of them emerged from the river wet and shaking, and some of them were only half-conscious. Afterward, Heston told Stevens, "If the Jordan had been as cold as the Colorado, Christianity would never have gotten off the ground."

In the Lazarus sequence, Ina Balin and Janet Margolin, the actresses who played the sisters of Lazarus, had to go barefoot and run down the steep steps of a desert mausoleum for six separate takes — in temperatures of 20 degrees. They, too, could have died. But it's only a slight exaggeration to say that Stevens would have liked that. Anything to impress the cast that, in this epic, no sacrifice was too important.

One morning, in the original Palm Sunday sequence, Stevens was out there revving up the extras like some USC cheerleader. "All right, you people. Get ready now for the arrival of Jesus. This is Jesus Christ, the Lord! Show awe! Show awe! 'Hosanna,' you people in the front here, joy! This is the Lord. Wave, wave, wave. Run, folks, run! Hallelujah! Hallelujah!"

John Wayne saved us from taking ourselves too seriously in this enterprise. Wayne, as I told you, was playing the part of the Roman centurion who presided over the crucifixion of Jesus. After Jesus had expired on the Cross and the sky grew dark, he, the centurion, was supposed to say, "Truly, this was the Son of God." And he did so, on camera. Sounded pretty good to us. He was a tough guy, a soldier, and to us bystanders, he sounded, in his rough-hewn way, convinced, and convincing, enough.

But Director Stevens wasn't satisfied. He stepped in, took Wayne aside, and told him, "Look, Duke, this is Jesus Christ, the Lord. Let's shoot it again. And put a little awe in it."

"Awe?" he said. "Gotcha, Pappy." He nodded, and strode back to his spot in the scene and adjusted the sword at his hip. Stevens set up the camera again. This would be an extreme close-up. Stevens wanted to capture all that Wayne was capable of. Many of us crowded around to witness this. Maybe we'd learn something from the great John Wayne. Finally, Stevens said, "Okay, cameras, roll 'em and — action!"

Wayne said, "Aw, truly, this man was the Son of God."

There was, then, just a short moment of silence, then an astounded look on the face of George Stevens, then an unholy roar of laughter — from Stevens, as he cried, "Cut! Cut!" Once we saw that Stevens was laughing, that meant that we had permission to laugh, too. (We kinda needed that, since it was Stevens himself Wayne was putting on.) And then we were slapping each other on the back and saying, "Aw, truly! Aw, truly!" and almost rolling on the ground with laughter. Through all this uproar, Duke Wayne just stood there, with a mischievous, manly grin on his face, obviously pleased that he'd figured out a way to score one on our esteemed director.

After that, Director Stevens went a little softer on the awe-ful instructions. By then, of course, we didn't need too many more reminders about the historic importance — you might say the awesomeness — of what we were doing.

12

Married

We wanted to believe that making this picture might help make some of us better Christians. Bobby Blake was my roommate in our little Quonset village, and I remember one freezing night, a couple of Navajos — some of our extras — came knocking at our door asking if we had some blankets for them to borrow. Bobby and I looked at each other, surprised to find Navajos unprepared for the cold night way out here in the middle of nowhere. And we turned them away empty.

Then we looked at each other again, and Bobby said, "Hey, we just finished shooting a scene today where we were in rapture over Christ's sermon on the mount. 'Blessed are the poor, for they shall see God?' Well, these are God's poor comin' here and asking us for help. And we turn them away?" We each grabbed a blanket and ran out looking for the guys. We found them and lent them the blankets, and told them to bring them back the next day. We never saw the guys again. But Bobby said he had a biblical verse that was appropriate for the occasion. "No good deed goes unpunished."

"Oh, yeah," I said skeptically. "Where does that come from, the Old Testament or the New Testament?"

With a dead pan look, he said, "My testament."

For the rest of the shoot, we lived the Gospel according to Robert Blake. At times, Bobby was another St. Francis of Assisi. Other times, he was King Herod.

One day, we found a lost calf wandering not far from our digs. Bobby wrestled it into our stretchout, which is an elongated limousine. (Yes, we had stretchouts to take us to various shooting locations near our camp — near, but too far away to walk to — and, according to our Guild contract, we had to be driven not in trucks or buses, but in cars.) And we got the driver to drive us around, looking for the wrangler in that area. When we couldn't find him, Bobby insisted we take the calf into our billet for the night. We woke the next morning to find cow dung all over the place, but we pulled and shoved the calf back into the stretchout and went out looking for the wrangler again. We finally found him. He took the calf, but he kept his distance from us, because we were dung all over. "Crazy actors," he muttered. "Crazy stinking actors."

Well, we took showers, so we didn't stink for long. But we were still crazy — stir-crazy. (The only one who wasn't going stir crazy was Sal Mineo, who had been hired on at the last minute. He got a special contract, one that stipulated that he was to receive $10,000 a day for every day he had to work after a certain date. I think it might have been February 15. As it turned out, at our pace, Sal worked many, many $10,000 days.)

We all had to stick around, but there was so little work to do. Some of us learned the art of photography from Roddy McDowall. We learned charcoal sketching from Robert Loggia. One day, somebody came up with a dozen copies of a famous play by Reginald Rose, "Twelve Angry Men," and we twelve apostles spent our off hours reading (that is, rehearsing) "Twelve Angry

Men." Our own beards began to grow, which lessened our time in makeup every morning. But so did our frustrations. Bobby Blake and I got into an argument one night about absolutely nothing, and it reached such a pitch that he said, "Well, hell, I'll just move outta here."

I told him that'd be just fine with me.

"Yeah?"

"Yeah!" (It was that kind of argument. We were like two second-graders.)

"Okay, then," he said. He gathered his things, looked up at the mural he'd been painting on one of our paneled walls, stalked out, and came back with a carpenter's saw. He proceeded to start sawing off the mural.

I said, "What are you doing?"

"What's it look like?"

I shrugged. Obviously, he intended taking a piece of the wall with him, but then, realizing he couldn't do it without tearing down the whole Quonset, he went and got a wet towel and tried removing the mural by rubbing it out. Finally, he was finished. When he staggered back toward the door, I couldn't resist a crack of my own. "It's a good thing," I said, "that Michelangelo didn't get into an argument with Pope Julius II. Otherwise, the Sistine Chapel wouldn't have the ceiling it has today."

He didn't think that was funny.

We went home, most of us to Los Angeles, for Christmas. Thanks to our jobs on "The Greatest Story," I suspect Christmas had a little more meaning for many of us in the cast. I know it had a lot of extra meaning to me, because it was on Christmas Eve that Joy and I determined to set a date for our wedding. We'd been seeing each other for more than a year now, and we wanted to get married and have children, but we hadn't been able to make a move, because we thought we couldn't afford it. But now, now that I was working steady, and stood to win more movie parts as a result of my appearance in this prestigious picture, we could at last afford to tie the knot. We set the date for our wedding, February 14, 1963.

131

After Christmas, when I got back to Utah, I told the cast to save Valentine's Day. Didn't know exactly where. But they'd all be invited.

I phoned Joy and told her the good news and the bad news. The good news was that practically everybody in the cast was going to be at our nuptials. Even Max Von Sydow and Dorothy McGuire said they'd come. "Uh huh," she said. "He's Jesus? And she's Mary?" Joy paused.

I got ready for one of her zingers. She has always had a pocketful of wry. "That's good," she said. "If we run out of wine, I guess we know what to do, huh?" For a wild moment or two, we both laughed over the fantasy — Dorothy McGuire going up to Max Von Sydow and saying, "They have no wine." And Max telling the waiters to fill up seven large urns with water.

The bad news was that Father James Meena was not going to be there to marry us. Father James had long been the pastor at St. Nicholas, but he was being transferred back to Pittsburgh. Joy had liked Father James, probably because he had been a real buddy to me and to my roommate Adeeb Sadd. (And maybe because he always used to compliment her on her legs. "Joy," he would say, "You got ring-a-ding legs.")

Father James was a big man, looked a little like Ernest Borgnine, and he was full of life. He'd often come over to the apartment I shared with Adeeb, lugging a bottle of retsina, to shoot the breeze, talk about music and film, or even go to the movies with us, where his seat of choice was in the balcony — so he could toss popcorn on the folks below.

What a story he had. He wasn't born with the name James. He was baptized Camille. His brother's name was James, and it was James who was aiming for the priesthood, according to a long family tradition. Both his father and his grandfather were priests, and James would be, too. That was okay with Camille. He had always wanted to be a songwriter and a musician.

But, come World War II, both of the boys were drafted and sent to Europe, where James was killed in action. Camille was wounded in another battle, so badly that he needed radical plastic surgery. The doctors had no picture of Camille, but they found a picture in his wallet of his brother James, and used that, as a kind of blueprint for their reconstruction of Camille's face. Now when Camille recovered and found his brother is dead, he stepped in, for the historic traditions of his family, took his brother's name, opted for the priesthood, and renounced his dream of a career in music.

The rest of the story, as Broadcaster Paul Harvey would say (and he'd love to tell this one, I think), is this. Camille (who took the name James) eventually married, became a priest and had a son. And that son grew up to fulfill his father's failed dream. He became a conductor of the Toledo Symphony.

After our Christmas break in LA. we were back on location again in Utah, just in time the catch the biggest snowstorm they'd had there in years. It snowed for two days, and then, when it stopped snowing, we were surrounded with two-and-three-foot drifts. Stevens announced that we'd just have to wait till the snow melted.

We were then shooting some footage near what was supposed to be the Wall of Jerusalem. The script certainly didn't call for snow. But the entire cast and crew rose up as one man and told Stevens, "Nothing doing. We will just sweep all this snow out of the area." And we did. For one whole weekend, we used brooms, we used shovels, we used rolled up Levis, we used anything we could to move that snow off 22 acres of land, to start shooting again on Monday morning. Ed Wynn added to the general hilarity when he found a little red wagon and a child's pail and shovel. While we were all slaving at a furious pace to sweep up the snow and haul it off the set, Ed Wynn was using his little shovel to fill his little red wagon, and then cart it off, and add his load to our mountain of snow.

It was a tremendous effort, something we all felt very proud of, something we felt we had to do for Mr. Stevens, who had by now convinced us that we were engaged in a holy enterprise that we'd never forget for the rest of our lives. And on the more practical side, we'd saved jobs for 1,500 extras, mostly locals, including 600 Navajos. We celebrated our goodness at dinner that night, toasting ourselves, and telling one another what a marvelous bunch we were.

I had mixed feelings about all this. If we cleaned up the snow, we could stay in Utah and keep shooting the picture. But if we kept shooting, then Joy and I would have to postpone our wedding — and lose a big deposit on our reception besides. Well, I enjoyed the dinner and tried to repress my mixed feelings.

But Bob Blake repressed nothing. He was bored here on location. He wanted to go back to LA. And he didn't see why Joy and I should have to postpone our wedding. We could easily come back to Utah later in the spring, when the weather was nicer. So Blake goes out and does a little rain dance in the moonlight after dinner, fully intending to bring down another snowfall. Of course, we all laughed.

You know what? We woke up the next morning to find another big blanket of snow had fallen on Moab and its environs. Now we knew Blake had called down the power of the rain gods. What astounded us was that they listened to him. I remember going out and seeing the snow about 7 a.m. and, blinking my eyes, stumbling over to Blake's Quonset hut and shaking him awake and telling him, "We had another big snow. Your dance did it."

He grunted. Before he covered his head with his blanket, so he could get some more shut eye, I think I heard him say, "Well, dat's da name a dat tune."

The storm wasn't expected to stop for days. Because of the snow, we struck camp and returned to Los Angeles, and when Stevens announced that we'd probably shoot interiors in Culver City for the rest of January and February, Joy and I firmed up the date and place for our wedding. We'd been aiming for February 14, Valentine's Day, but had to settle for February 16 — at St. Nicholas Antiochian Orthodox Church on West Third Street in Los Angeles.

We had the full Orthodox nuptial mass, conducted by our pastor, Father Paul Romley. He wore no beard. But the groom, and so many of his friends from the film, we were all wearing beards, and when we entered the church, many of my fellow apostles tried to pick themselves out of a painting of The Last Supper that hung over the entrance to the altar.

I tried to wink at everyone in the church as I stood at the altar with Father Romley, waiting for the bride to make her appearance in the back of the church. Our families were there — lots of my family, and my mom, now living in the Phoenix area, and Joy's family, the Richards, from Danville, Illinois. So was practically the entire cast of "The Greatest Story," including Max Von Sydow, who played Jesus, and Dorothy McGuire, his mother Mary.

I was quite comfortable being the leading man for a change. But Father Romley was nervous. I leaned over and whispered, "What's the matter, Father?"

He looked over at Max and said, "I never worked in front of the boss before."

My old acting coach, Jack Kosslyn, remembers that the ceremony was very long. But everybody had a great time at the reception afterward. Great music. Great food. And, since we'd ordered quite enough champagne, Max Von Sydow didn't have to tell the waiters to fill up seven large urns with water.

For our honeymoon, Joy and I went to Las Vegas. We picked Las Vegas because Mitch DeWood worked there, and Charlie Najjarr, another friend of mine, and his wife Tootsie, said, "We're going to Vegas. You should go to Las Vegas, too." The implication was that Mitch and Charlie would get us a special deal at a posh hotel on the Strip. Instead, the Najjarrs have a big view-suite at the Stardust. Joy and I have the cheapest room in the place. I guess Charlie was just trying to save us money.

Joy had never been to Vegas before, so, while I was talking to Mitch in the lobby of the Flamingo (where he was now entertainment director), I encourage Joy to go off and try her luck at the nickel slot machines. Soon, Mitch and I hear this scream from Joy. "I won!" she cries. "I won." Well, everyone in the casino thinks she's broken the bank, or at least hit a million dollar jackpot.

"What did you win, honey?" I asked when she came running up.

"Two cherries," she said, holding out her big winnings, three nickels.

A highlight of our wedding trip came when Joy and I went to a show at the Sands, where Danny Thomas was doing a show. He introduced us to the audience, and told the people we'd only been married a day. "Yes," I shouted out, "and they said it wouldn't last!"

My heart has always been touched on my trips to Las Vegas when I see all these prosperous business executives out on the town, showing such a good time to their beautiful daughters. Our first night out on the town, I had a young woman on my arm who looked like she could have been my daughter. Except that she was my beautiful, witty wife. Her witty presence made me bold, I guess, when quite by accident, we ran across Joey Bishop right outside the Flamingo. He was just coming out of the hotel with not one, but two young women, one on each arm. He took one look at me, still bearded for my role as the Apostle Thaddeus, also known as Jude, and said in an unnecessarily loud voice, "Hey, I tried your cough drops, and they stink."

Okay, so I did look like one of the Smith Brothers. But now that I had a couple of nickels to rub together and beautiful Joy on my arm, I felt I didn't have to take this. I said, my voice equally loud, "Well, you shouldn't shove 'em up your ass before you put 'em in your mouth."

Bishop was speechless. How could he top that spontaneous piece of vulgarity? He couldn't. I cannot remember any other time when I let myself go to that extent. Oh, I have gotten angry. But I have invariably been able to swallow my anger and get on with life. But I will not be anybody's patsy, either.

I recall one time, when I was traveling with Red Skelton, Red and Georgia were invited to a midwinter party at Hugh Hefner's mansion on Chicago's North Side. Red and Georgia went out and bought me a beautiful raglan overcoat made by Aquascutum, especially for this party. So I go off to the Playboy mansion, feeling like quite the man of the world. I am even smoking my new pipe, with a special blend of Dunhill pipe tobacco that I got from Jack

Paar, the longtime host of The Tonight Show on NBC, before Carson.

I was enjoying myself, schmoozing with all the nice people there, including some quite stunning girls. Then Hugh Hefner and a friend come out to the main room, each of them with a girl on each arm. The six of them proceed to sit together on a large sofa right across from the armchair where I am sitting.

"Mr. Hefner," I said. "What kind of pipe tobacco do you smoke?" (I knew he was a big pipe smoker.)

He mumbled something.

I said, "Well, I'm smoking a special Dunhill blend that Jack Paar —"

One of Hefner's ladies broke in. "What's with the kid with the pipe tobacco?"

"Oh," Hefner said. "Maybe he thinks I can do something for him." He said it sneeringly, loudly, just as if I wasn't there.

I said, "Excuse me, Mr. Hefner, I've gone 25 years of my life without you. I can go the rest of the way without you, too." And I got right up and retrieved my coat and left the mansion.

But that wasn't the end of it with me and Hefner. There was a showgirl at the Chez Paree whom I used to take to the movies. And Hefner had met her along the way and made some moves on her, moves that she always rejected. One night, at the Hotel Maryland, a favorite after-hours place in Chicago, I'm at a table, not far from where this girl and Hefner are having an argument. Finally, she stands and gives Hef a piece of her mind. "And furthermore," she says to him (with a surreptitious wink at me), "I don't like your pipe tobacco." It was her way of helping me score one on Hefner.

Back on location with "The Greatest Story," we finished shooting near Moab, Utah, on a site our craftsmen and designers made stand for the city of Bethlehem. Then we moved up to Nevada's Pyramid Lake, which became our Sea of Capernaum. Then we began to put all the finishing touches on the picture on a back lot in Culver City.

Until we had a wrap, I had to keep my beard. By now, I had a marvelous, luxurious growth. I looked like a real patriarch. Or, in the malls of San Fernando Valley, where we lived, like some kind of religious nut. Or a hippie.

One weekend, Joy and I made a quick trip to Phoenix to visit my mom. And then, on our return, we had to detour through Yuma. Just west of Yuma, about dusk, we were driving along when we noted what looked like a beacon ahead of us. Only, finally, we figured it wasn't a beacon, because it was moving. Sometimes it would zigzag, then it would hover. It was dome-shaped and it had red and white lights on it. Then it zipped across the sky and hovered right next to us, maybe ten yards away from us. It was now about 50 feet above the ground, kicking up sand below it, and it stayed with us, just off to our left, for five miles or so.

We didn't know whether to stop, or keep on driving. Joy wanted to stop. She believed in extra-terrestrials and I think she wanted to chat. I believed in them, too, but I wasn't as curious as Joy. I wanted to keep on driving. And then, all of a sudden, this thing zipped off, soundlessly, like a streak of light. I don't know. Maybe they were more frightened of me, wearing the beard of a patriarch (or a religious nut or a hippie) than I was of them.

This was on a Sunday night. By the time we got home, we were very tired and sleepy, and we went to bed, Joy in her baby doll pajamas and her hair in giant rollers, and I in a new pair of pj's, called "Great Zeus." They were horrible pajamas, pumpkin colored, with great flashes of lightning printed all over them, a gift from my sister, Yvonne. (I didn't have my hair, or my beard, in rollers.)

Well, we'd just gotten to sleep (despite the deafening sound of my pajamas) and the phone rang. Now who would be calling at this hour? We decided not to answer it, and soon we were back asleep again. Suddenly, I woke up. I wasn't sure what time it was, but there was a commotion outside, so I put on the light.

Then I heard a voice, maybe amplified on some kind of bullhorn, saying, "There's a light on inside."

I said to Joy, "There's something goin' on in our neighborhood tonight."

Then I heard a voice saying, "There's somebody in the house."

I said to Joy, "There's somebody in the house."

Then I peeked out the front window. Another voice said, "There's somebody looking out the front window."

I said to Joy, "There's somebody looking out the front window."

Joy joined me and peeked out the window, too.

"There's two of them in there," said the first voice.

I said to Joy, "They say there's two of them in there. Wait a minute!" I did one of my best double takes. "It's the cops, Joy, and they're talking about us."

"All right," said one of the policemen, "come on out of there with your hands up."

So I opened the door, and we stepped out on to the porch — Joy in her baby doll pajamas and I in my Great Zeus pajamas, with my long hair looking like a busted mattress and my beard down to here. We had our hands up.

I said, "Don't shoot officer. I'm an actor."

The police looked puzzled. What did being an actor have to do with anything? "What are you doing here?" said one of the cops.

"Officer," I said, "we live here. This is our house."

"Well, why didn't you answer your phone?"

I said, "Gosh, officer, we didn't know it was against the law."

We made Page One of the National Enquirer as sighters of a UFO, and we are listed on a special registry in Washington, D.C., of those who have seen UFOs. But none of our friends would believe our UFO story. Naturally, after awhile, Joy and I stopped telling it. But we know it happened.

On July 31, 1963, we had some one million feet of film in the can. By now, Stevens had spent not $12 million, but $16 million. It was, surely then, the most costly picture of all time.

Naturally enough, it would take Stevens and his film editors many months to cut and shape all of this footage. In fact, the final cut of the film — which ran some 245 minutes — didn't have its world premiere in Washington, D.C., until mid-February 1965, almost a year and a half after we finished shooting.

And some premiere it was. President Lyndon Johnson and the entire U.S. Cabinet were there. So were most of the members of the U.S. Supreme Court, U.S. Ambassador Angier Biddle Duke, Sen. Jacob Javits, Sen. Robert F. Kennedy, and Mayor Robert Wagner of New York.

The *Boston Globe* added to the importance of the occasion by telling its readers that this was "probably the most outstanding production to come out of the United States during the history of the motion pictures." The *New York Daily News* gave the movie four stars. A group of Southern California ministers agreed, after a screening at the Cinerama Dome in Hollywood, that this was "the finest religious picture ever filmed." The syndicated columnist, Jim Bishop, a Catholic, said this was "the most important movie I've ever seen." Even the Vatican daily, *L'Osservatore Romano*, chimed in with its blessings on the effort.

But the film was "too pious" for Bosley Crowther of *The New York Times*. The world "had already had enough," he said, of these great big biblical films. *The New Yorker* called it "a disaster." *Time's* reviewer said this was "as literal and conventional as religious calendar art." Indeed, he said, Stevens had borrowed the table setting at the Last Supper from Leonardo da Vinci's famous painting. Shana Alexander wrote in LIFE magazine that she was looking for a flash of irreverence during "four hours of reverent pomp." All she felt was boredom, and irritation, because the picture had "no point of view."

Only time will tell whether George Stevens' hopes will come true for his film — that it will help humankind commemorate the 2,000th anniversary of Christmas in the year 2000. In that year, George Stevens may not be around to see whether the film was "something for the ages" or not, or whether it will "play" in 2000. It certainly was a movie that stuck very close to the literal words that we've all read in Matthew, Mark, Luke and John. So, in that sense, it may last as long as the Gospels.

My guess: that someone in 2000 will try to re-tell the story of Jesus on film in a way that will excite people in the year 2000, as I suspect Jesus himself did with the story he told, almost 2,000 years ago. Anyway, I'd like to see someone try it.

140

13

Danny Kaye

Because of the mixed reviews for "The Greatest Story Ever Told" — and a disappointing box office — I found that my role in "The Greatest Story" wasn't exactly my yellow brick road to fame and fortune in Hollywood. Huge, new offers did not pour into my agent's office. Writers did not inundate me with new scripts. Producers weren't waking me up in the middle of the night. (No cops, either, 'cause we started answering our phone.)

One of Jesus' modern apostles did call, however. It was Father Ellwood Kieser, a happy giant of a priest who was then producing a weekly TV series called "Insight." I'll never forget how happy I was, during this period, just to get one week's work on Father Kieser's "Insight."

Father Kieser belongs to the Paulists, a kind of missionary order, but their mission is in the U.S., one that tries to reach the vast number of unchurched people who have lost any sense of

141

meaning, people who have no religion, or did, once, but lost it. To reach these kinds of people, the Rev. Pat Robertson, the Rev. Robert Schuller and others have turned to preaching on television. Father Kieser found ways of preaching without really seeming to preach.

Father Kieser did that by producing first-rate, dramatic stories on videotape, stories designed to get people thinking (and feeling) about ultimate values that were common to all religions. The values Father Kieser was pushing, through his stories, were "love, freedom and being human." And he invited all of Hollywood — writers, directors, producers and actors and actresses — to come and help him do these stories. Then he gave the videotapes away to any station in the world agreeing to play them on a regular basis every week.

Father Bud (as we learned to call him) never made a pitch on the air for money. His "Insight" wasn't about money. Consequently, he asked all the professionals who helped him to work for minimum union scale. At the time, minimum scale for an actor doing a week's work was $300. And even there, there was a catch. Most of the writers, directors, producers and actors would receive their checks from Father Bud in a kind of Friday afternoon ritual, just before the last scene of the show was shot. Then they'd endorse the checks and give them right back to the good Father. It was their contribution to the cause. Who didn't want to promote "love, freedom and being human?" By the mid-1960s, most of the Hollywood community considered it a prestigious thing to go in and work a week for Father Kieser.

On this particular week, however, my call from Father Kieser happened to come when my checking account was very sick, my pockets empty and the cupboard bare. I told Joy, "At the end of the week, honey, Friday night, we'll go shopping."

She said, "You're not going to give your check back to Father Kieser?"

"Well," I said, "I got it all figured out. I'll endorse the check and give it back. But he'll say, as he always does, 'Oh, no, I couldn't.' And then I will say, 'Oh, Father, I insist.' And he will say, 'Oh, no, I couldn't.' And will say, again, 'Oh, Father, I insist.' And he will say, 'Oh, no, I couldn't.' And then, I won't follow the script. I won't say, for the third time, 'Oh, Father, I insist.' I'll say, 'Okay, then, Father.' And I'll walk away. With the check."

Joy said, "You think that'll work?"

Well, Friday afternoon, we were ready for the ritual. Only one more scene to go, and we all crowded around Father Kieser, had some Cokes and cookies, and allowed him to go around the room and thank everybody. When my turn came, Father Kieser gave me my check, and I said, "Oh, no, Father, I couldn't." Then I endorsed it and handed it back to him.

He said, "Oh, no, Jamie, I couldn't."

And I said, "Oh, Father, I insist."

And he said, "Oh, no, I couldn't."

And I said, "No, Father, I insist."

He said, "All right then. Thanks, Jamie." And then — he — put my check — in — his — pocket.

"Wait a minute," I thought. He didn't follow the script.

When I arrived home to our little house in Studio City, Joy knew from the look on my face that it didn't work.

From my nine months' work on "Greatest Story," we had saved enough money to put a substantial down payment on a house in Studio City. So we had our first home — but no cash and very little furniture. All we had was a refrigerator, a sofa-bed, some TV trays and a big television, a secondhand model that we bought from Lynn Stalmaster, the casting director for "Greatest Story" (who got it from George Montgomery, the husband of Dinah Shore, and one of the great leading men of the 1940s, who taught himself how to be an expert cabinetmaker). I used to get up in the morning to bake bread, just to give myself something to do. But Joy was still working and I went for a full year without getting another part.

But then, after knocking on a lot of doors, I landed an ongoing role on "The Danny Kaye Show," a show written by, among others, my old friend, Paul Mazursky, the actor from "Blackboard Jungle," now a writer. His longtime partner, Larry

Tucker, was another one of the writers. Also on the team: Herbie Baker, Sheldon Keller, and Mel Tolkin. These writers were good. Many of them had worked in TV's early golden age with Sid Caesar. And, in Kaye, they also had a lot to work with, a very physical entertainer in the Ritz Brothers mold, a guy who could do almost anything: sing ditties, do silly sketches, dance.

As a kid, I'd loved all of Kaye's movies. "The Secret Life of Walter Mitty," "The Kid from Brooklyn," "Hans Christian Andersen," "White Christmas," "Knock on Wood," "The Court Jester." (You may remember Kaye's search, in that movie, for "the flagon with the dragon and the vessel with the pestle and the brew that is true....") And now, lucky me, I thought, I was getting to work with Kaye. I loved this kind of comedy.

We did a lot of sketches — the kind of stuff contemporary audiences sometimes see on "Saturday Night Live." I got my first shot in the first year of the show. I played an Arab in a spy-counter-spy sketch with Kaye and Peter Falk. My best line was a stage whisper to Kaye: "Don't touch the coals. They're hot." (It brought down the house. The writers took note of that. From that one line, I wound up as a regular in Kaye's first season. I had no contract, but I got $650 a week, whenever I worked the show that season.)

And the shows were fun. I remember one sketch we did, a takeoff on "The Three Musketeers." I did that one with Kaye and Harvey Korman. We marched down this long staircase together, the three of us, chanting, "Fight, fight, fight, fight, fight fight" in unison, but almost drowning in our oversize, over-the-knee boots. And then we doff our big, feathered hats with a flourish, and I am wearing mouse ears. "No, not Mouseketeers," they said, "Musketeers!"

We did a takeoff on the Steve McQueen movie, "The Great Escape." Danny was one of the English officers, along with John Mills and Terry-Thomas. Harvey Korman and I were Nazis. He wore his elegant overcoat like a cape, and I wore an oversize helmet. The only thing that kept it from resting on my shoulders was my nose. Harvey and I would always burst in on the men in the stalag to foil their attempts at a getaway. One night, Korman appeared and told a room full of prisoners, "Gentlemen, your escaping days are over. Ve haff barbed wire outside. Ve haff mines. Ve haff machine guns. Und a great big, mean doggy in the yard. So, you understand. You cannot escape. All right now. Lights out!" My character douses the light. But the Korman character has a second thought. "Oh, vun more thing." I turn the lights back on. Everyone is gone. Nothing there but an empty room.

I also have a fond memory of the three of us doing a sendup of "The Student Prince." We sang parodies of some of those marvelous tunes by Sigmund Romberg, in something we called "The Student Dentist." We sang, "In Vienna. In Vienna. Vot a vonderful shpot is Vienna. In Vienna. In Vienna. So how come ve're not in Vienna?" We were in Heidelberg.

But I do not have fond memories of another sketch, a takeoff on the movie, "Viva Zapata." In that one, Kaye whacked me so hard with his hat (adorned with Mexican silver) that he almost broke my hand. (That was part of Danny's shtick, hitting people. Other comedians have done this for laughs. Leo Gorcey slapped around other Dead End Kids. In "The Three Stooges," Moe was always poking his partners in comedy. Far as I know, they didn't break people's hands.)

My hand wasn't broken. But it was pretty badly bruised. I went off to the dispensary at CBS's Television City, and came back wrapped in a big bandage. Kaye didn't even notice it, didn't even care. I was shocked. So this wasn't Hans Christian Andersen! Or even Walter Mitty.

Kaye's self-absorption came out in other puzzling ways. He was not nice to Art Carney, a frequent (and highly paid) guest star on the show. Now Carney was a sweet fellow, charming as all get-out, but he'd irritate Kaye, just by winning laughs. That's what he was being paid for, but it made Danny angry. I couldn't figure this. I thought to myself, "Danny is an American institution. He doesn't have to worry about this. He has the job. He should stop with this already." But he didn't. Maybe he couldn't.

I said to myself, "So this is how you have to be if you are going to be a success in this business!" I flashed on a piece of advice I had gotten one day from Steve McQueen. He told me,

"Every morning, before you go to work, don't forget to take your asshole pills." So, from then on, every morning, I looked in the mirror and told myself to remember McQueen's advice, and figuratively speaking, take a couple of McQueen's pills, trying to change my inner image. But I really couldn't do it.

I know. I know. Being in the business, I should know the difference between real life and a movie script. But I had worked with so many marvelous people in the past, people whose better elements often came out in the characters they played up there on the screen. In fact, I was meeting some nice people on this very show. I remember meeting a young extra named Raquel Welch. She was a mother of two, but so beautiful, with such a fantastic figure, that I had to go home and tell Joy about her. "And such a nice person, too, honey."

But the Kaye show was one of the greatest things for me, because that is where I first met Howard Morris. We did a sketch together. I think I played a Boy Scout. And, whatever it was we did, we really hit it off together. How lucky! I thought, to be working with a legend. Like many of the writers on the Kaye show, Howie Morris was one of the comedy gang who surrounded Sid Caesar in television's earliest years.

Howie first got his job with Caesar in 1948, when Caesar's producer, Max Leibman, was casting something called "The Admiral Broadway Review." Max brought Howie into a tiny room high up in a New York skyscraper, where Caesar was doing auditions. "I got the job," says Howie, "because I only weighed 106 pounds. That meant that Sid could lift me up by the lapels." Which, as fans of "Your Show of Shows" and "Caesar's Comedy Hour" will remember, happened frequently.

The day of his audition, Howie remembers being introduced to two of Caesar's writers, Lucille Kallen, Mel Tolkin and "an observer" from France named Monsieur Brie. Howie was recruited as a performer and a writer who would help put together the show. That involved long days and nights, with the whole gang working furiously to outline the sketches that helped define a new form of comedy, television comedy. But for the life of him, Morris couldn't figure out what Monsieur Brie was doing there. He and Monsieur Brie communicated, if at all, in pantomime.

Then, several days later, Howie is in the men's room, standing at the urinal, next to Monsieur Brie. "How they hanging, Howie?" Morris looked around. Wha? Yes, it was Monsieur Brie, talking to him. Monsieur Brie was a put-on. And the guy doing the put-on was Mel Brooks. Howie didn't know who Brooks was? Well, at that time, according to Howie Morris, "Brooks was a nobody. So were we all."

But Howie Morris soon learned one thing about Brooks. He was a real practical jokester. For laughs, he used to steal Howie Morris' wallet. Sometimes, he would even give it back. As movie fans know, however, Howie Morris later became part of Mel Brooks' repertory company. He appeared in "High Anxiety," "History of the World, Part One" and "Life Stinks," all part of the Brooks' oeuvre. (I thought you'd like that word, Mel. Is that a $10 word, or what?)

Howie Morris went on to become quite a celebrated TV and movie director. And so, he was able to hire me, and did, on a number of occasions. It seemed that, in those days, whenever we were down to our last peso, I'd get a phone call from Howie asking me if I could work for him. Then one day, he called me and said he wanted me to play the part of an Italian in a comedy caper-movie at Columbia called "Who's Minding the Mint?" with Jim Hutton, Dorothy Provine, Joey Bishop, Bob Denver, Milton Berle and Walter Brennan, and written by R.S. Allen and Harvey Bullock. According to John Halliwell's encyclopedic film guide, it's still worth seeing,

In "The Mint," not only did I have to look like an Italian, I had to speak Italian, too. It didn't seem to matter to Howie that I only knew two words in Italian, *si* and *no*. He knew that I was smart enough and energetic enough to learn my lines if I could just get the part. And then Howie helped me get it with a little piece of trickery. He waited until the casting director was away from the studio; then, on the day before shooting was to begin, he took me in to see the assistant to the head of the studio. (I believe the hated Harry Cohn had already departed Columbia Pictures. Which reminds me of Red Skelton's remark after Cohn's funeral. They had a huge crowd there, and Red said, "Well, you give the public what they want, they'll show up.")

"This is Jamie Farr," Howie said to Jerry Tokofsky. "He's gonna play the Italian brother of Joey Bishop. I swear he can do it. I stake my life on it."

"Well," said Tokofsky, "if you stake your life on it."

After an introduction like that, what else could I do but go out and learn Italian? I signed up at Berlitz, and got my lines down perfectly. My big scene: I am Mario, a cousin to the Joey Bishop character, Rafael, and I am just off the boat from Italy. Mario can't speak a word of English, but he's delegated, as his part of the caper, to handle the boxes of $100 bills — $7 million worth — that the gang has just stolen from the U.S. Mint. Trouble is, Mario bungles. When a garbage crew pulls up, he thinks they are police, raises his hands and turns his face to the nearest wall. The two garbage men are puzzled. But they don't check inside the boxes. They just toss them into their truck and drive off.

Then Mario has to tell the gang. He tries to do so, in Italian, using all the body language he can muster, until he gets to Bishop, when Bishop is supposed to say: "Hey, Cousin Mario. *Ma come successo?*" Or, in other words, "What happened?"

At which point, Mario is to tell him what he's been trying to tell the others — that the money has gone off in a garbage truck. It's a two-page scene that Howie Morris wanted to do without a cut. So I had to do everything in one take.

Trouble is, first time I do the scene and get to Bishop, he takes it upon himself to abort. He says to me, "You're standing in my key light." A "key light" is the piece of lighting equipment that is supposedly focused exclusively on him. If I am standing in his key light, well, this demands a re-shoot.

So, we re-shoot the scene. I go through the whole thing again, because Howie Morris wants to do it in one take, and I do it again, without a hitch. Until I get to Bishop. Again, he stops the action. "You missed your mark again," he says.

Hey, I am furious, but I am not saying anything. I refuse to let Bishop get to me. The star, Jim Hutton, is sympathetic. He takes me aside. "Use it, Jamie," he says. "Use it." In other words, funnel the real aggravation into the role, to help give it more passion.

So we try a third time, the whole thing from the top as before, because Howie Morris still wants to shoot it without a cut. Result: same kind of nonsense. Bishop breaks up the scene again, this time with another charge that I have screwed up.

Howie Morris, the director, who knows Bishop is a schmuck, comes up to me. "It's okay, Jamie." He tells me the same thing Hutton told me. "Use it."

Well, on the fourth take (or maybe the fifth or sixth), we finally got the whole scene in the can. I am exhausted and unnerved. But what can any of us do? Bishop gets away with murder because, it is said, he's a friend of Frank Sinatra.

After doing "Mint," I got another part from Howie. I played a hippie leader in "With Six you Get Egg Roll." This was Doris Day's last film. I didn't have lengthy conversations with her. But she was very kind to me, very approachable, very nice on the set. There were some nasty rumors about her, to the effect that she was difficult to work with. None of them were true. In fact, I learned one thing — about the way the star in any production, or TV series, sets the tone for everyone else. Here, the tone set by Doris Day affected the entire cast and crew. Working with all of them, then, was a pleasure. I couldn't wait to go to work on this set.

I also had a good chemistry with Brian Keith. I had met Keith sometime before this, at a party in honor of Father Bud Kieser and all the Hollywood professionals who were then helping him with "Insight." I remember the night Joy and I pulled up in front of the Keith mansion on a hill in Bel Air for that party, ashamed of our old Corvair, and hoping no one would notice us amid all the Rolls and Mercedes and Jaguars that were up ahead of us. We planned to hop out of our car as quickly as we could, then hand the thing over to the valet parking people and disappear quickly into the crowd.

So what happened? The worst. We climbed out of our old Unsafe At Any Speed Corvair all right, but, before the parking valet could take control of it, the brake slipped. Now our heap was rolling back down the hill. So now Joy and I became a spectacle, chasing the car down the hill, trying to stop it before it crashed. Well, with the help of the parking guy, we did stop it, and we brought it back to the party — to the cheers of the crowd. Joy's heels were trashed, of course. But she was happy, not nearly as humiliated as I was, because, after all, she had helped save the only car we had. Furthermore, she enjoyed the party — in her stocking feet.

But Joy is like that, genuine and unpretentious and funny. Years later, she agreed to go on a TV talk show being hosted by the wife of Allen Funt. It was called "Are You Anybody?" and it was about the spouses of famous people. Well, the producers sent a limo for Joy, but when the limo started smoking on the Ventura Freeway coming toward Hollywood, the driver pulled on to the shoulder to investigate. He couldn't fix whatever was wrong, and walked off to find a phone and call for help. By then, Joy, standing there in the kind of windstorm that is generated on your average LA freeway, went looking for a phone herself to tell the producer of the show, Roz Doyle, she was stranded.

"It's okay," said Ms. Doyle. "Come whenever you can. We'll wait."

So Joy went back to the limo, deciding to wait and see how long it took for someone to come and fix the limo. Not too many minutes passed before Joy looked up to see a cement truck pulling off the freeway. By chance, the driver of the truck knew the driver of the limo. Once he sized up the situation, he said to Joy, "Look, if you don't mind, I'll take you into Hollywood in my truck."

Joy regarded the cement truck. "Okay," she said brightly. "I don't mind."

So she climbed up in this guy's truck and off they went, looking for the TAV Studio. They found it on Vine Street, near Sunset, and they found Roz Doyle standing outside, looking for Joy. "Mrs. Farr?" she said incredulously, as Joy hobbled down from the cab in a tight, black skirt all covered with cement dust, hair wildly windblown.

Airily, Joy said, "Yeah." Just as if she always went places in a cement truck. After all, this was a show that called itself, "Are You Anybody?" And she thought she ought to fit right in because she guessed that, after all, she wasn't anybody. But of course she was, she was Joy Richards Farr, and she gave a great interview.

They asked her what she called that hairdo of hers.

"Freeway breeze," she said.

Besides being a very very resourceful broad, Joy is also clairvoyant. Not long ago, Joy and I were watching some of the preliminary heats for the Indianapolis 500. Then, before the big race, she left to go see her mom and dad in Danville. "Enjoy the Five Hundred," she said, "but whatever you do, don't go anywhere near the track."

Sure, Joy. I never gave her warning another thought. Until after the wreck.

Here's what happened. I was safely up in a tower overlooking the race with the actress Adrienne Barbeau and Jackie Cooper, the former child star turned director. But we got antsy and decided to accept an invitation to go watch the race from Tony Holt's luxury box with James Garner, Barry Goldwater Sr. and Jr. and a few other folk, enjoy some of the food and drink being laid out, and find a spot on that box's balcony. So, right in the middle of the race, we made our way to Tony Holt's box, and just as we set foot on the balcony, Tom Sneva's car kissed another car's wheels. His car went end over end and hit a chain link fence just below us, sending hunks of metal and chain link flying up directly at us.

Everyone scattered. It was like a stampede. In fact, the footprints of the Goldwaters, Sr. and Jr., were on my back, when I got up off the deck to see what and who was damaged. (I always thought politicians were quick on their feet. Now I knew it.) Fortunately, though there was debris all around me, I was okay. And I wondered about Joy and her premonitions. She told me to stay away from the track. And I didn't listen.

14

A Loaf of Bread

One day in 1968, Joy told me we were going to be parents. We didn't know what to do. I was hoping to get work, preferably in something that would last awhile. But, when Joy's time drew near, I still didn't have anything. And she knew she would have to quit her accounting job very soon. We were worried. Almost from the beginning, our family unit needed her salary to survive. And soon that unit would be augmented by one baby and diminished by one salary.

I went to George Sadd, a man who had known my parents way back in Toledo. He was now living in Los Angeles, and I told him about the baby, and said, "Mr. Sadd, what are we going to do?"

Mr. Sadd didn't lend me money. (I didn't ask for that.) But he gave me something more valuable. He gave me hope. He said, "Remember, Jamie, a newborn baby always brings a loaf of bread." That may have been an wise old saying in Lebanon. I had never heard it in Toledo, much less in Hollywood. But it was just the thing I needed to hear, now, and it helped me not give up hope. I continued to work hard. I kept making the casting calls and phoning my agent every hour on the hour, and then, when our first-born, Jonas, made his entrance into this world, he brought a loaf of bread.

In fact, I was in Yuma on the day he was born, Dec. 17, 1968, making a Coca Cola commercial slated for national distribution, a job that could bring me at least $10,000. I was there with Naji Gabay, an Iraqi Jew, on the Sahara-like sands west of Yuma when a sheriff's car pulled up to our location. A deputy got out to ask for me, and then tell me, "Mr. Farr, you're the father of a seven-pound, eight-ounce baby boy. Mother and baby are doing fine."

I had gotten my mother to stay with Joy, and the morning Joy went into labor, they called a cab to take them downtown to the Cedars of Lebanon Hospital. The cab driver wasn't quite sure where Cedars of Lebanon was. He set out anyway, in the general direction of downtown, hoping he'd stumble into it somehow. My mother didn't help much. As soon as she found out the driver was Lebanese, and that he had lived in New York, she engaged him in an intense question-and-answer session about who he knew in the old country, and who he knew in New York City. Meanwhile, Joy was groaning in the back seat, wondering if she would make it to the hospital on time.

They finally pulled up in front of a hospital. "It's practically Christmas Eve," Joy said. "If there are three Wise Men on the front lawn, then this must be the place." It was the place. Her doctor's nurse was standing outside waiting for her when she climbed out of the cab.

The commercial featured me and Naji, two Arabs, riding camels, looking for succor in the burning desert, and finding it in the shape of a glistening bottle of Coke. My camel, whose name was Clyde, kept throwing me off his back, and spitting on me, with spittle that smelled like skunk. "Look," I said, trying to reason with Clyde. "I'm one of your people!" Then I climbed back on, to let him know who was boss. I knew — and he knew that I knew — that he was boss.

We thought that this commercial would be on the air in no time. No such luck. Renewed hostilities between the Jews and the Arabs in the Middle East suddenly forced Coca-Cola to withdraw their plans to air that particular commercial, one that tried to show that even Arabs know things go better with Coke. So, as it turned out, the only fortune I made on that Coke commercial was my day rate, plus ten percent, nothing more. If the thing had gone national, I'd have been in the money.

Nevertheless, Mr. Sadd's loaf of bread kept multiplying for us. Not long after Jonas landed, I landed, too, with another regular series slot — this time in something called "Chicago Teddy Bears" at the magnificent sum of $1,000 a week. And, you know, since Jonas was born, I have never been out of work.

"Teddy Bears" ran 13 weeks on CBS, and deserved to last longer. It was a comedy starring Dean Jones (who went on to have quite a career with Disney, making good, clean family movies), and John Banner, the actor who played Schultz in "Hogan's Heroes." In the script, Jones was the owner of a legitimate night club in Chicago during the 1930s. He had a rivalry with a not-so-legitimate night club, owned, of course, by the mob, which was so stupid as to hire four comic idiots as their musclemen: Mickey Shaughnessy, Huntz Hall, Mike Mazurki and me. I was always the driver of the getaway car.

Film buffs know all three of these character actors. Mickey Shaughnessy always played punch-drunk Irish fighter-types. He was most well known for his roles in "Designing Woman" with Gregory Peck and MGM's "Don't Go Near The Water." Huntz Hall was one of the original Dead End Kids. And Mike Mazurki was one of the guys who was so firmly established as a big, dumb tough guy in countless B-movies that no fans had to wonder what they needed to do when he appeared in a scene: laugh.

I think that "Teddy Bears" didn't get extended, or renewed, because Warner Brothers had decided to produce it cheap. That was not what Director Hy Averback, who did the pilot, intended at all. He had made the pilot into a marvelous period piece, with antique cars in an antique streets of an antique Chicago. When the studio nixed that, Averback quit the show. Hy refused to cut corners as Warner Brothers insisted he do. Which I think is the main reason why it did not win the ratings it needed to stay on the air more than 13 weeks.

So now it was 1971, and I was out of steady work again. I began to doubt myself, wonder what the hell I'd ever come to Hollywood for. The acting jobs were dwindling down, as the song goes, to a precious few. What now? Well, energy had always been my middle name. I wasn't afraid of work. I certainly wasn't afraid of rejection. So I teamed up with one of my best friends, Eddie Carroll, whose real name was Eddie Eleniak. We had met in 1959, in Jack Kosslyn's acting class in West Hollywood (Clint Eastwood was also a member of the class) and we found that we had some things in common. He had come from Edmonton, Alberta — a place, like Toledo, with a large immigrant population.

Leslie Nielsen, an actor who won great success as a comedian late in his career, was one of Eddie's classmates. I have since come to know Leslie as one of the world's great imps. I first met him when he was a serious leading man at MGM — and then later at golf tournaments, where I found him making mischief with a little machine that made very vulgar noises, big ones, little ones, farts for every occasion. Leslie Nielsen called himself "the Toscanini of farts." He'd turn them on in the middle of a game show, or in an elevator full of nuns, sometimes with a straight face, sometimes apologizing profusely with, "Oh, I'm terribly sorry. I'm afraid it was the beans." Or, with the same words, accuse someone else by inference.

Eddie Carroll and I had both worked in grocery stores, I for my dad, and Eddie for a Chinese gentleman. Unlike my dad, who spoke without a foreign accent, Eddie's boss struggled with his English.

One day, Eddie's boss sent him to the stockroom to get "my cheese" for a customer. Eddie hustled to the basement storeroom and scanned the cheese department. Velveeta, Edam, Gouda, Stilton, Swiss, Philadelphia Cream Cheese. What was "My Cheese?"

"Eddie," shouted his boss. "My customer here wants my cheese. Hurry, hurry!"

"I'm looking, I'm looking," Eddie hollered back. Now he was getting flustered.

Another tirade from the boss. "My cheese, Eddie." Or was he saying, "Mai cheese?" No matter. He couldn't find either one.

Frightened now, and embarrassed, Eddie emerged from the stockroom. "Gee, I found Velveeta, Edam, Gouda, Stilton, Swiss, Philadelphia Cream Cheese. But I just can seem to find Mai Cheese."

His boss glared at him. "What's the matter with you?" he said. "Can't you understand English. I don't want cheese. I want my cheese — you know, to light the cigarette?"

"Oh," said Eddie. "Matches!"

"Yes, that's what I said, 'My cheese.'"

Through the years, Eddie Carroll and I had become close. In fact, I met his wife, Carolyn, before he did. She was dancing in a show at Lake Tahoe when I was doing a show with Red Skelton at the same hotel, and soon after that, Carolyn had become a part of our crowd in Hollywood.

As some unemployed actors will do, Eddie and I started writing scripts of our own. We did some scripts for a TV series, "Swiss Family Robinson." We did some scripts for Hanna-Barbera, the animators who created the Tom and Jerry cartoons. And we formed a production company of our own, taking office space with our mutual lawyer-agent, Harvey Palash, on 7715 Sunset Boulevard.

Any time you ever read about anyone in show biz who is described as "an overnight sensation," don't you believe it. Most people who make it in Hollywood work long, hard hours at their craft (whatever it be) before they finally start getting mentioned on "Entertainment Tonight." If ever. And even after all the hard work, an actor or an actress may never become anything close to a household name. I have always tried to follow the example given me by my hard-working mom, and my hard-working dad. The harder they worked, the luckier they got.

But sometimes I worked hard and got nowhere. I recall the words Orson Welles once said to the actress, Cissy Spacek: "Give up a whole lot of talent to have one little bit of luck." I think Mr. Welles could have been thinking of me when he said that.

In my life I have had a lot of luck. My friend, Eddie Carroll, on the other hand, is still waiting for his lucky star to shine. You may yet take special notice of him when he puts the final touches on a new show he is mounting on Jack Benny. (He plays Jack Benny.) Eddie is a fine actor, with great comedic gifts. In his time, he has landed some nice jobs. For several seasons, Carroll was one of the sidekicks of Don Knotts on "Hollywood Palace," a popular variety show in the 1950s. But when Eddie goes to Ireland, as he did last spring, nobody knows him. Now, I can get off a plane in almost any international airport and people will come up asking for my autograph.

Anyway, as partners in our production company, Eddie Carroll and I had one object: to sell and produce a great new game show, one that would capture the imagination of America. We made more than a good stab at getting four different game shows mounted. "The Millionaire," "Trademark," "Fact or Fancy" and "Double Take." We came close. We took each to what is known as the "run-through pilot" stage. That is, we produced and taped the shows for the benefit of potential buyers at the networks. But they never appeared on national TV, where the public could decide.

I won't try to describe here the intricacies of the game shows. Needless to say, they were all fun, they all involved celebrity panelists, and all four of them "almost made it."

One never really knows why a network does or doesn't buy a show. But I think that "Trademark" didn't quite come up to the mark because we had an emcee named Jack Carter who'd been around so long that he had come to the conclusion that "nothing is funny anymore." More than that, he seemed to hate everyone in sight. I can remember one of his own writer-producers, Marty Roth, practically in tears, screaming back at him one day, "You can't hurt me any more! You understand that? You can't hurt me any more!"

Though he was a tortured Hollywood producer, maybe a guy in the mold of John Patrick Shanley's producer in "Four Dogs and a Bone," Marty Roth was a dear, dear man, who suffered through all the ups and downs that many parents were faced with in the 1960s and 1970s. I heard that, after he returned from our shoot in Palm Springs, he arrived home to find his kitchen in an absolute shambles. His 14-year-old daughter had been making chocolate chip cookies, and the kitchen looked like someone had lobbed three hand grenades into it moments before he had arrived. Egg shells on the floor. Flour on the light fixtures. Milk spilled on the counters, all of them. Melted chocolate slopped over the edge of a half-dozen pots and pans.

Marty started yelling at the top of his lungs. "What is going —"

His daughter stopped him. She said, very calmly, "Dad, I am not on drugs. I do not sniff cocaine. I don't smoke pot. I do not drink. I am not pregnant. And I'm getting straight A's."

Marty Roth blinked, and then the light of an absolute love suffused his entire being. "Stop," he said. "Say no more." He reached into his pocket, fished out a $50 bill and said, "Here, honey, make all the cookies you want."

Carter treated me and Carroll like he treated Marty Roth, like used Kleenex. For one thing, he never seemed to know our names. To him, Carroll was Dumbo. I was Schmucko. "Hey, Dumbo and Schmucko," he would say, "Come over here." But of course he knew who we were.

But why should I belabor the negative? Let me tell you about our sports show, "Man to Man." That was fun. That was something else again. Eddie and I sold it to MGM, and it ran in 60 markets for 26 weeks in 1971 and 1972.

It was hosted by Merlin Olsen and Roman Gabriel. In the early 1970s, they were the two biggest names on the Rams. Gabriel, the big, strapping, dark-haired, handsome quarterback out of North Carolina State. Olsen, a down lineman, one of the Rams' famous "Fearsome Foursome" and a perennial performer in the annual Pro Bowl. More importantly, they were both very intelligent, both very well spoken. (Since his retirement from pro football, Olsen has made a great, second career on network TV. Some of you may remember him in "Little House on the Prairie.")

Gabriel and Olsen knew other sports, too. They had to.

Each of our shows had a theme, revolving each week around a particular sport that was then in the news. One week, pro football, maybe, hockey, the next week, and tennis the next. And for each sport, we got one of that sport's superstars as a studio guest. What made it special, though, was the presence of yet another show business celebrity who was also a fan of that particular sport. We had guys like Ricardo Montalban, Clint Eastwood, Arte Johnson, Peter Lawford, guys who might otherwise have been unavailable for a show of this type — except for the fact that when we had a great golfer coming on, someone like Sam Snead, it wouldn't be too difficult to get a guy like Bob Hope to sign on, too.

That, at least, was the theory. And, for the most part, it worked. We brought on Mickey Mantle, one of the greatest Yankees of them all, and had no trouble persuading Rock Hudson to come in and shoot the breeze with him, on national television. And then, when we persuaded the great golfer, Sammy Snead to come aboard, we got right on the horn to Bob Hope's agent, Jimmy Saffier. "Sure," said Saffier, "Mr. Hope will be glad to come on your show. When is it?"

We always wanted to be as topical as we could. We told Saffier it would be next week, the week of the Los Angeles Open.

That's when Saffier started to laugh.

I said, "What's the matter?"

Saffier said, "Hey, Mr. Hope's booked solid for the next year and a half."

Our hearts sunk. But, what the heck. We tried. So then we went looking for someone else, another celebrity who was also a golfer. And we came up with Forrest Tucker. Younger readers may not flash on his name right away. But Tucker had been in some fine movies in the 1950s and 1960s. And he was the main man in a TV comedy series called "F-Troop," good enough to still be in re-runs. And he was also a fixture at many a pro-amateur tournament around the country. Would Tucker come on our show? Of course he would.

So, there we are at TAV Studios, at Sunset and Vine, ready to tape our show with Sammy Snead and Forrest Tucker. Gabriel and Olsen are all smiles. They anticipate another good go-round. We, and they, are well prepared. And then we're aware of a terrific commotion outside. A big chopper is landing in our parking lot, right in the middle of Hollywood. Who? What?

It is Bob Hope. "Hey," he says, as he breezes in, "there wasn't anything good on TV tonight, so I just thought I'd drop by."

"Jeez!" I say to Carroll. "What are we gonna tell Tucker?"

Carroll said, "Tell him the truth, I guess."

So that's what we did. We went into the Green Room together and tried to explain to Tucker. "We'd asked Hope first. He couldn't come. So we got you, and felt lucky you said yes. But now...."

Tucker was a trouper. "Hey," he said, "if it was anybody but Hope, I'd be pissed off. But, well, just get me a bottle of Jack Daniels and I'll watch."

But Hope stuck his head in the door right then and he got the picture right away. "Whaddya mean, 'watch?' No big deal, you guys. All you have to do is pull up another chair. We'll do it together." They ended up throwing away the script. All of 'em. They all just ad-libbed the whole show together, including Gabriel and Olsen. To them, all of them pros, it was indeed "no big deal." And, as a matter of fact, it turned out to be one of our best shows, ever, a helluva show.

But we didn't carry on with "Man to Man." Eddie Carroll got another regular, high-paying spot with Don Knotts.

And Gene Reynolds thought he could use me in M*A*S*H.

15

M*A*S*H

When I arrived for my first guest shot on M*A*S*H, the producers already had a half-dozen shows "in the can." But M*A*S*H hadn't made its debut on CBS, and Maxwell Klinger — the corporal who was trying to get out of the Army on a Section 8 — still hadn't been introduced to the American people. Few of the workers on the Fox lot knew what a "Klinger" was, and that got me into some very awkward situations at first.

When I was brought back for my second show, the script called for me to wear a very chic, very tight black dress, with a black hat, high heels — and pearls. The pearls were a set-up for an old gag. Alan Alda — Capt. Hawkeye Pierce — was to challenge me. The script had him saying, "Pearls? In the afternoon?" To which Klinger would reply, "Well, what else goes with basic black?"

As it turned out, they didn't get around to shooting my scene until late in the day. After we'd done it, there was no one left in wardrobe to help me out of my dress, which was fastened with a tricky little hook in the back, and a zipper. So I ducked into a convenient men's room, where I could use the mirror and try to figure out a way to undo the snap and the zipper. At that moment, in walks one of the maintenance people, or maybe a truck driver — a rather tough, burly guy, as I recall. He looked surprised, and he didn't try very hard to hide his surprise.

"Excuse me," I said, in the straightest of voices, and with the straightest of faces. "But you would you please help me get this undone in back?"

Gingerly, and with some difficulty, he got the snap undone and he got the zipper started. We did not talk, we did not trade pleasantries. And when he was finished, he just high-tailed it out of the men's room, forgetting why he had come there in the first place. I could only imagine what he told his wife that night when he got home. If he told her anything at all....

I could go on here for a good long while, telling you stories about the 4077th Mobile Army Surgical Hospital — M*A*S*H for short — and about the people behind the scenes at M*A*S*H. And I think I will. M*A*S*H's fans are legion, and judging from personal appearances I have made over the years since the series ended in 1983, people never seem to get enough of these stories.

M*A*S*H, as you know, has become a legend in America. For eleven seasons, some 32 million people watched it every week, and they go on watching it in re-runs, not only in places like Chicago and Denver and Des Moines, but all across the world, wherever English is spoken, and in some places, like Spain, The Netherlands and Germany, where it is dubbed. The Dalai Lama, now living here in exile, says he watches M*A*S*H "to relax." I hear that somebody is trying to bring M*A*S*H back as a Broadway play.

And because M*A*S*H lasted for 251 episodes, it made television history. From September 1972, until February 1983, this half-hour series was just simply among the best things ever done on television. You don't have to take my word for it. In April

1993, *TV Guide* tried to sum up 50 years of TV history. The editors said M*A*S*H was the sitcom of the 1970s. "We said The Mary Tyler Show in our heart and All In the Family in our head, but M*A*S*H came right from the gut." *TV Guide's* editors also declared M*A*S*H "the best sitcom in history" because, among other things, "M*A*S*H made us laugh till we cried."

People cried when we presented the last M*A*S*H on Feb. 28, 1983, a two-and-a-half hour special that turned out to be the highest-rated show in TV history, with a Nielsen rating of 60.2, a 77 share that translated into 125 million viewers. It is a record that still stands. (By comparison, the biggest Super Bowl audience ever — in 1982 — had 110 million viewers. And the most-watched segment of Roots had 99 million. The last episode of "Cheers," in 1993, had 93 million.)

Younger readers who weren't watching much TV in 1983 still know M*A*S*H, because 1983 wasn't the end. There would (always) be the re-runs. People still tell me, "When my children hear that theme music (referring to Johnny Mandel's now-very-familiar "Suicide Is Painless") they run to the TV." They still sell bubble gum cards with our pictures on them. People still have M*A*S*H bashes, costume parties where everyone comes as a character from M*A*S*H. *The New York Times* crossword puzzle still has clues like "Jamie of M*A*S*H."

For an actor, getting caught up in Re-run Land is the closest thing to immortality. Long after I'm dead, new generations will be laughing at me in my pitiful efforts to get a Section 8 and get out of the Army. If that's not immortality, what is?

I think we achieved this immortality because we were able to suspend Murphy's Law — for a change. According to Mr. Murphy, "Whatever can go wrong, will go wrong, and at the worst possible moment." On the Stage 9 of the Fox lot, and out in Malibu Canyon — "on location" — almost everything went right with our little war.

Our little war? Well, we were in the Korean War, a little war as far as 20th century wars go, and not even a declared war at that. But we didn't show the war itself. Not the ground war that brought American soldiers and American Marines face to face in firefights with North Korean and Chinese troops. Not the air war, either, what there was of it. We staffed a field hospital in that war, where we could show the blood and the violence of war without ever actually taking viewers to the front lines. We showed the inside of the battles. We showed the underside. We showed the effects of the war by trying to tell stories about the casualties of the war — and not only the wounded and the dying, either. We dramatized the absurdity of the war — stitching men up so they could go right back out and get torn up again. We dramatized the loneliness of the war, we dramatized the fear, we dramatized the psychosis of it all. We dramatized death.

It wasn't easy. M*A*S*H, you see, was, first and foremost, a comedy. We made our field hospital — often crammed with some very very bloody wounded men — into a comedy. That was no small feat.

In life, comedy may be easy, especially if you pay attention to the all the incongruities of the world we live in today. But in theater, comedy is not easy. Edmund Gwenn found a way to say this most winningly on his death bed. Gwenn was one of Hollywood's great character actors, most famous for playing the Santa Claus character, Kris Kringle, in "Miracle on 34th Street." Let me recap the scene. Gwenn is lying there in the hospital, gasping, and then he says to his loved ones gathered around: "It's hard to die." Well, that just tears his family apart. But Gwenn is really setting them up. He gives it a beat. (Even as he was dying he knew the importance of a good gag — and of good timing.) Then he delivers the punch line, with a merry twinkle in his eye: "But comedy's harder."

People in the business like that story. In fact, other people say it was Morris Tomashevski, the great star of the New York Yiddish theater, who delivered the line first, and on his deathbed, too. Maybe other comedians can't wait to regale their families on their deathbeds with this good, last joke.

Fact is, that everybody in the business knows that comedy is hard — hard to write, hard to bring off on stage or on film. And our M*A*S*H was even a little harder than straight comedy, because it was a mixture of comedy and drama, something close to what they call "black comedy," a literary form that started to come into vogue in France after World War II with the theater of the absurd.

One of the finest American examples of black comedy is not a play, but the novel by Joseph Heller, *Catch-22*, written about the madness at a U.S. Army Air Corps base, where U.S. pilots ended up divebombing their own airstrip under contract to the Germans, at cost-plus-ten percent.

Catch-22, opens with a hospital scene that could have played on one of our M*A*S*H episodes. A terribly wounded patient, so wrapped with bandages that he looks like nothing so much as a mummy, has one IV bottle dripping fluid into his body from above. Another identical bottle receives fluid running out of the body below. When the upper bottle is empty, an orderly comes along, and switches the two bottles. That is a piece of black comedy.

Most of Heller's action takes place on a fictional island called Pianosa in the Mediterranean, on a base run by an absurd group of officers in the U.S. Army Air Corps. The closest thing to a sane person in the book — Capt. Yossarian, proves his sanity by continuing to appeal for reassignment stateside, out of the war zone. Those in charge will send a man home if he is crazy. But according to another rule, he first has to ask to go home; and if he asks, then that's ipso facto evidence that he is not crazy. Only crazies, you see, would want to stick around. And that's "the Catch." That's *Catch-22*.

In a way, then, even though the writer who created my Klinger character says he wasn't thinking of *Catch-22* when he brought me to life, Klinger was a kind of spin-off from Capt. Yossarian. I was sane enough to want out of Korea, but none of my insane ploys was ever taken seriously enough by the men in charge to merit more than a glance of amusement, or a little chuckle. Within the 4077, in fact, everyone completely ignored my daily changes of wardrobe and treated me like anyone else in the unit.

(When my son, Jonas, was six, he thought that dressing up in women's clothes was part of a game called "Army." One day he slipped on one of his mother's bras, and said, "Look, Mom, I'm playing 'Army.'")

The fact that everyone in the 4077 paid little if any serious attention at all to my couture, of course, was part of the fun. Only visitors to the unit were allowed to do an occasional double take (but hardly ever more than that). In every other respect, you see, I was a good soldier, and I demonstrated a wide variety of skills that were useful to my compatriots in the M*A*S*H unit.

Being from Toledo (both in real life and on the show), and being presumably connected, therefore, to some fringe elements of Toledo's notorious and lawless underworld, I was also a fixer and a conniver. In real life, I have no connections to the Toledo underworld. And I am not much of a conniver. But on M*A*S*H, that was my shtick: Klinger was an ingenious guy, often able to help Hawkeye Pierce and B.J. Hunnicutt come up with the props they needed to pursue their almost-weekly round of mischief and practical jokes. He was also inventive enough to put together a rather astounding collection of gowns, dresses, skirts and blouses (and wild, wild hats). On the show, Klinger had established the fact that he was a pretty darn good seamstress. But how he managed to come up with some of his more-elaborate creations was always a mystery that never got an explanation in any of the shows. Klinger would just show up wearing them.

I got most of them from a big department at Fox called "Wardrobe," with help from a former talent scout for the Los Angeles Dodgers and from Producer Burt Metcalfe. Metcalfe still looks back on those moments as a highlight of his years on M*A*S*H — to spend time each week with Jamie Farr, selecting outfits, hats, shoes, earrings. It was something that Metcalfe looked forward to every week, and come to think of it, if you wanted to ask who was the most spectacular character in the show, I was. I was the only one on the show who could really dress up. Loretta Swit wore nothing but olive drab uniforms or surgical gowns in the operating room (what we would always call "the OR"). She said she envied me.

It was kind of ironic. When I was at Warner Brothers, doing "Chicago Teddy Bears," I had used costumes that had been made for George Raft, Dane Clark and Anthony Quinn. (I saw their names sewn in the lining of the suits I wore.) Now, at Fox, I was getting into costumes made for Alice Faye, Betty Grable and Carmen Miranda.

You may remember some of those costumes. The one on the jacket of this book, of course: celebrating the moment when Klinger showed up one day as the Queen of the Nile, Cleopatra. My yellow pinafore with a hoop skirt and parasol. My Scarlett O'Hara costume, a print chiffon in lavender and green, with jewelry, purse and gloves to match. The flowing purple Victorian frock with the big summer hat that I wore at Maj. Margaret Houlihan's wedding. My flowered Japanese kimono. My simple evening gown in silver lurex, with a fruit-covered turban to match (my Carmen Miranda statement). My blue-and-white checked Judy Garland, Over-The-Rainbow jumper (which I wore with a white blouse when I appeared on a bicycle carrying a wicker basket, presumably with my own Cairn terrier inside). My full-length mink coat with the feather boa. My Scotch-plaid woolen skirt, with the cashmere red sweater set and the matching tam o'shanter. My little black cocktail dress with the matching pumps and purse. And pearls. My unending supply of colorful babushkas. One day I entered the camp on horseback, playing Lady Godiva. I was naked, except for the yards of surgical cotton wrapped around my torso.

As an exceedingly clever operator, I also happened to be following in the footsteps of another character from *Catch-22*, Milo Minderbinder, the great procurer of Pianosa, who ran his own astounding private international cartel — wheeling and dealing all over Europe and North Africa, forever buying long staple cotton in Egypt and trading it for hams in Poland, to be bartered, in turn, for Pfefferkuchen in Berlin, or baby lamb chops from Portugal. Milo's mess hall was a dream. There, pilots who cooperated with the enterprise feasted most sumptuously, and so did the generals who went along with the plan. Breakfast on

Pianosa? They had the best white fresh eggs fried in pure creamery butter. Tangerines, too, and casaba melons, honeydews, filet of Dover sole, baked Alaska, and cockles and mussels.

Milo was a benevolent wheeler-dealer. He always made sure that, in this squadron, "everyone had a share." There were parts of Milo in my Klinger. And our whole M*A*S*H unit, in fact, carried something of the flavor of *Catch-22*. We also did absurd things, things that moved audiences to laughter. Laughter was the only antidote to the chaos of the Korean War, and that laughter, I must add, generally came amid tears, as the doctors and nurses and staff of a Mobile Army Surgical Hospital worked furiously trying to patch up the casualties of a senseless war. We were people who cared. And we tried to make everyone else care, too, in the middle of absolute absurdity. Which was one reason why someone called our work "dramedy."

I give most of the credit for all this to Larry Gelbart, the real "creator" of the show. But Larry, for all his genius, didn't exactly start from scratch.

Our TV series was a spinoff from a very successful movie called M*A*S*H, produced by Twentieth Century Fox, from a novel by the same name that almost never got published. Dr. J Richard Hornberger had 17 rejections from 17 publishers, but his book finally found an 18th, William Morrow, who took a chance on it. The book, polished by a former sportswriter named W.C. Heinz, and published under the pen name, Richard Hooker, became a best- seller. Then, one of the truly great directors of our time, Robert Altman, hired a fine screenwriter named Ring Lardner Jr. to turn the book into a movie. That M*A*S*H, Altman and Lardner's M*A*S*H, won a place on everyone's list of the top ten movies in 1967.

Cut to 1972. Critics could only react with dismay when they heard that Fox, which was in deep financial trouble, wanted to translate that story to the cultural wasteland called television. Critics said, "They want to sitcomize M*A*S*H? Never!" But never underestimate the power of real talent when that talent is willing to take extra-special pains.

Fox found a lot of talent willing to take pains, first in the person of Gene Reynolds, a former kid actor-turned-administrator, whom Fox hired as executive producer, and second, of writer Larry Gelbart, brought back to the U.S. by Reynolds from a kind of expatriate status in England.

Gelbart, who was born in 1925, was already writing jokes for radio comedians in 1940, before television. As a teen-ager, Larry sold jokes to Danny Thomas, who was then coming into his dad's barbershop on Fairfax Boulevard in LA. Then he graduated into television in the 1950s as a writer for Bob Hope, Sid Caesar and Art Carney. Gelbart wrote one classic Broadway musical comedy, "A Funny Thing Happened on the Way to the Forum" in 1962, and one classic movie comedy, "The Wrong Box," in 1967. And then he sort of retired, moved to England, and was doing something called "The Marty Feldman Show" on English TV when Reynolds called him and asked him whether he wanted to be the principal creator on M*A*S*H. (Marty Feldman, you may recall, was the bug-eyed cretin in the Mel Brooks' classic, "Young Frankenstein." When he wasn't working as part of Brooks' repertory company, Feldman was an English comic with a solid following in Great Britain.)

Gene Reynolds had run into Gelbart not long before on a trip to England. When Fox handed Gene the assignment of finding the creative genius who could make M*A*S*H work as an extended piece of television fiction, Gene immediately thought, "This is Gelbart's."

Gelbart told Reynolds he wanted to do more than make M*A*S*H work on TV. He wanted the TV show to transcend the movie, "to make people laugh and cry and, through the laughter and the tears, reconsider their whole lives." In other words, Gelbart didn't want to be the chief writer on an old-fashioned Abbott & Costello, Gomer Pyle service comedy. If Reynolds wanted to give him the encouragement to reach for the TV stratosphere, Gelbart said, "Fine, I'll try it." Otherwise, Gelbart wasn't interested. Well, since Gelbart was ready to do something special, Reynolds told him to go for that special something.

Gelbart took his time. Writers almost always take their time — to the distraction and the frustration of their wives and agents, who never quite believe they are working when they just seem to be looking out the window. I suspect that Gelbart spent a good deal of time looking out the window before he sat down to bang out the pilot for TV's M*A*S*H. In any event, Reynolds didn't get the script he wanted, not right away.

He finally phoned Gelbart, still in England, and asked him how he was coming along. He got the answer many impatient producers get from many writers: "Oh, it's in the mail." Of course, it wasn't. But then, facing Fox's deadline, Gelbart holed up for three days and produced a pilot script that was everything Reynolds was hoping it would be, because it not only introduced all the major characters in the series, but it did so inside a suspenseful story that demonstrated the heroic, life-dealing professionalism of some Army surgeons who, for all that, would never make sainthood.

For instance? Well, in the pilot, Hawkeye wants to raise $2,000, so he can send his Korean houseboy to medical school in the states. To raise the two-grand, he and his partners-in-crime raffle off a weekend in Japan with a voluptuous nurse named Dish, but they are caught red-handed by the two early villains of the 4077, Capt. Frank Burns and Maj. Margaret Houlihan, the head nurse, and they are almost court-martialed for the caper. Except that the arrival of many wounded puts them all into the OR for a medical marathon that goes on for 12 hours. Their heroic work so impresses the general in charge that the Army drops the court-martial.

As a matter of historical fact, when the pilot aired for the first time, the critics didn't know quite what to make of it. *Time* magazine called it one of the biggest disappointments of the 1972-73 season. Maybe the *Time* critic was expecting something that had the satirical bite of another then-popular TV series called "All in the Family." Eventually, he would see that bite on M*A*S*H, and more, but it would take time

But, as I have said, Reynolds loved the script for the pilot. He told Gelbart. "Come to LA. Time's awasting. We've got work to do. There'll be some re-writing. I want you to do it." Reynolds was also aware that, as soon as the pilot was in the can, he'd have to start shooting the next 12 shows. He didn't have scripts for a single one of those. He wanted Gelbart to get cracking on more of them. He also hired other writers; in fact, 12 other writers (plus Alan Alda himself) had a hand in the first season's 24 shows. But Reynolds wanted Gelbart to exercise an editorial role even on those.

As far as Reynolds was concerned, he wanted this to be a classy show. It was standard in those days for TV shows to be videotaped in front of a live audience. This was the way they had done the big shows on network radio, in front of live audiences. Since network television was a spinoff from radio, television simply followed the old radio pattern. But Reynolds wanted M*A*S*H to be different. One way to do that was not to videotape the stories, but film them. On film, the actors had to relate to a camera, not to 300 people sitting in the studio bleachers.

You may wonder how that helped the show. Here is why.

By working on film, we, the actors on M*A*S*H, didn't have to project out to a studio audience. All we had to do was project to the other actors (which, of course, was picked up by the camera). That made everything much more intimate. When I was talking to the other actors, you see, I was, in effect, really talking to each and every member of the TV audience. That made M*A*S*H much more believable. That is the main reason why Reynolds insisted that Fox give him a film budget, not a tape budget, which would have been cheaper.

In retrospect, this was a happy decision. Now, with all 251 episodes on a film master, instead of on old videotape, technicians can make excellent new prints of those shows — something that Fox is doing, paradoxically enough, by digitizing the original films and putting the results not on new film, but on tape.

Since this was a TV sitcom, however, CBS (the network that bought this idea from Fox) couldn't quite depart from the norm for all sitcoms: CBS said M*A*S*H had to have a laugh track.

Reynolds didn't fight too hard against the old radio (and now TV) convention. Sure, he resented the network presumption — that audiences were so dumb they needed to be told when to laugh. But he struck a compromise with CBS: there'd be no laugh track in the 4077's operating room (called the OR for short). Laughs just didn't belong in the OR (particularly if it was canned studio laughter, some of it often recorded decades earlier in the heydays of Jack Benny and Fred Allen).

On occasion, Reynolds was also able to negotiate with the network on a given show. There was no laugh track, for instance, in one episode when some members of the 4077 were stranded on a bus in the demilitarized zone, a place where they were in great danger. Reynolds says, "I was able to convince the network people at CBS Television City that it didn't make any sense for an audience to be 'there' with Hawkeye and the others in a bus in the middle of the DMZ. Of course, it didn't make any sense to have an audience in the M*A*S*H compound either." (The DMZ, kids, was the Demilitarized Zone at the 38th Parallel, which was the line that separated South and North Korea).

It was interesting to me that English television eliminated the laugh track entirely, a twist that has prompted some critics to note that the "purest form" of M*A*S*H is still to be found on British television, where audiences are still watching the re-runs, and apparently, don't need the laugh-cues.

Reynolds had other ideas that would make the show look classy and, well, more real. He didn't want to simulate helicopters, trucks and ambulances on some kind of sound stage. He wanted to use standard helicopters, trucks and ambulances, which meant we couldn't do our exteriors on a sound stage. All exteriors would be shot on location, at the old Fox Ranch in Malibu Canyon.

Finally, Reynolds sought out the best production people he could find — cameramen, editors, set designers, costume people and the like. And Hollywood being Hollywood, a place teeming with film talent, he found them. One of his best finds was a former actor named Burt Metcalfe, whom he hired to serve as casting director and associate producer. (In year six, Metcalfe would take over for Gene Reynolds.)

16

The Cast

Burt Metcalfe's first job was all-important: to find the right
actors. He and Reynolds knew that, on a TV production budget,
he couldn't sign the principals who had played in the movie
version of M*A*S*H — Elliott Gould, Donald Sutherland,
Robert Duvall and Sally Kellerman, who were then all very high-
priced movie stars. At that time, once a star made it big in the
movies, he didn't step backward into TV. So Reynolds and
Metcalfe got one and only one principal from the movie, Gary
Burghoff, who played the boyish company clerk, Radar O'Reilly, a
very small part in the movie, but one that would turn into a very
big one in the TV series.

Reynolds and Metcalfe had to search for the rest of the cast
— five other principal roles in the beginning: Capt. Benjamin
Franklin Pierce, Capt. John McIntyre, Col. Henry Blake, Maj.
Margaret Houlihan, and Maj. Frank Burns. Father John Mulcahy,
the chaplain, was a kind of afterthought. (At that time, no one

ever thought of Corporal Maxwell Klinger. He wasn't even an afterthought. He was just an accident.)

But Metcalfe didn't have a very long, or very difficult, search for the principals. Hollywood has a million actors. Only a small percentage of them ever gets a fighting chance. And so, while Metcalfe came up with a group of fine actors and actresses who were relative unknowns in middle America, he made some fantastic choices — people who were not only good in their own right, but people who could, and did, work well with the others in the cast. As Reynolds and Gelbart were to say, many times, without this particular cast, M*A*S*H never would have made the history it did.

Only the two leading roles Capt. John McIntyre (Trapper John) and Capt. Benjamin Franklin Pierce (Hawkeye) gave Metcalfe pause. He had no immediate favorite for either job, so he put out the word that he was looking for two leading men to play Hawkeye and Trapper John McIntyre. Some 75 men read for the parts, which were considered of equal importance at the time. Somewhere along the way, Alda's agent indicated that Alan might be available for the part. So, Metcalfe put off a decision about Hawkeye, and ended up filling the Trapper John role first.

To play Trapper, he selected Wayne Rogers, a really handsome, curly haired guy with a winning smile, who had been starring in a daytime soap, "The Edge of Night." Rogers had a good deal of stage experience before he joined the M*A*S*H company. In M*A*S*H, Wayne Rogers would be Hawkeye's irreverent sidekick, Trapper John, the show's second lead. He shared a sleeping tent, called The Swamp, with Hawkeye (and Maj. Frank Burns), and presumably helped Hawkeye build the homemade distillery that produced the gin for the very regular cocktail parties held by Hawkeye and Trapper John. He was also Hawkeye's partner-in-practical-jokery that enlivened life in the 4077.

Next, Burt Metcalfe went looking for someone to play the role of the 4077's commanding officer, Col. Henry Blake. CBS made it easy for Metcalfe. The network had been wanting to cast an actor they had liked for some time, a man with too much talent

not to be working on a regular basis. His name was McLean
Stevenson, who just happened to be the nephew of Adlai
Stevenson, twice a candidate for the American presidency. So
when the network people suggested him to Metcalfe for the part of
Col. Blake, Metcalfe met Stevenson, and liked him, and done was
done.

Metcalfe never considered anyone else but Larry Linville for
the part of Maj. Frank Burns. Let me say this about Linville from
the start. In no way was Larry Linville like his M*A*S*H
character, Maj. Frank Burns (the character played by Robert
Duvall in the movie M*A*S*H). I know: you find this hard to
believe. This is because Larry was such a darn fine actor that he
could command your belief in just about anything. That he did
this so well in M*A*S*H was, to be sure, a byproduct of the
show's longevity. Those M*A*S*H characters were with you in
your living rooms for years. By the end, they had become real
people. And if Maj. Frank Burns was so consistently obnoxious, so
unreasonable, so petty, so hypocritical, then why wasn't Larry
Linville? No one could invent such a character as Frank Burns.
But Larry Linville did.

Metcalfe had even less trouble hiring Loretta Swit. He knew
some of what Loretta Swit had done on the Broadway stage before
she came west in 1969 — and, after one interview with her, Burt
knew she, too, was right for the part of Maj. Margaret (Hot Lips)
Houlihan. She got her job without a test. And she never looked
back. Others would quit the show. The thought hardly ever
crossed her mind. She was the only gal on the show. She was
absolutely unique. And she was able to take the role of this hard-
bitten, often angry Army officer — a very one-dimensional part
in the movie M*A*S*H as played by Sally Kellerman — and
humanize her.

Sure, she was a spit-and-polish officer who went by the book.
Sure, she was a terrible taskmistress for the other nurses. Sure, she
was a spoilsport and a fink and a tattletale. Sure, she had an affair
going on the side with Maj. Burns. But underneath all that, Maj.
Houlihan began to emerge, over the length of the entire series, as

someone who had to put on much of her toughness simply in order to survive in her command. In one of the shows, "The Nurses," which ran in our fifth season, she revealed that she was not an officer who only went according to the book, but a human being.

"Did you ever show me any friendship?" she shouted at the other nurses. "Ever ask my help in a personal problem? Include me in one of your little bull sessions? Can you imagine how it feels to walk by this tent and hear your laughter and know that I'm not welcome? When did any of you ever even offer me a lousy cup of coffee?"

"We didn't think you'd accept," said one of the braver nurses.

"Well," said Maj. Houlihan, "you were wrong."

For the part of Father Mulcahy, Metcalfe tapped an actor named George Morgan. He did the pilot. But, on second thought, he wasn't really the chaplain that Gelbart wanted. Bill Christopher, with whom I had worked in the movie, "With Six, You Get Eggroll," who had also had an ongoing role in the Gomer Pyle TV series, turned out to be the man they needed. So good a choice, in fact, that his part grew and grew with the passing years, and he became the longest running religious character in prime time.

After Bill Christopher went off to do his own research about priests, and about chaplains, he concluded that priests are very human and that many of them had a sense of humor like his own: whimsical. He tried not to play his priest as any kind of holy man — rather as a simple man, as confused as anyone in the TV audience about what was happening here. For that reason, Bill thought that Father Mulcahy represented the point of view of the audience.

So now Metcalfe was down to the other leading man, the Capt. Pierce role. Could he get Alan Alda? That wasn't too clear. In the first place, Alda himself needed some convincing. He and his family lived in New Jersey, and he wasn't going to move them to Hollywood. He'd have to commute, and an LA-New Jersey commute is pretty tough. He'd have to catch the redeye from Los Angeles International Airport (often referred to as LAX) on

Friday nights, then leave Newark International on the last flight
west every Sunday night so he could begin another episode on
Monday morning. Subjecting himself to that meant that this role
better be good. And he had his reservations about the future
exploits of Capt. Benjamin Franklin (Hawkeye) Pierce.

Alda was shooting a picture in Utah at the time Reynolds
approached him, and he had some hard questions for Reynolds. He
liked the pilot script very much. But he was afraid Gelbart would
go back to England after the pilot, and that the war would just be
treated by the writers and the production staff "as a backdrop for
lighthearted high jinks." Alda didn't want any part of a series that
critics might call "Abbott and Costello Go To War." He said, "I
wanted to show that war was a bad place to be, that people got
hurt in war and that it was not the occasion of hilarity. The way
people reacted to it might be hilarious."

I can't imagine how any other actor alive could have brought
off the part half as well as Alan Alda did. Alda was never content
to come in every week and just read the lines. He tried to help
shape the show, as well as to shape the character of Hawkeye
Pierce. Three or four of the early shows, for instance, did fall into
the style of light, Gomer Pyle, service comedy, and Alan (along
with others) objected to that, and their input helped steer the
show into another attitude, the seriocomic stance, the dramedy,
that led to its great success. "It wasn't clear to many people,"
recalls Alda, "that we wanted to have two levels going on at once.
I don't mean two story lines. I mean two levels of intent, with
light on top and serious underneath."

Gelbart would be the first to concede that. "That first year,"
he would have been the first to say (and did): "We were really
feeling our way."

Gelbart first followed cues from CBS, which wanted a show
with "the greatest possible appeal." But that was like asking
Gelbart to cut back his own genius to the lowest common
denominator. Under CBS guidelines, he felt he couldn't kill
people on the show (even though it was about a battlefield
hospital!), and that he had to be too careful with sex, sacrilege and

language. The upshot was that M*A*S*H got poor ratings that first year, trying, as Gelbart said, "to be as wholesome as possible at 8 o'clock on a Sunday night, when wholesomeness was a direct contradiction to what the show was all about."

Gradually, Gelbart and Reynolds found ways of making the show more real. Seventeen shows into the first season, they had already gotten to a kind of an apex with an episode called "Sometimes You Hear the Bullet." Not many laughs in this story. The episode started out with a soldier named Tommy Gillis stopping by the 4077 for a joyful reunion with Hawkeye, whom he'd known since the fifth grade. He was writing a book about life in the infantry, one filled with vignettes — like the time a young blond kid who was mortally wounded told Gillis on the battlefield, "I never heard no bullet." Gillis was going to call his book *You Never Hear the Bullet*.

But Gillis never finished his book. After an all-night drinking session in Hawkeye's quarters, Gillis went back to his unit, only to return to the 4077 some 12 hours later dying of severe gunshot wounds. Gillis said, "I'd give you a kiss, Hawk, but I can't lift my head."

Hawkeye tried to cover his pain with a joke: "You'd just get my mask icky," he said.

"I heard the bullet," said Gillis. Then he died.

Tears streamed down the face of Hawkeye. "This is the first time I've cried since I'm in this crummy place," he told Col. Henry Blake.

Said Blake: "All I know is what they taught us in command school. Rule Number One is that young men die and Rule Number Two is that you can't change Rule Number One."

As you can see, we were beginning to mix the dark with the light. But some network people said, "What is this? A comedy or a tragedy?" They were afraid audiences wouldn't accept it. Gelbart has made it clear that the network people "were not anti about our being anti-war. But they were anti-heavy and anti-serious. Most of our battles with them stemmed from the fact that we wanted to veer so far from what was considered half-hour comedy. They called us periodically to have it out with us. While the cast and the crew were out at the Fox Ranch fighting the elements, Gene and I fought two of the most unnatural forces in the world — the networks and the studio — for the right to deal with bolder and more serious subjects than they were inclined to allow, like the effects of violence, adultery, amputation, derangement, impotence, homosexuality, transvestitism and interracial marriage."

(In this, I think Gelbart was only putting his interviewer on. We were doing a comedy, for God's sake, and, though we could touch on some serious themes, neither our producers nor our writers wanted to screw up a good thing by getting into stories about impotence, homosexuality or interracial marriage.)

Fights with network censors revolved around far more trivial matters. Gene Reynolds remembers, for instance, that the network censors refused to allow Radar O'Reilly to use the word "breasts." We could show bras on screen, but we weren't allowed to show athletic supporters. Once, Gelbart was told to take the word "virgin" out of one script. (Gelbart says he got it back in the next week, by introducing a soldier who was from the Virgin Islands.) The only story that was ever completely rejected by the network told of Hawkeye's simultaneous affair with two different nurses, each on a different shift. CBS's censors might even have allowed that. But when the nurses each announced they were pregnant, that was too much. That would have implied that Hawkeye wasn't just flirting with the nurses, but going a little further than that.

I guess CBS had a point. They didn't want to have Hawkeye doing anything that would make audiences hate him. And that policy worked. Capt. Benjamin Franklin Pierce quickly became the most beloved character in American television.

17

Hawkeye

I just don't know how Gene Reynolds or Larry Gelbart could have predicted Alda's great celebrity. In fact, they never foresaw what a success M*A*S*H would be. Nobody did. A TV series is a crapshoot, and more often than not, some very creative people in this business will enter the crap game with a new series idea — and end up rolling snake eyes. But both M*A*S*H — and Alda — were one of the stunning show business surprises of the 1970s.

To be sure, everyone knew that Alda was a good actor. He had a great background. His father, Robert Alda, had been a star of stage and screen in the 1940s. He was Broadway's first Sky Masterson in Frank Loesser's "Guys and Dolls." And he played the main man in a pretty good Hollywood biography of the great (perhaps the greatest) American composer of them all, George Gershwin.

But Robert Alda never "went Hollywood." He raised his family in the East and sent his son, Alan, to college at Fordham

University in New York. Young Alan started out like his dad, on Broadway, won some critical notices, and then took the usual trek to Hollywood to do some television. (In 1972, he got an Emmy nomination for the portrayal of a serial killer named Caryl Chessman.) By then, he had done eight movies and a lot of theater work, but his work in those productions, though good, didn't win him any box office awards, or bring him anything like the commercial success of a Clint Eastwood.

In fact, Alan Alda got little critical (or popular) acclaim until he joined the M*A*S*H unit at Fox. Then he won every award there was — for writing and directing, as well as acting.(He is, in fact, the only person ever to win Emmies for all three.) He became, and will be identified forever, as "Hawkeye" Pierce, a terribly skilled, smart-cracking, emotional guy who loved the underdog and hated authority, especially when it was vested in pompous military types who insisted on following the rules, even when doing that tended to get people crushed, or killed.

So, yes, he also drank, and he also flirted with the nurses, both of which would be activities no doubt proscribed today by the networks as just too politically incorrect. But M*A*S*H was supposed to be about the 1950s, and it was written with a '70s sensibility. Few complained that this TV hero was addicted to martinis, made with gin distilled in his sleeping tent. Or that he chased most of the attractive women who ever passed through the 4077. This was a hero who wasn't perfect. In fact, in M*A*S*H, nobody was perfect. They were human beings. And M*A*S*H was probably the first sitcom to paint both its heroes and its villains in varying shades of gray. Or crack wise about Gray's Anatomy, the famous medical text.

NURSE: I thought we were going to talk about Gray's Anatomy — not mine.

HAWKEYE: Gray has a fabulous personality, but no body whatsoever. You really want to talk about surgery? How 'bout if I show you my appendix scar?

If you had the feeling that there was something of Groucho Marx in this Hawkeye character, you are absolutely right. Gelbart admits he owes a debt to Groucho. A good many of Hawkeye's lines ape the manic, up-tempo non-sequiturs of that were so characteristic of Groucho in all those old Marx Brothers comedies in the 1930s and 1940s.

Here is a scene from "Duck Soup." Groucho is the prime minister of a mythical country called Fredonia, which is at war with Sylvania. Under artillery fire, and in the midst of falling debris, Groucho gets on the short wave radio. "Calling all nations. Calling all nations. This is Rufus T. Firefly coming to you courtesy of the enemy. We're in a mess, folks. We're in a mess, folks. Rush to Fredonia. Three men and one woman are trapped in a building. Send help at once. If you can't send help, send two more women."

Can't you just hear Alda-as-Hawkeye delivering those lines? I can. In more than one episode, in fact, Hawkeye looked more like Groucho than Groucho. One notable show, "Dear Sigmund," written and directed by Alda himself, didn't have much of a plot. Rather, it was a series of sketches that attempted to epitomize each of the M*A*S*H principals, in turn, and the sketches were cinematic realizations of a letter that the visiting psychiatrist, Dr. Sidney Freedman (played by Allan Arbus), was writing to Sigmund Freud. Wasn't it kind of crazy, asked B.J. Hunnicutt, for Dr. Freedman to be writing to Freud? Dr. Freedman, who paid more than one visit to the 4077 during the run of the show, said, "Who, better than he, would understand?"

The rest of us in the cast were more than fascinated to find that Alda had written a sketch for himself that was almost pure Groucho. Alda romped and clowned his way through the entire sketch, doing a sendup of an Army medic much as Groucho might have done. In one part of the sketch, Alan was making bedside calls wearing evening clothes and swimfins on his feet. "Nurse, nurse!" he cries at one point.

She comes and says, "Did you call me, Doctor?"

He says, "Why would I call you doctor. I'm the surgeon." Then he gallumphs over (how else would describe a man trying to walk in swim fins?) to a soldier's bed and scans his chart. "Well," he says, "your feet seem to be coming along just fine."

The patient says, "It's my head, Doctor."

Hawkeye rotates the chart, which he had been reading upside down. "Oh," says, Hawkeye, "for a minute there, I thought you had athlete's scalp." Is this Groucho, or is it not Groucho?

Alda, of course, was the magnet for everything on the show. That isn't the way it started out. His character, that of Hawkeye, and the character played by Wayne Rogers, Trapper John, were supposed to be equals. But Gelbart began to identify with the Hawkeye character, and since he was the creative genius who had a hand in 97 M*A*S*H episodes in four years, Hawkeye became the sun, and every one else a planet.

As in any successful enterprise, the bosses had to give their support to the creators. Boy, did Gelbart create. He was a pure writer, totally devoted to the show. He would hole up in his office and stay there, throughout the day and throughout the night, until he was sure he had it right. He might well have looked at his bank account and said, archly, "I'm Larry Gelbart," and turned in some things that were "good enough for TV." But he never did that, never said that.

Because Gelbart was such a pro, the Fox management said, "Gelbart's the creator. Let him create."

And so, after three seasons, Wayne Rogers left the show. He just got caught in the creative downdraft. He was a terrific guy and a real pro, and I think he could have stayed with us if his character had been allowed to grow, along with that of almost everyone else. That was one of the secrets of the show's success: each character grew through the months and years, often with assists from the actors themselves. But Rogers never felt his character was allowed to change. Instead, he saw Trapper John diminish in depth, until he was just a happy-go-lucky foil for Capt. Pierce.

It didn't take long for Wayne to become disenchanted with his diminished role. "Very early on," Rogers recalls, "it was obvious my time wasn't being used well. If you read the book or saw the movie, you know that Trapper John was the thoracic surgeon, the chest cutter. Then one day they made Hawkeye a thoracic surgeon. They took away Trapper's credentials, his identity!" After the third or fourth script of the second season, Rogers went to the producers and said something like, "It appears this part is getting smaller. What are the plans here?" He said he had a solution to their problems. "I can do less shows and be more involved in those. That saves you money, and I won't feel like I'm wasting my time, and I won't feel like I'm being treated in some half-assed manner."

They told Rogers they were going to do more for the Trapper John character. But, by the middle of the third season, it was clear to Rogers that Trapper John was "an ancillary character plastered onto the script. It didn't matter who was playing him, me or 'Chaim Kanipganop.' It could have been anyone. My creative talents weren't being used."

After the final segment of our third season, he would be gone, on to better things. For five years, he had a TV series at Universal, "House Calls," with Lynn Redgrave, and had part ownership in it. He had another good, though short-lived, series called "City of Angels," where he played a stylish, LA private eye of the 1930s.

And Gelbart was busy, creating another character to fill his shoes at the 4077 — Capt. B.J. Hunnicutt — who would be married, and something of a straight arrow. Trapper John had been a rakish guy. By contrast, B.J. was devoted to his wife and child, which made him a better straight man for Alda's Hawkeye. Many of us were sorry to see Wayne Rogers leave. We thought things would never be the same without him. How could they ever replace him?

As it turned out, they didn't exactly replace him. But they brought in someone we quickly learned to like. His name was Mike Farrell, and what was not to like? He proved to be a perfect foil for Hawkeye, and eventually, he became somewhat more than just a foil.

18

Klinger

Now, this all happened toward the end of our third season and the beginning of our fourth, just about the time the show was really beginning to stun people, and start winning slews of Emmy awards. (In 1975, M*A*S*H won the George Foster Peabody Award, the first time that any sitcom ever won this prestigious prize.)

It was the time I became a regular on the show, which meant, for me, among other things, that there would be something for Klinger on almost every show. Unlike Rogers, I never felt that my character was being given short shrift. To the contrary. Gelbart and the other writers began to give Klinger more of a personality. He wasn't simply a one-joke character any longer, but a complicated individual, someone who had what writers call "a back story" — a history of his own — that would come out from time to time.

And, to make things even nicer for me, Klinger's back story was, in part, my back story. I came from Toledo. So, too, did Klinger. I never forgot some of my old neighborhood haunts, like Packo's Hot Dogs. Neither did Klinger. I rooted for a minor league baseball club called the Toledo Mud Hens. So, too, did Klinger. I was Lebanese. So, then, was Klinger. And this helped the humor along a little — as long as no one minded the stereotyping that went along with my Middle East background. I certainly didn't.

Stereotyping is an old, time-honored tradition in the American theater, dating back to vaudeville, and I can only deplore the super sensitivity of certain spokespersons for certain groups who seem to have lost their sense of humor. I saw one M*A*S*H re-run recently, "Margaret's Marriage," originally shown at the end of our fourth season, and found Klinger wishing that Maj. Houlihan and her groom, Lt. Col. Donald Penobscot, would have a married life blessed by many camels. After awhile, Gelbart and the other writers looked for ways to insert Arab jokes wherever they could. But they'd also invite my suggestions from time to time, too. I was only too eager to help. This would generally happen on rehearsal days.

In fact, our rehearsal days (generally Mondays) were marked by an openness to the cast that was, up to that time, at least, unique in the television business. In most shows, the actors simply read what's been written for them. In M*A*S*H, the producers and the writers and the director seemed to have a special regard for the sensibilities of the actors, so much so that they embraced us as collaborators in the enterprise. I'm not saying that the actors wrote the shows. No. Except for that rare occasion when one of us was given the chance to write a show, the writers wrote the shows. But Gene Reynolds set the kind of climate on rehearsal days that invited input from us that could only make the show better.

It worked like this. First thing Monday morning, we'd gather around a big rectangular table and read out loud the script that we were going to be shooting that week. That gave us all a chance to see how the lines felt to us. Then we'd have another reading, and during that second reading, each of us had a chance to make suggestions about the script. Alan might say, "You know, that's a great line, but I think it would be better if it were to come from B.J."

We were not a bunch of saints. We had our tiffs like any other group of human beings. But Reynolds set the rules. "Fight all you want," he'd say. "But I'm the guy who makes the final decision. When I make it, you all have to live with it, okay? And what we say in here doesn't go out of here." So, yes, we had our differences, and sometimes we'd get all heated up and even call each other names. But when the discussion was over, it was over. That's what it meant to be a pro. We were pros. And getting the job done — that is, doing the best possible show — was always more important than seeing who would have the upper hand.

Maybe it was because the show was so successful. But the fact is that the M*A*S*H cast displayed an extraordinary amount of selflessness. Each of us was quite secure over our place in the scheme of things (inasmuch as actors can be secure about anything). We didn't fight over how many lines we had in a given show. If I didn't get many lines in this script, I'd be sure to get more of a play in the next one. We used to say, quoting Bill Shakespeare, "The play's the thing." Working together on M*A*S*H, the play was always the thing. Sometimes it was hard to remember, because we all wanted to be special. Ego sometimes got in the way. An actor has to have ego, or he will never make it. But he has to know how to control it. Otherwise, his ego will destroy him.

So we all had input. Each of us tried to add a bit of ourselves (or a bit of our own original invention) to the characters we were playing. The result: more nuance, more of a sense of the real, more fun. Mike Farrell might say, for instance, "B.J. is being such a straight arrow here. Let's curve him a little bit — have a little more fun here, round him out a little." And if he could find a way to do that, with a different word here, or sometimes just a frown or a grimace, there was no reason for the producer (or the writer) to veto the suggestion. Every reason, in fact, to go along with the new notion, because it only made the show better.

191

Later on, Mike Farrell would write and direct some episodes himself. Harry Morgan, and David Ogden Stiers and I also directed. (More about David later.) Alan Alda wrote and directed no less than 14 episodes, and he had a big hand in the last show, the two-and-onehalf-hour show that capped our series in February 1983.

Radar O'Reilly was another good example of a character who grew through the years — within the confines, at least, of his place in the ensemble. He was the 4077's little innocent, shy around the nurses, unable to sleep without his teddy bear, and sensitive to a fault. He was clairvoyant — able to anticipate his CO's needs, often before the CO even realized what his needs were. And he never drank anything stronger than grape Nehi.

In real life, however, he could have his ferocious moments. I remember early one morning, about 7 a.m., when Raquel Welch came to the lot and parked in Gary's parking place. It even had his name on it. Well, he needed that place. There was, in fact, no other parking place within a half-mile of Stage 9. So he collared me. He knew I knew Raquel when she was just an extra on "The Danny Kaye Show." And what a great gal I told Gary she was. We went looking for her together.

When we found her, she was in makeup, just across from Stage 9. She was sitting there, looking at herself in the mirror, and she didn't turn around to talk to us. She kept dabbing on this makeup and talking rather abstractedly to us through the image in the mirror. Could this be the same young woman I had known years before? Yes, but I guess she had learned that, to be a success in this business, you had to be tough. Maybe she'd been taking Steve McQueen's pills.

I said, brightly, "I'm Jamie Farr. You remember? From 'The Danny Kaye Show.' We used to work together."

She had no interest in that at all.

So now we tried to tell her about this new TV show called M*A*S*H. It wasn't clear she'd ever heard of it. I said I played a character named Klinger. Gary said he played a character named Radar. That didn't ring any bells either. She was barely listening

Once I'd made it in M*A*S*H, I was a frequent guest on many talk shows. Here I am, serving as a co-host with Mike Douglas. That's a young Billy Crystal between us. He was marwelous, marwelous.

Jaye P. Morgan and I were regular guests on NBC's daytime version of "The Gong Show." Here we are with a gong that has, obviously, been bonged too many times.

This was a milestone in the history of inter-faith relations, Arab and Jew together — me and Sammy Davis Jr., having fun on the set of "Cannonball Run."

In May 1981, I went to Washington to emcee a celebration commemorating the 100th anniversary of the Red Cross. There, I presented Vice President George Bush with a M*A*S*H jacket.

Grip and grin with President Reagan. From the look of us, you'd think we'd just won the California Lottery, but, as I recall, we were feeling relief after a campaign rally because no one had taken a shot at us.

When President Gerald Ford left the White House, he joined the board of Twentieth Century-Fox. He was a frequent visitor to the set where we used to trade taunts about the upcoming Ohio State-Michigan games every year. He was an alumnus of Michigan and I was still an Ohioan at heart.

In September 1980, I was privileged to be among the members of the 1980 U.S. Olympic Team when they were invited to the White House by President and Mrs. Jimmy Carter. That was the team that didn't get to go to the Games in Moscow.

Here is the greatest hockey player in the world, Wayne Gretzky, visiting the set of M*A*S*H. My son Jonas was there for the occasion.

This was an even more distinguished visitor, Prince Charles of Great Britain, who told me that his mother, Queen Elizabeth, was a M*A*S*H fan. That's Bill Christopher on the left, David Ogden Stiers, the Prince, Mayor Tom Bradley (in the background), Harry Morgan, and, just over his shoulder, Ron Beckman, the executive from whom I demanded a raise, at gunpoint.

When I joined "The Love Boat" company in the early 1980's, Joy and I found ourselves on a camel (what else?) near one of the pyramids.

Here's my daughter, Yvonne, in a contemporary photo with my wife, Joy. Like mother, like daughter, right?

In April 1985, I got my Star on the Hollywood Walk of Fame, on Vine Street, right next to Merv Griffin's Theater. That's my family in the back row, Joy, Jonas and Yvonne, with Mike Farrell (kneeling down). Front Row: Johnny Grant, me, and Bill Welsh. (Photo below) For ten years now, I have promoted the Jamie Farr Ladies Professional Golf Association Toledo Classic, played every summer at the Highland Meadows Country Club in nearby Sylvania, Ohio. Here I am presenting first prize money to our 1994 champion, Kelly Robbins.

In 1994, I made my Broadway debut in a prize-winning revival of "Guys & Dolls." Here I am with the other stars, Martin Vidnovic, Kim Crosby, and Jennifer Allen. (© Martha Swope 1994. Photo: Carol Rosegg.) (Photo below) This is Jerry Zaks, director of "Guys & Dolls" at the Martin Beck Theater in New York. As an actor way back when, Jerry did some day work on M*A*S*H, but then turned to directing plays, and he is now one of the best directors on Broadway.

Current family portrait. Me and Joy and my sister, Yvonne in the back row. Jonas and my mom, Jamelia, sitting down. My mom and my sis live in Phoenix, but we visit them all the time. And they visit us. (Photo below) And, finally, two very happily married folks, me and Joy, in the backyard of our home in Bell Canyon. It's been nice being on Broadway, but seeing this picture makes me yearn to be back in Bell Canyon, with Joy.

to us. As soon as I saw the situation, I wanted out of there, because I didn't see how I could help Gary.

"Yes, I know, I know," she said when Gary explained why he needed that parking spot. But she didn't know, didn't seem to understand.

Then Gary blew, and I saw a new side of Gary. "Listen," he shouted. "Get your effing car out of my spot, or I'll have the studio police do it." Now she understood. She moved her car.

Eventually, the confines of the M*A*S*H ensemble proved too restrictive for Gary Burghhoff. He was good enough to win Emmys every single season he was on the show. But then, he began to burn out. He talked about it very movingly in an interview with Suzy Kalter: "For seven years, no new person in my life called me Gary. Only Radar. A name is a very important thing. It's one of the first elements of identity. It's primary, and if you're missing your name, you're in trouble.... It took me a long time to figure out what was going on those last years. I thought it was only me, but know now that's not true. I had to leave. In Year Seven, all I could really think about was being able to take a year off to be with my daughter. That's what I did."

And so, Gary, too, would leave the show. (It took us two episodes during our eighth season to say goodbye to Radar O'Reilly.) Now Burghoff was the last of the original regulars to depart.

By then, it only seemed fitting that Klinger take Radar's place as company clerk. By then, the eighth season of M*A*S*H, Klinger stopped wearing women's clothes. Nobody seemed to miss his pinafores. Or his babushkas either. So Klinger evolved. When Gary left, Metcalfe and the writers got the idea of having Klinger take over as Col. Potter's clerk (rather than replacing Radar with someone else). That worked, too, and it gave Klinger some new life on the show. And anyway, Metcalfe knew that, "Sooner or later, the one-joke Klinger character was going to wear thin."

So now, even though Klinger wasn't wearing his own couture any longer, he was still inventing wacky ways to get a Section 8. Once, Klinger decided to pretend he was going to immolate himself, by seeming to ignite a can of water that was masquerading as gasoline. But Col. Potter discovered the ploy in advance, and substituted real gas for the water. When Klinger poured the gas-water over his head, he realized that someone had pulled a switch. He may have been crazy. But he wasn't stupid. He hightailed out of there, pronto.

Another time, Klinger planned to float home (all the way across the Pacific) in an inflatable boat. When the military police caught him with the boat, they collared him and brought him to Col. Potter's office, wearing a Florence Chadwick bathing cap, with the boat under his arm. "Son," says the colonel, "You never would have made it."

"Oh, yes sir, I would have made it," said Klinger. Then he threw the boat down, and pulled the inflating pin. Suddenly, the two of them (plus the company clerk and the MPs) were engulfed by a huge rubber boat. It knocked Harry Morgan right back off his chair and pinned him to the wall. Knocked me down, too. We hadn't rehearsed this. We were both surprised. Neither of us had to do much acting.

Klinger also sat a flagpole. He tried to go AWOL in a hang glider. He put on civvies and pretended he was already home, selling aluminum siding. He tried to eat the colonel's jeep, piece by piece.

When I first broke in as a regular on M*A*S*H, I got my own dressing room. Well, it wasn't exactly a dressing room. It was a tiny trailer not far from the dressing rooms of the others, and naturally, it didn't have any air conditioning. Some summer and fall days, it got so hot in that dressing room that I imagined myself as that Alec Guinness character in "The Bridge on the River Kwai," who was put in a sweat box by his captors to make him crack.

But when Gene Reynolds saw where I was, he prevailed upon the studio to give me a real dressing room. It, too, was tiny, and it didn't have many amenities. Everyone else had a little refrigerator. I had none. When I noted this in the presence of Wayne Rogers, he told me he was leaving the show. Why not take his?

Well, I knew I wasn't supposed to do that without a requisition from Mark Evans, the administrative producer at Twentieth Century-Fox. But, what the hell, I said. I remembered a famous old Errol Flynn movie, where he played the role of Don Juan. In a final scene, Don Juan is supposed to have learned his lesson. He's not going to chase women any more, right? Wrong! He spies a beautiful woman climbing aboard her carriage and he says, "There's a little bit of Don Juan in every man. And since I am Don Juan, there's a little more of me in me than there is in anyone else." And then he mounts his horse and rides after a new conquest.

And so, given a shot at a modest new fridge for my little dressing room, I thought of my identity as Maxwell Klinger, a scammer, a con man and an fast operator who would have finagled his own grandmother out of her walker if he thought he could make a profit on it. And so, at this juncture, I say to Wayne, remembering Flynn, "You know, there's a little bit of Klinger in every man. And since I am Klinger, there's more of me in me than there is in anyone else." And then I went in and commandeered the mini-ice box.

But, one day, I am coming back to my dressing room for lunch, and I see some workmen hauling my refrigerator out the door — with my lunch just sitting there on the carpet. When I wonder to them why they are taking my fridge, one of them says, "Mark Evans says one of Fox's executives has just been allocated a refrigerator. He told us to take yours."

I said to the men, "Uh, guys, don't walk too fast." Then I stormed down to Stage 9, where I told one of the assistant directors, "If my refrigerator isn't back in my room in ten minutes, you'll be able to find me at home. I'm outta here." I stalked back to my dressing room and started my countdown. They brought back the fridge.

Now, let me tell you why this whole refrigerator caper was important to me. Though I was now appearing in every segment of M*A*S*H, I was still a second class citizen, salary-wise. And so, to save money, I made it a habit to bring my lunch every day. And I needed a fridge to store it in.

Was the studio cheap? Sometimes that was the only conclusion we could make. Once, Mark Evans sent down a directive to cut off our peanut butter. Peanut butter! Yes, you see we were in the habit of taking breaks at 4 p.m., at our crafts-services cart inside the cavernous Stage 9, where everyone — cast, crew and extras — could gather, talk things over, let their hair down, have a snack. Our breaks weren't elaborate. Far from elaborate. We seemed to like crackers and peanut butter, for example, and we paid 25 cents a cup for our coffee. But now the studio was telling us it could no longer supply our club house with free peanut butter.

"Using too much peanut butter!" Our first reaction: We took up a collection to buy our own peanut butter and had almost $100 in the kitty until Alan Alda heard what we were doing. "Wait a minute!" he said. "Here's where we take a stand." He led all of us, all seven principal actors on the show, in our costumes, over to the office of Sy Salkowitz, who'd just become head of production. We went unannounced, and Sy's secretary, flustered and puzzled, led us into Sy's office. "Now, Sy," said Alda, "We have one of the top shows on television. We alone are keeping this studio in the black. And the studio wants to cut off our peanut butter?"

Sy clapped his palm to his forehead, a gesture that said it all. Unthinkable. How could we? Idiotic! He looked at Alda. He looked at me. He looked at every one in turn. I could almost see the wheels turning in his mind. "These people are keeping Fox afloat. Without M*A*S*H, I wouldn't have my job. And all they want is peanut butter?" But I also suspect that he, too, was a comedian, and he was milking the moment. Finally, he spoke. "Regular or crunchy?"

Before the end of the week, some men arrived in a big truck and offloaded enough cases of peanut butter to panel one of the walls in Stage 9. And from then on, we also got free coffee and tea.

One other time, I think it was in our fourth season, we marched together in protest. CBS had been playing games with our time slot. First season, we were on Sunday nights. Second season, Saturday nights — which was probably the best Saturday night in the history of television. I think this was the exact batting order: "All In The Family" led off. Then came "M*A*S*H." Then "The Mary Tyler Moore Show" followed us. Then came "Bob Newhart." Then "The Carol Burnett Show." After that exposure, we had people tuning us in, no matter where we were scheduled. Third season, they put us on Tuesday nights, where we held our own. Fourth season, Friday nights.

But, ratings-wise, Friday nights were not like Tuesdays. And so, in the middle of the fourth season, in the fall of 1975, we decided we'd go to CBS and demand another night, almost any other night, and keep it. Alan led us again, this time to Robert Wood's office at CBS Television City. Wood was president of CBS at the time.

We tried to make the meeting as painless as possible for Wood. Alan remembers that, "as actors, we weren't expected to act like grown-ups. We were all over him, with a lot of antic energy."

For a moment or two, we had a reasonable discussion. Wood tried to make the point that all the network really wanted us to do was win our time slot, against the competition of the other networks.

Wood said, "What do you want us to do? Turn out the lights on Friday night? Somebody's gotta do Friday night."

Then, as Alan remembers it, "We attacked Wood. He ended up sprawled on his desk — proving to us that he could have fun, like us. So he just got up on his desk. I don't think any of us threw him on the desk. But I can't be certain of that. Maybe it was Jamie Farr who threw him on his desk."

Well, the upshot was that Wood caved in. "M*A*S*H," he said, "is the jewel in the crown of the CBS eye. What night would you like?"

We thought Tuesdays would be just fine. And so, Tuesdays it was — from December 1975 until January 1978, when CBS asked if we'd mind moving to Mondays at nine o'clock — where we stayed until the end of our series in 1983.

19

Col. Henry Blake

McLean Stevenson, our humorous, easygoing Col. Blake, our in-over-his-head-most-of-the-time-but-trying-to-make-some-kind-of-reason-and-order-out-of-the-chaos Col. Blake — McLean left the show, too, after three seasons. I think McLean was sorry he left. He talked about the war he was having with Twentieth Century-Fox. He talked about the war he was having within himself. "It was terrible. Sometimes, I think I won the battle and lost the war. Sometimes, I think I won the war and lost the battle. I'm not sure."

One thing I am sure of: he made a huge contribution to the show. Another thing I am sure of: that it was hard to figure out where the personality and the character of McLean Stevenson ended off, and the role of Col. Blake began. McLean made Blake a mirror image of himself, and he signalized the informality of his command by wearing a fishing hat much of the time, a hat decorated with dozens of trout flies. This was a clue that, though he ran a very good M*A*S*H unit, he also liked to have a little fun.

I think people like to see authority figures who are also real human beings. Henry Blake was a human being. He sucked in his pot belly when a pretty woman passed by. Though he had a wife in the U.S., he fell in love with a clerk typist in Toyko, who was half his age, and still a cheerleader at heart. (Their romance didn't survive one weekend visit to the 4077.) He let Radar run his command. He allowed himself to be intimated by Maj. Margaret Houlihan, and irritated by Maj. Frank Burns. He let Klinger amuse him (and get away with everything short of murder). He treated Trapper and Hawkeye with embarrassing kindness. He once said, "I really represented what most young people wished their own dads, or their bosses, or their commanding officers had been like."

Offscreen, McLean Stevenson was even more likable. He had a great gift of pantomime, and he could entertain the whole cast with a single prop, something as simple as a fly swatter in his hand. One moment, the fly swatter would be baseball bat, then a butterfly net, then a spatula, than a canoe paddle.

It was partly because McLean was so darn likable that we in the cast concocted some of our best practical jokes for his benefit. I am sure he would amend that to say, "Well, I would hardly say for my benefit." You will understand why when I tell you about one trick we played on McLean during our second season. CBS had brought a number of reporters to the set to do interviews with the cast. There was one particularly lovely woman in the group, and McLean made it very clear to all of us that he was looking forward to his interview with her.

Well, the interviews were all set up for a particular corner of Stage 9, in director's chairs printed with our names on them, each lined up next to an empty chair for the visiting reporter. So, of course, we had to booby-trap McLean's chair. We undid the seams that held the chair together and put a whoopee cushion on the seat. When McLean plopped himself down next to this very attractive reporter, everything happened just the way we planned it.

No, better than we could have planned it. First, the whoopee cushion made a loud, very vulgar sound. Startled and embarrassed, McLean tried to get up off the traitorous chair. It fell apart, and McLean tumbled onto the floor. As he lay there wanting to die, listening to the howls of the cast, the lovely young reporter immediately sized up the situation, and joined in on the fun with us. She leaned over and said, "Mr. Stevenson. That is not only the loudest fart I've ever heard, but possibly the most dramatic one I've ever seen."

Speaking of that f-word, reminds me how I used to have a little fun with it. Sometimes, when a visitor would come by the set, I'd go over and shake hands and tell him my name. "I'm Jamie Farr," I'd say. "The 'T' is silent in Farr." Sometimes people would get it. Sometimes they wouldn't. But I always wanted to give people what I liked to call "the twinkle and the tickle."

McLean didn't leave the show because he wanted more money. In fact, Fox offered to double his salary if he stayed for the run of his five-year contract. He refused that, but did come back for a third year at his original salary, if they would let him leave at the end of that year. His problems with Fox were based on the studio's almost total disregard for some very basic comforts for cast and crew. "I was asking for a place to dress. I was asking for some kind of air to be pumped into the stage to combat the 110-degree heat we endured there during July and August. I was asking that we might have a place to sit when we were on location that wouldn't be 150 degrees inside. I wasn't asking for a special place to park my car, I just wanted a place to go to the bathroom. We had to go all the way to the makeup department to use the bathroom. I couldn't understand why we even had to ask for these things."

McLean Stevenson reached his breaking point with M*A*S*H one frosty morning out on location in Malibu Canyon. We all got there at dawn, only to discover there was no heat, no water and no coffee. We were nothing but philosophical about this. What else did we expect from Fox?

But McLean was not in a philosophical mood. He bolted, drove over to a diner off the Ventura Freeway, and phoned Fox, leaving a message with a studio guard to tell Bill Self, the head of Fox Television, to phone Stevenson at Al's Diner. Well, Self called him there, and McLean told Self he was going to sit there until they got some heat and water and coffee out here in Malibu Canyon, and he didn't give a damn if it cost the studio money, or if the show fell behind.

He later realized he was talking to the wrong man. The studio was then undergoing some kind of reorganization. It wasn't Self who was running things, but a committee. And McLean didn't foresee any change in the near future. Besides, he'd been hosting the Tonight Show on NBC, and actually making more money there than he was making with Fox. So he didn't need the aggravation of M*A*S*H. He told Gelbart and Reynolds he was resigning from the show, effective at the end of the season, our third.

The only thing Gelbart could do was write him out of the script. He had to figure out what plausible plot turn he might use to explain Col. Blake's departure from the 4077. And so, for the last show of the season, Gelbart had Col. Blake going home because he'd accumulated enough points for a discharge. (Which was an anachronism, since the point system was used in World War II, but not in the Korean conflict)

We shot a farewell scene with him at our helipad. He was in civies, looking a little ridiculous in a natty blue suit, a fedora and brown and white shoes. I was looking a little ridiculous, too. I wore my Carmen Miranda outfit, the one with the fresh-fruit headdress. Then I went home, thinking I was through for the week. So did Loretta. Then we got this mysterious phone call. We had to come back for one extra scene. So, next day, we were back in costume, but in the dark. No one had given us any extra pages of script. We wondered what was going on.

We soon learned. Gelbart took the principals — no others — behind closed doors and told us he was going to make the colonel's departure more dramatic. He would have him killed in a plane crash on his way home from Japan. We were to learn of it through Radar. He would read out a cabled message, and we would react.

Well, there was quite a discussion about this. It seemed a cruel thing to do. To us, Col. Blake had assumed the status of a real person. Kill him off! I didn't like the idea, but I was low man on the totem pole. I said nothing. I just went out with the rest of them to shoot the final scene, whether I liked it or not.

And so, when Radar read the cable, he was all choked up, just as if it was McLean Stevenson who had died, and not the fictional Col. Henry Blake. At 1900 hours, Radar entered the OR where the doctors were doing their jobs. "I just got a message. The colonel's plane was shot down over the Sea of Japan. It spun in. There were no survivors."

We were choked up, too. And our eyes showed it, over our surgical masks. Sure, we were acting. But the feeling we conveyed brought things home to the American public, which was up in arms over the death of Col. Blake.

McLean Stevenson was more matter of fact. That plane crash made it impossible for McLean to ever come back on the show, if he were to have a change of heart. It also prevented him from doing his own show, where he might continue being Henry Blake, MD. But McLean really never thought about doing that. He accepted his TV death philosophically. "It did make one hell of a show," he said, "one that a lot of people won't forget."

20

Harry Morgan

Some of us thought that we'd never have another CO like Henry Blake. Well, we were right. We never did. But, for my money, we got someone else who was different, and just as good, a new CO, Col. Sherman Potter, a regular Army surgeon who, according to the back story, had once been part of the U.S. cavalry, now fighting his third war, cutting and stitching a third wave of wasted youths. The U.S. Army still claimed his loyalty. But his tired eyes had long since failed to see any glory in battle.

That man was Harry Morgan, a familiar figure in network television, most renowned as Joe Friday's sidekick on the LA cop show, "Dragnet." He was a TV veteran, one of the most consummate pros in the history of network television, and talk about McLean's fatherliness! Harry was father and mentor to almost all of us — but most especially to me and to Loretta Swit.

Ever since he made his Broadway debut as a broken-down fighter named Pepper White in "Golden Boy" in the early 1930s,

Harry Morgan had been in show business. ("Golden Boy," you probably remember, was a prize-winning play written by Clifford Odets, about a promising violinist who becomes a boxer. It was a huge hit on Broadway, and it starred Karl Malden, Lee J. Cobb, Luther Adler and Martin Ritt. "Golden Boy" also became a film, and an historic one at that, because it was young William Holden's movie debut.)

But life for Harry Morgan wasn't one success after another. He remembers one year, after "Golden Boy," when he appeared in three successive Broadway flops, and didn't clear $1,000. That year, on Christmas Day, he and his wife dined on a can of crab meat and a can of potatoes. Even when he came to Hollywood in the late 1930s, he couldn't find work right away. But once he did land his first role, a juicy part in "To the Shores of Tripoli," and then another good part in the classic "Oxbow Incident," directed by William Wellman, he was off and running — doing more than 100 films, including "High Noon," "What Price Glory" and "Inherit the Wind" before he moved into television, into "Dragnet" — and a number of other series gigs, before and after M*A*S*H.

His series work — starring roles on 11 different series — may be close to a record. In order, he did "December Bride," and then "Pete and Gladys," which was a spin-off from "December Bride" — the first time in television history that one show evolved out of another show. Then came a long stint on "The Richard Boone Show" (an anthology done by Boone's repertory group, including Morgan), "Kentucky Jones," "Dragnet," "The D.A.," "Hec Ramsey," M*A*S*H, "After M*A*S*H," "Black's Magic," and finally, "You Can't Take It With You." He turned down a lot more series opportunities (and wished, later, that he'd taken some of them on, including a show produced by Burt Metcalfe featuring the characters that hung out at an interesting barbershop, a series called "Cutters.").

In fact, it was Bert Metcalfe's idea to hire Harry, one to which Gene Reynolds says he gave his enthusiastic approval. Harry had already done a guest shot on M*A*S*H, so Metcalfe and Reynolds knew what he might add to the show. And what was that? Reynolds says, "He had a great sense of humor. He was a great actor. He'd done some marvelous work through a wonderful career. He worked with me in 'Pete and Gladys.' And he had the kind of virility that this part demanded, so that people could see him as an Army guy. He was the kind of CO that McLean Stevenson was. He could be cranky, or obstinate, but he was not a martinet."

Yes. Harry had the kind of strength that would allow him to be a friend and a father to the rest of us and still maintain his authority. He could be stern with Klinger, but there was a kind of a not-too-veiled amusement with Klinger as well.

Off the set, Harry and I amused each other. Though we were invited to the dailies (noon screenings of the previous day's film), Harry and I hardly ever went to them. We'd rather go off together for a nice lunch at the commissary. The place was always jammed, because, in addition to the great atmosphere, walls covered with murals commemorating some of the films produced by Fox over the years, they had very fine food that was reasonably priced. Few on the lot ever went anywhere else. And theatrical agents would often come in for lunch. For years, our commissary had been a favorite place for Abe Lastfogel, the legendary head of the William Morris Agency, who would dine there with his secretary, David. Now, as Mr. Lastfogel was less active, he stopped coming. But David still came. And Harry Morgan and I would sometimes sit with him.

On this particular day, we lunched with David. And he picked up the check "on instructions from Mr. Lastfogel, who loves M*A*S*H so much." Imagine! We weren't even with William Morris.

After that lunch, Harry and I stopped by the executive dining room, to see if we could cadge a cigar from the head waiter, an amusing fellow from Germany named Hans. Hans liked me and Harry and had gotten used to us. We stopped by so often that Hans would be reaching into this large humidor for some of Alan Hirshfield's famous cigars as soon as he saw us coming. Alan

Hirshfield was a real big shot, number two man at Twentieth Century-Fox, well known for his taste in cigars.

On this particular day, I opened the door to the executive dining room, and, finding it empty except for Hans, I shouted, "Hey, Hans, how about a couple of those great Hirschfield cigars for me and Mr. Morgan?"

"*Jawohl*," he shouted back with a click of his heels.

Jokingly, I added, "Make sure Hirschfield doesn't see this."

Just as Hans was handing me the cigars, I heard this voice coming from a table behind a small palm tree. "Hirschfield can't see, but Hirschfield can hear." There was Alan Hirschfield, lunching with a client, peering at me now. He said, "Are you really going to smoke that shit?"

I thought the only thing I could do, now, was brazen it out. "Sure. I heard they were your favorite cigars."

He smiled, and said, "That's a rumor I started to get rid of them. You want a couple good Havanas?" He picked up the phone on his table and dialed a number (his secretary, I guess). He said, "Send Harry Morgan and Jamie Farr a couple of my best Cubans. Yes. On the M*A*S*H set." They were terrific cigars. Harry and I were grateful that Hirschfield couldn't see that day, but Hirshfield could hear.

While I'm on cigars, I have to tell you about meeting George Burns at a celebration commemorating CBS's 50th year of broadcasting. I was one of a hundred or more stars who were invited to this grand party. They included Roy Rogers and Dale Evans, Telly Savalas, Red Skelton, Alfred Hitchcock, Mary Tyler Moore, Carroll O'Connor, Walter Cronkite, James Arness, Loretta Swit, Lynda Carter, Eva Gabor, Danny Kaye, Arthur Godfrey, Danny Thomas, Mike Wallace, Dick Van Dyke, Ed Asner, Carol Burnett, Eric Sevareid, Art Linkletter, Lucille Ball, Dan Rather, Rob Reiner and, as Yul Brynner used to say, "et cetera, et cetera and so forth."

They wanted to take a large photograph of this group. Hard to get all these folk together at one time, easy to commemorate the occasion with a picture. So, while the photographer and his assistants were lining us up, I found myself next to George Burns. What could I say to the great George Burns? I was intimidated by this great man. But I summoned up my courage and said, "Excuse me, Mr. Burns." I was trying to be casual. "I know you're an avid smoker. Tell me, are your cigars expensive." He studied my face.

Was he angry at my question? I stuttered, "I, I mean, I imagine they run you six or seven dollars apiece." Oh, jeez, I wanted to bite my tongue.

He wasn't angry at all. He finally smiled and said, "El Producto. Cost twenty five cents apiece. Son, anything that costs six or seven dollars, I suck it first, and then I smoke it."

By now, I think you are beginning to realize that I am a real fan. I like people in the business, whether they're beginners or veterans who have proved their talent over the long haul. I remember encouraging some day players who used to get bit parts in M*A*S*H. "Hang in there," I'd say. "It wasn't so long ago that I was a day player, too." One of these actors was a nice young man named Jerry Zaks. Jerry would go on to become a highly regarded director on the New York stage, and as it turned out, someone who didn't forget the times on the M*A*S*H set when I had gone out of my way to be nice to him.

In this, I think I was only imitating the example of Harry Morgan. Harry, the TV veteran, went out of his way to be nice to me, rookie though I must have seemed in his eyes. I got to be very good friends with Morgan. And I felt myself very lucky to meet some of Harry's best friends in the business, people like Ralph Bellamy.

Harry had known Bellamy for years. He was a member of something known in Hollywood as the Irish Mafia: James Cagney, Pat O'Brien and Jimmy McHugh. When Bellamy showed up to visit the M*A*S*H set at Harry's invitation, I was thrilled to meet him. I don't know if many people know it, but Ralph was one of the founders of the Screen Actors Guild, and president of Equity, the theater actors' union, for 12 years.

In my book, he was a giant, an actor equally at home on the legitimate stage and in front of a camera. Talk about a self-made man. He never finished high school, played tent shows at age 17, started stock companies of his own in Atlanta and Des Moines, and eventually made it big on Broadway. He took the inevitable trip to Hollywood and played, among other things, in a series of movies that were memorable to me, "The Wolf Man" pictures, at Universal.

Then, one day, he realized he couldn't stick around Hollywood any longer. The realization came when he heard a casting director was looking for "a kind of Ralph Bellamy type who never gets the girl." He knew it was time for him to move on, to re-create himself on Broadway again. Which he proceeded to do with "Detective Story," and "Sunrise at Campobello" — the play in which he brought Franklin Delano Roosevelt back to life.

Bellamy loved the theater, loved to act. And when Joy and I were invited to have dinner with the Bellamys, Ralph and Alice, and the Morgans, Harry and Eileen, we accepted eagerly. Gee, I could sit around all night and listen to Ralph and Harry tell their stories.

One of Ralph's best stories happened in the early days of television. He was in a half-hour show called "Man Against Crime," which he was doing on live TV in New York while simultaneously starring on Broadway in "Detective Story." He'd finish the TV show, then hop in a limo waiting to take him to the theater. But not before his final turn before the camera on behalf of the sponsor, Camel cigarettes. At the end of every program, Ralph would announce that cartons of Camels would be sent to our armed forces all over the world. Ralph would take out his Zippo lighter and light his cigarette and then announce the names of the bases that would be receiving the free cigarettes this week.

Well, one night at the close of the show, Ralph appeared on camera, took out a Camel, put it in his mouth, lit up, and took a deep drag. But a flake of loose tobacco got stuck in his throat, just as he was about to announce the names of all these bases. Now understand: the show is live and it is sponsored by the R.J. Reynolds Tobacco Company. Ralph is about to choke, but he can't cough, or even clear his throat. What kind of p.r. is that for

Camels? But here's what kind of trooper he is: he neither coughs nor chokes. Instead, he exercises mind over matter, takes a deep breath and ticks off the bases as fast as he can. When he is finished, his voice is in the upper registers — practically falsetto. But he gets through the recitation, and is out the door and into the limo headed for Broadway. Now, in my book, that was an Emmy-winning performance.

So was Bellamy's quick thinking when he found himself in front of a TV camera — same show, "Man Against Crime,"— prepared to confront, and arrest, the man whom he'd been pursuing for the last half-hour on live TV. Only trouble was, the actor playing that man had already left the studio — thinking he was finished for the night. That didn't stop Bellamy. He had training on the stage, and he knew how to keep the show going, no matter what. Alone on the set, he spied a window, went over, threw it open, and shouted out, "I know you're out there, and I know that you know that I know. You're surrounded now, and you're under arrest. And let me tell you how I know you did it."

Another time, Bellamy told about a nighttime shoot at Universal, a movie starring Evelyn Ankers featuring the Wolf Man, Dracula and the Frankenstein Monster. The director on this one was one of those European types, the kind of guy caricatured in all the cartoons: beret, megaphone, jodhpurs, high riding boots, foreign accent. Get the scene: it may have been three in the morning in front of the castle's moat. There's a fine mist falling and the director is giving Evelyn Ankers her final instructions for the next shot. "Okay, ze Wolf Man eez chasing your boyfriend into ze woods. Dracula eez running for your muzzer. And ze Frankenstein monster, he eez about to capture your fazzer. Now, I vant you should have ze feeling that you are, you're just — you're just, uh, fed up vith it all."

Harry tried to top Ralph's stories. Sometimes he succeeded. Like with this one: In the early 1950s, Harry was in a Western with Jimmy Stewart called "The Far Country." Harry was one of the bad guys and, in the last reel, he and two other desperadoes are holed up in the town saloon when Stewart and the townspeople march right up to the saloon. They have seized their own courage, and Stewart is their spokesman. "All right," he says, his scratchy voice breaking up a little, "you men can fight us, or you can ride out of town."

Harry turns to his fellow villains, Jack Latimer and Steve Brody, and he says, "We can't fight the whole town. We'd better ride out."

So they mosey on out of the saloon and head for their horses. Latimer and Brody are on their saddles with ease, but as Morgan attempts to put his foot in the stirrup, the horse bolts on him, and Morgan gives up. Director Daniel Mann yells, "CUT!" and frowns at Morgan. "Come on, Harry, we've got to get this shot. We're losing our light."

Take two: Stewart and the townspeople come up the street, stop in front of the saloon, and Stewart says, "All right, you can fight us or you can ride out of town."

Morgan says to Latimer and Brody, "We can't fight the whole town, so we'd better ride out." They exit again, and once again, Latimer and Brody mount their horses. But as Morgan puts his foot in the stirrup, the cinch on the saddle comes loose, and the entire saddle slips down and into the dirt.

"CUT!" screams Director Mann. Now he is really getting mad. He turns to Morgan. "Harry, we've got to get this shot."

Take three: Stewart and the townspeople march to the saloon. Stewart says, "All right, you can fight us or you can ride out of town."

Morgan says, "We can't fight the whole town, so we'd better ride out." They exit. Latimer and Brody mount their horses (again). Morgan puts his foot in the stirrup, but he stumbles and the horse bolts. Before Mann can cry, "CUT!" Morgan turns to Latimer and Brody. "Oh, hell with it," he says. "Let's fight 'em."

I am sure that scene was shown again and again, at any number of Hollywood parties, in a blooper reel that is known in the business as "outtakes." These "outtakes" or extra, unusable footage, are legendary throughout the business. On M*A*S*H, we had our fair share of bloopers that never made the final print, but did make our annual outtake reel, put together every year by our longtime film editor, Stanford Tischler. He dubbed his annual reel "M*I*S*H-M*A*S*H." That reel was one long series of bloopers and flubbed lines, generally followed by gales of laughter from the guys, or gals, in the shot. Very amusing.

Some of the outtakes were breathtaking. We saw one riotous outtake when Klinger was standing there, naked to the camera from the waist up (and supposedly completely naked). McLean Stevenson's eyes go down, and he ad libs, "My God, look at the size of that thing!"

One year at Christmas, Tischler gave us a change of pace. He showed us a M*A*S*H episode that had been dubbed in Spanish. We found it real kick to hear ourselves speaking Spanish.

Harry Morgan absolutely loved M*A*S*H. He'd been around the business a long time, right? Yet, he has made no secret of the fact that in all his working years he'd never enjoyed anything more, or been prouder of, than his work on M*A*S*H. What did he find? "This was the best show I ever had. The most rewarding from every point of view. Special people. A loyal, endearing sweetness" — not from just one or two of the cast, but from everyone, and from the producers, Gene Reynolds and Burt Metcalfe, as well.

Harry says, "We were all working on such grand material, and with such great people. There has never been a congregation of actors put together that could come within a mile of this bunch. How the hell could you beef? Unless you were a real asshole. Of which there are some in this business. But there didn't happen to be any in this company. If there had been, I don't think it would have lasted so long."

The first meeting between Harry and me occurred the year before he came aboard M*A*S*H as Col. Potter. He did a guest spot on M*A*S*H, playing a dotty general named Steele, on a show called "The General Flipped at Dawn." Nobody knew Gen. Steele had lost it, until he happened upon me, or rather Klinger, at a morning inspection. He was making his way up the line. "Let's put a better shine on those shoes, Father," he said to the chaplain,

221

Father Mulcahy. "Stomach in, chest out," he said to Maj. Houlihan. "No talking in the ranks," he said to Radar. And then, oh-oh, here comes Cpl. Klinger, in drag, arriving in line, late, and gleeful over his big chance to get out of the Army on a Section 8. As soon as General Steele got a look at Klinger....

A close up of Col. Blake indicates that he's afraid something drastic is about to come down on his head, as soon as the general sees Klinger. But that doesn't happen. Gen. Steele spies Klinger, in high heels and a dress, and he bristles, like this is an intrusion. He says, "Not now, Bernice. I'm inspecting the troops." You see, when the general saw Klinger in drag, he thought Klinger was his wife. Flipped? I guess. A little removed from reality, anyway.

Once Harry became a regular on M*A*S*H, there was no shakedown period. He remembers that he had a great first script. "Hawkeye and B.J. and I got drunk together," he says, "and that set us up right away." Nor did he ever have problems "dealing" with Gelbart. "You didn't have to 'deal' with Gelbart," Harry said. "He was a courtly gentleman. Pretty funny, too. And that was also true of Gene Reynolds." He was astounded to find, for instance, that if, in rehearsal, a given line didn't sound like him, "All I had to do was say so. Sometimes, they'd convince me that I was wrong. But if I wasn't convinced, they'd change the line. That just doesn't happen in most of the television I've done."

Harry felt that his input was so welcomed by the writers that he felt like "a co-creator, of a moral universe, or a little island, at least, of a caring community." An overblown sentiment? An exaggeration?

I don't think so. Reynolds and Metcalfe and Gelbart (and all the other writers) had a great deal of respect for Morgan, for what he had done in the business, and for what he was still doing. He was a real pro. I will never forget the speech that he gave in a M*A*S*H episode called "Old Soldiers," written by Dennis Koenig. Harry did seven takes of that speech during a 6-hour session. (He did this, because the director wanted to get reaction shots from each of the principals, and, to get those shots, he had to ask Harry to repeat the speech. In some productions, these off-stage lines are read by an assistant director. But that wasn't good enough for M*A*S*H. In our quality show, the off-stage lines weren't read by a stand-in, but by the guy, or the gal, who was actually delivering them in the show.)

Well, this was a poignant speech, given by a Col. Potter who was close to tears. So, too, was the cast in tears — each time he did it. And so, interestingly enough, was the crew, too. The cameramen and the sound crew, everybody.

Here's the story: Potter had taken a phone call at 3 a.m., then departed immediately for Tokyo, muttering something about a sick friend. He returned shortly, but seemed caught up in a state of melancholy for a time, listening to old French records, and communicating with no one. Then came notes from Potter to each of the staff: "You are invited to my tent tomorrow night at 1900 hours. P.S. That's an order."

We were all were mystified. Was Col. Potter in trouble? Sick himself? What? When we got to the colonel's tent, we found him wearing his World War I uniform. That piece of nostalgia was a clue, but still a puzzle to us. What was up? Here is how Col. Potter explained his sadness:

"I guess you're all wondering why the get-up. Well, it was a long time ago, 1917, to be exact. We were in France under a heavy artillery barrage. Me and my buddies laid low in an old French château. We were quite a group, the five of us. Went through hell together and lived to get drunk about it. Anyway, there we were in this château. So Stein finds a cache of this fine brandy and we sat up the whole night. Shells were screaming and we were singing and toasting our friendship. Then we got down to the last bottle."

Col. Potter raised a dusty old bottle. "This bottle here. Do any of you know what a tontine is? It's a pledge. The five of us made a pledge. We'd save the last bottle, let some legal eagle store it for us. Whoever turned out to be the survivor would get the bottle and drink a toast to his old buddies.

"For good or bad, you're looking at the last survivor. I got the job when Grusky passed on in Tokyo. He had the bottle sent here, God rest his soul. I was feeling real sorry for myself, getting along in years and all. But I'm looking at it differently now. As much as my old friends mean to me, I think you new friends mean even more. So I'd like you to share this bottle with me."

I think Harry could deliver this speech (seven times!) with such feeling because they weren't simply "lines" that were written for him, but because Harry was looking at us when he delivered them. We really were new friends who meant a lot to Harry Morgan, and he used the feeling to make this speech something special. Over the years, I have talked to M*A*S*H fans about this particular scene, and they remember it, and say, "You know, there was a level of feeling there in Harry Morgan's performance.

"Yeah, well," said Harry, trying not to be too sloppy sentimental about it when we asked him about it, "you did mean a lot to me — but it's not what you mugs think. It's because I won an Emmy for that speech."

21

Comrades

At the beginning of the 1978-79 season, Larry Linville left the show. He just got tired of doing the same thing all the time, being the butt of everyone's jokes, being the obligatory villain. But that was only on camera. Off-camera, Linville couldn't have been more likable. And so, none of the cast wanted him to leave. We thought his leaving had something to do with money. So Mike Farrell and I went to Ron Beckman and tried to persuade him to ask Fox for more money for Larry. Farrell and I think Beckman even succeeded in getting more money for Larry. But not even that did it. Larry just wanted to go.

Which reminds me of a story about my old friend, Bill Holden, and his old friend, William Powell. For those of you who weren't going to the movies much in the 1930s and 1940s, Powell was a fine actor, distinctive good looks, dark hair, pencil-thin mustache, with a special gift for comedy. He did a series called

"The Thin Man" with Myrna Loy, another actress with very distinctive good looks, including, as a I remember, a dimpled chin. He and Loy were a husband-and-wife team, private detectives, with an amusing Airedale named Asta. Anyway, sometime in the 1950s, Bill Holden ran across a dynamite script — perfect for him, with a part in it that was made to order, he thought, for Powell.

So Holden drove out to the Springs one Saturday morning bearing the script. Powell was fiddling in his garden. "This script," said Holden. "It's you."

Powell frowned. "I can't do it."

"But, Bill," said Holden. "It's not only you. It's also big money. A lot of money."

"Look," said Powell. "You just don't understand. I — can't — do — it — any — more."

Ah yes, said Holden to himself. He would soon hear a voice within himself that said, "I can't do this any more."

I guess Larry Linville had reached that point — at least with the role of Maj. Frank Burns.

And so, Larry Linville was written out of M*A*S*H. The writers replaced him with an aristocratic Bostonian, Maj. Charles Emerson Winchester. Metcalfe found a perfect Winchester in David Ogden Stiers. Like most of the cast, David had experience in the legitimate theater. He began his career little more than a year out of high school at the California Shakespeare Festival in Santa Clara, then went to New York to study in the acting division of the Juilliard School. He returned, briefly, to appear in some Actor's Workshop productions in San Francisco, then caught on with John Houseman's City Center Acting Company in New York. Eight plays with Houseman and he was ready for his Broadway debut as Buck Mulligan in "Ulysses In Nightgown" with Zero Mostel. He had a good many Shakespearean roles at San Diego's Old Globe Theatre. Metcalfe found him playing a television executive in an episode of "The Mary Tyler Show," which meant that he was already known (and esteemed) by CBS. With Larry Linville gone, the Maj. Winchester character had to become our fall guy, the butt of all the jokes formerly aimed at Maj. Burns.

You may recall that, in many a M*A*S*H story, Maj. Winchester preferred nothing more than classical music. Our writers didn't have to invent that; David was, and is, an accomplished musician in his own right, and has served as a guest conductor with symphony orchestras in Portland, Oregon, and in San Diego.

From this account, David sounds like a starchy guy. He wasn't. He had a superb sense of humor, and he fit in gloriously with our funning troupe.

How can I explain the spirit of camaraderie, the good feelings that came over our little M*A*S*H troupe? I don't think I really can. I can only tell you a few stories — about how we were when we were together, how excited we were after a vacation period to come back together again, how eager each Monday morning to plunge into the new theatrical adventure that each script promised us. And then, at the end of every week, on Friday nights, instead of scrambling off the lot, we stuck around to have a drink or two, order in some pizzas, and mainly, to review the week and the episode that we'd just shot.

Alan would usually buy the pizzas, from a little place on Pico Boulevard. Metcalfe's office would buy the beer and the wine. Writers and crew, cameramen and makeup people, as well as the cast, we had a hard time leaving the set. To unwind, we'd shoot the breeze, talk about anything and everything, the Dodgers or the Lakers or the Kings. (In fact, it was one of the writers, Thad Mumford, a Fordham alumnus from New York, who introduced me to hockey and remained a friend long after our M*A*S*H days together. He and his girlfriend and Joy and I used to go to some of the Kings hockey games together, and root, of course, for our friend, Gretzky.)

Television could be hard work. We normally worked from 7 a.m. to 7 p.m., five days a week. It wasn't unusual to shoot ten pages of script in one day; by contrast, actors and actresses in a feature movie are lucky to shoot two or three. And so, those Friday night parties were a welcome release from some of the tensions of the week.

One Friday lunchtime, however, we overdid the release a little bit. It was a kind of potluck affair, served in the mess tent of our set, and somebody made the mistake of bringing in several gallons of margaritas. Well, to make a long story short, almost the entire company got bagged. It looked like a triage scene, bodies slumped all over our mess-tent area. The only ones left standing were Burt Metcalfe, Mike Farrell and I, the camera operator, the director of photography and a couple ADs. Knowing we had one more scene to do that afternoon, we didn't do the margarita bit. But then, that was typical of the work spirit on our sets.

Often enough, even when the week was ended, we couldn't let go. In some Friday night pizza parties, I would catch myself re-playing a scene with Gary Burghoff, one that was already shot, but still one that we thought we could improve upon, if given the chance. Or I would find Alan Alda actually re-doing a scene with Mike Farrell. The scene was already in the can. But here were the two of them, doing it over, trying one last time to get it right, if only for themselves. I think part of our collective joy came from the fact that we were all creating something together. Anybody who builds things or makes things — it could be a novel or a play or a poem or a painting, or it could be a new construction business, or a paint store — must understand this.

Our occasional guest stars were agog. One of them, John Randolph, spent a rollicking week with us, and said, "I can't believe this. I'm getting paid for this?" Yes. For having fun. And if anyone came in and made it clear he didn't want to have fun, we'd tell them there wasn't room here for vanity or pretension. If a guest-actor came in and tried to lord it over a crew member, or speak disrespectfully, one of us would take the actor aside and tell him, "We don't do it that way here."

Outsiders didn't seem to understand how serious we were. In fact, Alan Alda remembers that we became more and more disciplined, but you couldn't tell it by looking at us. "They would scream for quiet on the set, but nobody would stop talking. Then they would say 'Roll 'em' and things would go down to about half-volume. Then the guy would hit the clapper and most of the talking would stop. Now the scene is running and the guy would say, 'Action' and there would still be one or two people mumbling. And there would be absolute quiet just before our first line of dialogue.

"What we were doing was keeping our off-stage energy going, right into the scene, so that the relating we were doing and the energy that we had was immediately transferred to the characters' energy. Also we were testing this unspoken sense of communication that we had. We were saying, 'We know when we have to shut up, and that's when we will shut up.'"

Loretta Swit remembers now: "People were running to get to work, happy, happy to be there. A blessed way to make a living. I was usually the first one to get there in the morning. Harry was the only one to ever beat me there. We even saw each other on weekends. I took an actor friend to a M*A*S*H party once, a party to open the season. He took me aside. 'You're all crazy about each other?' Loretta nodded. The actor said he was really impressed. She said, "Yeah, it's like kids coming back to school after vacation."

Loretta also remembers that the men in the cast always gave a good deal of scrutiny to her dates. "They were all like so many elder brothers, looking the guys over. It was even better than family, because we chose to align ourselves with these people. And new people who'd come along were entranced when they saw us together. We thought that Wayne and McLean were the ultimate. And they were. But, those who came along to take their places were also ultimate. If they hadn't killed off Col. Blake, McLean would have come back. I know he would. He loved us. The day he left, McLean told me, 'I know I will never be in anything this good again. Because there will never be anything this good again.'"

Loretta remembers how at the end of a difficult, long day, the group would end up in the CO's office, punchy, suffering from a kind of battle fatigue. She says she was terribly impressed with me the day we were sitting around during one of those sessions, and someone said of someone else who was absent, "Oh, he's so limited." She remembers my quiet comeback: "Aren't we all?"

I do not remember that. What I do remember are all the laughing fits we had. "We'd stay on at the end of a day" she says, "and we'd get crazy. We couldn't stop laughing. Harry and Jamie would start joking around and crack everyone up. I remember one time Mike Farrell was actually rolling on the floor, laughing so hard that tears were rolling down his cheeks. He was totally out of control. And everyone else was laughing and screaming. Harry and Jamie would do routines together, often with the big cigars they loved so much." (Loretta's dad used to smoke cigars. She says being with Harry and me made her homesick.)

Some of the most inveterate M*A*S*H fans were always expecting that, someday, Hawkeye and Maj. Houlihan might fall in love. And then, in the sixth season, in a show called "Comrades in Arms," she and Hawkeye (her most vocal tormentor for years on the show) found themselves alone together in a shelled-out house during an artillery barrage.

She and Hawkeye turned to each other, were forced to admit that they didn't really hate one another, and — well, they were suddenly very close. The morning after, she made him breakfast from K-rations while he made small talk. "Well, here we are," he said, "two sleepy people by dawn's early light hoping they don't get shot before lunch."

They started to walk homeward, and spent the next night under a palm tree in a rainstorm. Margaret snuggled next to Hawkeye. "You know," she said, "all the time when we were insulting each other, every once in a while I'd wonder what it would feel like to be, you know, close to you. And there you were, wasting time with other women."

"Waste not, want not," quipped Hawkeye. When they were finally rescued, Hawkeye laughed, with tears in his eyes. "Margaret, we're safe. It's all over."

"Oh no, it isn't," she said. "Not by a long shot!"

Margaret and Hawkeye did not become a romantic twosome after that. Even so, they were in a new phase together; now, they couldn't take back the closeness and affection that they found for each other, either.

That pretend romance between Margaret and Hawkeye was symbolic of the love we all felt for Loretta in real life. There wasn't a man in the cast who didn't have the warmest feelings for this woman. She was, after all, the only woman among the principals, and she helped make more gentle the life of our little world. Harry Morgan used to say that her presence was "like that of any girl in a family of boys. She helped smooth our rough edges. And she brought some flowers and some light to Stage Nine."

Loretta got Emmys every year from 1974 through 1981, for OUTSTANDING SUPPORTING ACTRESS IN COMEDY, and she was always very generous, probably overly generous, in sharing credit for her Emmys with those of us who gave her support. Loretta says I was a key character in one show that won her an Emmy. It was the show where she was headed off for a birthday rendezvous in Tokyo with a general. She grabbed Klinger and insisted he drive her to Kimpo Air Base to catch her plane for Japan — even though he was all involved in making book on when a difficult calf was going to be born in the M*A*S*H compound.

But then, she insists he take a shortcut on a very rough road; because of that, the jeep gets a flat, and they are stranded. Another non-tough side of her character emerges. She confesses to Klinger that it is her birthday — and this is one further reason why she is so sad to think that she will not catch the plane for Japan. Klinger responds by bringing out a little cupcake, putting a match on it and presenting it to her as her birthday cake. At first, she is angry. "Don't you dare feel sorry for me," she cries. Then she is touched, and in those moments she, Loretta, is given a chance to surprise audiences with another side of Maj. Houlihan. She says, now: "Jamie won that Emmy for me." Hardly. But it is typical of Loretta to look for a way to hand credit on.

She also gave great credit to the show's writers. "In the beginning was the Word," she says. "If you don't have the words, you don't have anything."

But the writers wouldn't have anything without the actors and actresses, either. There is something called "the craft of

231

acting." I say "craft" advisedly. Most of us actors aren't born. We're
made. Or, rather, we make ourselves. We work at our craft. We
learn how to use our eyebrows, our mouths, our teeth, our twitches
and spasms and groans in order to help tell the stories that reflect
the glory and the agony of life. When those stories and those
enfleshments on a stage or on a piece of film really work, then we
are reflecting the glories and the agonies of the entire human race.

What I am saying is that we actors work at our craft. In time,
if we keep on working, we get pretty good at it. Occasionally, an
actor comes along who can also write. I am thinking, most
obviously, of Orson Welles, who co-wrote, produced, directed and
starred in what some consider the greatest movie ever made,
"Citizen Kane."

Alan Alda is made of the same stuff. Over time, he earned
the admiration of everyone in the M*A*S*H cast. And one of the
things we admired about Alan was his enthusiasm for the stories.
He himself could hardly refrain talking about the excitement he
felt making a contribution to M*A*S*H as a writer. It kind of
captures the excitement that we all felt as we proceeded along our
creative way.

It seems that Alan was writing a particular show — I can't
remember which one it was, nor can he. But he was so bursting
with the ideas that he wanted to cram into this piece that he
asked Larry Gelbart to have dinner with him. It might have been
at one of our favorite hangouts, a Chinese restaurant on Pico
Boulevard called King Foo. Or it might have been a place on
Wilshire Boulevard.

Well, wherever it was, anyway, they talked furiously all
through dinner, with Alda trying out one scene after another on
Gelbart, and Gelbart reacting, adding to the imagined action
whenever he could, feeding new ideas back to Alda. They went on
at a great rate, all through dinner, through dessert, and the check.
I think they closed the place. Then they continued their
conversation in the parking lot for a while, and then they
proceeded homeward, probably west, on a deserted Wilshire
Boulevard.

But that wasn't the end, either. Each time they stopped for a red light (and there were a good many of them on the way home to Beverly Hills), they were still trading ideas, shouting them out now, back and forth from their separate cars.

You can run into the most interesting people stopped at red lights in Beverly Hills. My writer friend, Sherwood Schwartz, found someone who kept waving at him as he drove up Rodeo Drive one day. He didn't recognize the guy. He didn't wave back. Finally, at the third red light, the guy rolls down his car window, points an index finger to his teeth, and smiles.

Schwartz still doesn't get it, but now he pushes a button to roll down the window on the passenger side of his vehicle, so he can learn who this fellow is.

"It's Dr. Goldberg," the man cries. "I'm your dentist."

Schwartz said, "Thank goodness you weren't my proctologist."

Which reminds me of another red-light-in-Beverly Hills-story. It seems that Hal Linden, the actor who was such a big hit in "Barney Miller," was taking a golf lesson in Toronto early one summer morning, and enjoying himself, until he realized that if he didn't leave for the airport right away, he was going to miss his plane to LA. So he threw his clubs in his golf bag and zipped back to his hotel and packed and made it to the airport in time to catch his plane. Only trouble was, in his rush, he left his three-iron behind on the driving range.

His golfing companions told the pro, George Knudsen, "Hey, we'd better get this club back to Hal Linden."

"Why?" said Knudsen. "He doesn't know how to use it anyway."

But of course Knudsen was just funning. Eventually, he found someone to take Linden's club back to LA — a broadcaster named Len Bramson, who was going to Southern California to cover a hockey game between the Maple Leafs and the Kings.

So, Bramson packs Linden's three-iron. But then, he gets to LA on a Saturday morning, and he can't find anyone who knows how to get in touch with Linden. He covers the hockey game that

233

night, and then on Sunday morning, he leaves his hotel in his rental car, still lugging Hal Linden's three-iron. He stops for a red light on Wilshire Boulevard. And then he turns to look at the car that pulls up next to his. Hal Linden is behind the wheel. This is quite a coincidence. It is Sunday morning, and there is absolutely no one on the entire boulevard except Len Bramson and Hal Linden.

Bramson rolls down the window on the passenger side and makes a rolling motion with his free hand. Linden is puzzled. He doesn't know Len Bramson from Len Dawson. But he rolls down his window.

"Hal Linden?" says Bramson.

Linden nods.

"I've got your three-iron here." He reaches into the back seat, grabs the club and hands it over to Linden. Then he drives off.

Linden is stupefied.

I wonder if, or how, he ever figured out what happened. (If you didn't ever figure it out, Hal, now you know!)

Where was I? Oh, yes, I was talking about the morale at M*A*S*H. Our good feelings about what we were doing even extended to the office employees at Fox. Once, when they went out on strike, we went to Burt Metcalfe and told him that, as SAG members, we had problems about crossing a picket line. Besides, these people were all our friends.

Metcalfe noted they were also the people who write our checks every week. He solved the problem by giving us all a two-week vacation. But then Murphy's Law kicked in. Something always goes wrong, and at the worst possible instant. I got a phone call from one of the editors. There was a scratch on an important piece of film or something. They could fix it. But they needed me to come in for a re-take. That's right. I was the only one needed.

Well, I revved up my fire-engine-red Cadillac (the only Cadillac I ever owned), the one with the license plate that read, TOLEDO 7, and drove in to the studio. I stopped and chatted with the pickets for a while. I explained what I was doing there and asked them if they would allow me in — "just for a couple of hours, maybe less. I'll be in and out, I promise you."

I kept my promise. And they cheered me on the way out.

For me, this picket line was a classic conflict situation. I'm a firm backer of the notion that working people have a right (and a duty to their families) to organize. But I also had this great love for the show. Alda once said, "There was a kind of ecstasy about our work." And I have to agree. I was excited about M*A*S*H, and I never lost my enthusiasm for what we were doing. Nor did the others. We found what we'd been looking for all our lives. And we found it here on M*A*S*H, together. Working on that show was so much fun for me that, sometimes, I'd head for home with my sides hurting from all the laughing. I could hardly wait to get up and go to work the next day.

Harry Morgan says that was one of my great contributions to the M*A*S*H troop, my enthusiasm. He told my collaborator, "Jamie was a real spark plug. Those frosty mornings on location, when we could think of a lot of other places we'd rather be. Those long evenings, when we were behind schedule and trying to finish. Jamie was never down, always up, happy doing what he was doing. His sunny disposition radiated over everyone."

I can report this praise from Harry without embarrassment — or pride. If I have a sunny disposition, it is because of my genes, a gift from God, not something I need to take credit for. But it is something to give thanks for. Lord knows, I have needed a positive attitude, through the ups and the downs of my professional life, before M*A*S*H, after M*A*S*H.

22

Practical Jokes

As far as anyone else was concerned, however, I never had
any problems. My shtick: To be upbeat, to enjoy the people
around me, to let them enjoy me. Work on any picture — even on
a television series — isn't all drudgery. There's a lot of kidding
around on a set. And with the M*A*S*H troupe, there was more
kidding around than I had experienced before — or since. We
brought practical jokes to the level of a fine art. And because
practical jokes have a way of drawing retaliation, they never
seemed to end.

One day, at lunch time, some four or five of us M*A*S*H
people were in the commissary, and, lo and behold, the waiter
comes up to our table bearing frozen chocolate yogurt deserts for
each of us, compliments of Richard Attenborough, who was sitting
at another table way across the room. We had no idea he even
knew we existed, and here was, sending us some frozen yogurt.

What a nice man! He was also one of the very finest actors we knew, and a pretty good director of movies in his own right. He did that great movie on Mohandas Gandhi, for one thing.

We waved at him. He didn't wave back. Maybe he didn't see us. We waved again. Nothing. Pretty soon, we were pointing at our desserts, grinning inanely, mouthing wide "Thank yous." I am sure we looked like idiots. Still no reaction from Attenborough. Then Mike Farrell noticed that David Ogden Stiers, sitting at another table and watching this scene, was choking with laughter.

"Hey, guys," said Farrell, "look at Stiers." We did. And then we knew we'd been had. Attenborough hadn't sent the desserts over to us. David had done so, with every expectation that we'd act like fools. Which is what we were doing.

But now, we had to put our heads together. How could we get even with David? We — Farrell was there, and Harry Morgan and Loretta — we had an idea. We had our sizable lunch check sent over to Stiers. Without a beat, Stiers signed it. We watched him. But we didn't know he'd signed the name of Gary Burghoff, none other than our own Cpl. Radar O'Reilly — who wasn't even there.

But we were soon made aware of this switch when we noted that Gary and David started snarling at each other on the set. Jeez, what was going on? Now it was clear to us that Gary hadn't appreciated paying our tab one bit. What we didn't know was that David and Gary were faking their whole tiff. It was David's way of turning the ongoing practical joke back on us, a joke that he had started.

By the end of the week, Gary and David were at each other with their fists. At least, that's the way it looked to us, watching their shadows going at it behind a sheet of canvas. When we broke in on them, the two of them were laughing their heads off — and pointing at us.

We got even with Stiers — by having David's dressing room painted a hideous orange and purple.

We had it done over a long Thanksgiving Day weekend, and could hardly wait until Monday to see David's reaction. He had no reaction at all. We couldn't believe it. "Did David say anything to you?" asked Alan.

"No," I said. "He hasn't said anything to anybody."

Finally, toward the end of the week, David sidled over to me. He wanted to know, "Did they do anything to your dressing room?" All innocence, I said, "No. Nothing. Why?"

"Oh," he said, "they seem to have painted my dressing room a beautiful salmon and mauve."

I blinked, speechless at the way he got even with us (he knew we had done it, or gotten somebody to do it) by pretending that he rather liked the "salmon and mauve" combination.

At lunch, I told Alan, Michael and Harry. "You know that hideous orange and purple paint we ordered up for David's dressing room? He loves it. Calls it salmon and mauve."

"Why that so-and-so!" said Harry.

"How dare he love it!" said Michael.

Alan laughed. "Guess we're just a bunch of slobs who don't appreciate a fine color combination when we see one, right?"

We got even, by — well, you get the picture. We loved practical jokes.

Only once do I recall that a practical joke went awry — although I really can't remember how or why the payoff was supposed to be funny. Maybe, on second thought, it wasn't a practical joke at all. Best I can recall, Harry Morgan was kidding Gary Burghoff about his frozen yogurt shop in Hawaii. But Gary got very peevish about this, and next thing we knew (we were in the Fox commissary), Gary was coming up behind Harry with a bowl of frozen yogurt in his hand. "Don't do it, Gary," I said, "don't do it."

Too late, he'd already done it — poured the entire bowl on Harry's head. There was absolutely nothing funny about this, and Harry was justifiably steamed. He was like a father to Gary, as he was to me. Gary had no reason to do this.

As Harry was doing a slow burn, two other actors who were visiting our commissary, Florence Henderson and Shecky Greene, sitting at a nearby table, couldn't help but see all this. "Hey," said Greene, "the stories about you guys are true! You really do have fun, don't you?" Because of Harry's forbearance, they never knew.

(P.S. Gary apologized.)

Michael Farrell may have concocted the most elaborate practical joke. It was aimed at Alan Alda, partly because Mike and Alan had a great competitive thing going. It was as if they were always playing a game called, "Everything you can do I can do better, I can do everything better than you." If Alda did 23 pushups, then Farrell would do 24. If Mike could win at Scrabble with a huge score, like maybe 350 points, then Alan would set out, next game, to get 400.

One day, Mike learned that Alan had been asked to invest in a wall of golden bricks in San Francisco. The idea was that each brick would be donated to this named charity by a famous person. The promoter, a guy named Lenny Schrader, said they were actually getting 10,000 celebrities to help build this wall. "Can you imagine the gall of this guy?" Alan said one day as he was sifting through his mail. "Have you ever seen a more transparent scam?" Alan proceeded to toss the letter into the trash.

But that was enough to tickle Mike's fancy. Later, he dug the letter out of the trash, and proceeded to concoct a series of follow-ups, each calculated to raise Alan's dander. He went to Scotty McDonald, who worked for our crafts services, and asked him to tell Alan that someone named Lenny Schrader had phoned. Would Mr. Alda please call him?

Mr. Alda would not, and did not. Not then, nor on any number of occasions when these messages would come to Alan (always when Farrell was in the room). Then, one day, another message, from Lenny Schrader. He wanted to know why Mr. Alda hadn't responded to his letter.

"Why," said Alda, "that miserable sonuvabitch!" Farrell was very sympathetic.

Two days later, Alda gets a telegram from Lenny Schrader saying, OBVIOUS YOU DIDN'T GET LETTERS OR PHONE CALLS PROJECT CANT GO FORWARD WITHOUT SOMEONE YOUR CALIBER. Alan goes ballistic, much to the amusement of the cast, all of whom are now in on the joke and enjoying it immensely. By now, Alan is a growing mountain of fury, a rumbling volcano.

A few days later, Farrell went out and hired an actor friend, Ernie Parmentier, to impersonate Lenny Schrader. He also inveigled our M*A*S*H publicist at Fox, Chuck Panama, into the act. "Just tell Alan," Farrell advised Panama, "that we have a very important visitor on the lot today, and Fox would like Alan to show him around the M*A*S*H unit."

So Ernie Parmentier shows up, and Farrell introduces him to Panama, and Panama takes him over to see Alan. Of course, Alan wouldn't mind showing him around. He is all charm. But imagine how his charm turns to pique when "the important visitor" turns out to be a man who introduces himself as Lenny Schrader!

Now steam is coming out of Alda's ears and, over in the corner, Panama is wringing his hands. Farrell trots over to calm Panama. "It's okay," Farrell tells him, "I'll bail you out if Alan comes after you."

Alan doesn't. With superhuman effort, his maxillary muscles working furiously, Alan Alda controls himself while this Lenny Schrader character proceeds to give one last, furious pitch about the importance of this wall in San Francisco.

Finally, Alda can't stand any more. He flags Panama, and says, through clenched teeth, "Would you get this guy out of here. Out! Off the lot!" And, then turning to Farrell, he says, "This was Lenny Schrader! Can you imagine the nerve of this guy? And how the hell did he ever get on the lot?"

All this happens at lunch time. It is all the cast and crew can do to restrain themselves until the four o'clock break. Then, Farrell has another surprise for Alda. He has hired another actor to come in, in a gorilla suit, like someone who is there to do a singing telegram. And what does the guy sing? A ballad that tells the whole story about Alan Alda and Lenny Schrader. Now, of course, everything is clear to Alda.

He screams with delight, he does a little dance, he goes over and hugs Farrell.

We played other games. For a while there, we were all doing a takeoff on the then current Pink Panther films, where Peter Sellars playing Inspector Clouseau engaged in mock karate fights with his faithful valet, Cato, who often lay in wait for him when he arrived home at night. We, too, would lie in wait for one another, and trade mock karate blows, one with the other. The trick was to pounce at the most unexpected moment. I think the game got old when we started expecting the karate blows at any and every moment.

Once, when we were walking back to Stage 9, Mike Farrell saw a bulldozer parked on a studio street. He hopped up in the driver's seat, and drove it to Stage 9. Farrell says now that it was "a silly, outrageous thing to do. But we were so appreciated on the lot that no one could get angry at us. All they'd say was, 'Oh, God, what'll they do next?'"

But Farrell was one of those all-around great human beings who had many sides to him. He had his fun side. And he had a serious side. Of all the members of our troupe, he was the most oriented to various causes around the world. We kidded him about this. "Hey, Mike," someone would say, "what country you saving this week?" The thing was, Mike Farrell was a caring guy, and he reached out in a particular way for Bill Christopher, our Father Mulcahy, when he learned of the Bill and Barbara Christopher's struggles with their younger son's autism.

The Christophers had adopted two sons, John and Ned, when they were six weeks old. But Ned wasn't normal. He was eventually diagnosed as autistic. Now, autism is one of those developmental disorders that medical science doesn't know a great deal about. They don't know what causes it. They don't know what cures it. But they have discovered ways to help parents help their kids afflicted with it. It just takes a great deal of time, patience, and obviously, devotion on the part of the parents.

In the case of the Christophers, they were ready to give that little boy all three. Bill didn't go around telling us all about it. But Mike Farrell visited the Christophers in Pasadena from time to time. He could see (and admire) what they were doing, and he couldn't help but tell us. To help enhance Ned's neurological development, Bill was crawling three miles a day with him on his hands and knees. (He was also walking and jogging more miles every week with Ned, teaching him with flash cards, flying off for days at a time to a special program in Philadelphia.)

A lot of the work paid off — to the extent that their little boy was able, as a youngster of 12, to join the family when all four of them went on a European trip in the summer of 1980, and enjoy London, Paris and Rome and other places. Eventually, the Christophers found they were unable to give Ned all the attention and treatment he needed at home. He lives now at the Devereux Foundation School in Santa Barbara.. He visits in Pasadena once a month, and the Christophers visit him every two weeks. Ned has restricted language skills, but he has people around him that he likes, he rides horseback, and he swims.

He also knows that he is loved. Bill and Barbara Christopher see the whole experience as a "Mixed Blessing" — which is what they titled their story in a book they published in 1989 with the Abingdon Press. One extra blessing: Because of Ned, Bill and Barbara have become very active in the annual conferences of the Devereux Foundation, and as honorary national chairman, Bill is able to help the Foundation gain moral and financial support in the drive to understand more about autism.

In many a M*A*S*H episode, you may remember that Christopher's Father Mulcahy evidenced a concern for the children of war. In fact, he put a lot of time and attention to an orphanage situationed not far from the 4077. Now, we never did go deeply enough into the whole orphan question on M*A*S*H. The orphans of that war, indeed of any war, are our little secrets — innocent byproducts of the liaisons that happen between warriors and the women of the warzone.

M*A*S*H, as I've said more than once, was the kind of television comedy that could go into a great many serious questions. This question, however, was difficult for us to handle. We avoided it for a while, then finally bit the bullet in our eighth season with an episode called, "Yessir, That's Our Baby!"

It may have helped contribute to a greater public awareness of the problems of Amerasian children, but it didn't help change the situation any. In the show, a baby girl was left on the doorstep of The Swamp, with a note saying the child had an American father. Father Mulcahy noted that "Korean babies with blue eyes are shot on sight. The child has no future here." So Hawkeye took her to the Red Cross, the Army, the Republic of Korea. With Maj. Winchester at his side, he even flew to Tokyo to talk to the American consul. No one could help get the baby out of Korea. She could not be admitted to the U.S. without a relative there. The solution was certainly not an ideal one: they left the baby on the doorstep of an old Catholic mission. Father Mulcahy's final blessing didn't seem to assuage our misgivings.

Other art forms, like opera, for instance, have been able to dramatize the problem of such children in Asia. I am thinking of Puccini's "Madame Butterfly," for instance, the story of a British naval officer, his Japanese lover and their love child. The contemporary musical, "Miss Saigon," deals with the same basic story — except that the officer is an American, his tragic lover a Vietnamese girl, and their baby destined to join a class of children called Bui-doi.

Rather than wait around for somebody else to do something about the Amerasian children, the Aldas, Alan and Arlene did a great deal on their own to help them. The term Amerasian was coined by the author Pearl S. Buck, who won both the Pulitzer and the Nobel Prize for her books on Asia, to describe these children of mixed race, and to fix co-equal responsibility for them.

Amerasian children are outcasts in Asia. There, the father is key to the record of birth, to citizenship, to education and to employment. Without a father, an Asian child has none of these, not even a legal standing without a proper birth record. In places like Korea and Vietnam, then, Amerasian children hold a kind of second-class citizenship — if they hold citizenship at all.

You may remember how they're described in the haunting refrain from "Miss Saigon."

They're called Bui-doi
The dust of life,
Conceived in hell

And born in strife.
They are the living reminder of all the good
we failed to do.
We can't forget, must not forget
That they are all our children, too.

Over the years, the Aldas have contributed a great deal of time, attention and dollars to the cause of these poor children. In December 1983, they produced a beautiful book, called *The Last Days of M*A*S*H*, with photographs and notes by Arlene Alda (a professional photographer) and commentary by Alan Alda. And they contributed their royalties on the book to the Pearl S. Buck Foundation, which is working to provide a hopeful future to these children of war in Korea, Okinawa, the Philippines, Taiwan and Thailand.

23

Anti-War?

Was M*A*S*H anti-war? In fact, M*A*S*H was ambivalent about the Korean War — much as the whole country, throughout the 1970s, was ambivalent about the Vietnam War. Just when Hawkeye Pierce was uttering words of despair about the utter senselessness of this "police action" in Korea, Col. Potter or Maj. Houlihan would come out with a telling remark about the utter rightness of what they were doing there.

By being ambivalent, the show was holding a mirror up to the U.S. at large, which was still undecided about our military presence in Vietnam. (According to Gene Reynolds, "M*A*S*H was more about Vietnam than people realized.). Over M*A*S*H's 11 years, however, and through another 11 years of M*A*S*H reruns, the nation would become less ambivalent on this question, so that now, in 1994, the country is less ready to send American youth to die in strange places like Somalia and Bosnia.

No one will ever know whether this change of mind and heart came about, in part, because of M*A*S*H. But the fact is M*A*S*H made a case against war. At a forum on M*A*S*H in October 1986 at the Museum of Broadcasting in New York City, Alan Alda was challenged by someone in the audience about M*A*S*H's attitude toward war.

Alda said, "The show... took the position that war is disastrous regardless of what reason you have for going into it. If you look at a war from the point of view of the people who have to stand ankle-deep in the blood, the young men who are fighting it, young men on both sides, then your reaction is liable to be, 'I don't care who started this, I don't like it. I don't care what reasons there were for it.' It's a little like the proposition that there is no reason for a man to batter his wife. It doesn't matter what she says or does, it's inexcusable. For those people who thought there was a rationale for that war, or any war, that might sound like an unpatriotic idea, and I think you're entitled to that opinion.

"I think we were entitled to take the position we took, though. I don't think it was conceived as a strategy designed to change any government policy. We were trying to do plays.... We were trying to show the human condition as we understood it, and we were talking about a human reaction to a horrible situation. I have to be candid and say that probably most of us on that program did not agree that we should be involved in the war in Vietnam that lasted through a lot of the series. I don't know if anybody had any illusions about affecting the course of the war, though, by virtue of a television show."

Alda's interlocutor suggested that M*A*S*H was taking a side that was in favor of the enemy.

"I don't think that's what we were doing," said Alda. "I think we did recognize some of what you're talking about. But we didn't go out of our way to say, 'Now, don't forget, we're basically patriotic.'" But he did concede this: "I think what we did was look at things differently from how you would probably look at them."

Patriotic Americans might be interested to learn that, as far as Larry Gelbart was concerned, he was "less influenced by Karl

Marx than by the Marx brothers." Insofar as he regarded war as a futile act, Gelbart probably saw things much as Alda did. I think this was one of the reasons why he took on the assignment in the first place. I think he was challenged by the idea of trying to top Robert Altman and the movie M*A*S*H — which, according to Altman, wasn't so much anti-war, but anti-pro-war films, or any entertainment that made war seem acceptable.

I don't think Gelbart ever believed that M*A*S*H had changed the political landscape. In October 1984, in his own four-day seminar at the Museum of Broadcasting in New York, he said, "I haven't seen any wars averted because of M*A*S*H's success or message; none are going to be. One young man wrote us, 'God, I love your show. I'm joining the Army next week.' I don't know what lasting effect the show had — as people have said, television is bubble gum for the eyes."

Still and all, the anti-war message was there, if you were looking for it. "By the way, what war is this?" Col. Potter asks Hawkeye during a moment when the two of them are so exhausted from hours at the operating table that they can hardly talk.

Hawkeye says, "The latest war to end all wars."

In that same episode, Col. Potter are motoring home from surgical duty on the front line, getting tipsy on some brandy that Cpl. Klinger has thoughtfully provided for them in a canteen, to ease the pain of their mission of mercy to the front. As they are driving along, Col. Potter toasts Klinger. Hawkeye toasts Klinger's nose. "That's a double!" says Col. Potter, taking a double swig from the canteen. But then they are forced out their Jeep by enemy gunfire.

From a ditch, Col. Potter takes out a sidearm and fires back at the enemy. Then he hands his gun over to Hawkeye and tells him, "Fire that weapon."

"All right," says Hawkeye, the pacifist. He addresses the weapon. "You're fired."

Col. Potter puts on a stern face. "I said fire that weapon. That was an order, Pierce."

"Oh, waiter," says Hawkeye, "would you take this man's order, please?"

Now Col. Potter is mad. "Fire the gun, Hawkeye!"

Hawkeye says, "Look, Colonel, I'll treat their wounds, heal their wounds, bind their wounds. But I will not inflict their wounds."

"But you can't just sit there," says Potter.

"I may be sitting on the outside, but I'm running on the inside."

"You love life that little?"

"I hate guns that much."

When they weren't being cynical about the war, they were being irreverent about practically everything else.

Our doctors and nurses (and those of us like Klinger and Radar who supported them) were there to treat the wounded, but it seemed we always had to do so under the most insane conditions — sometimes because of the insanity of the war, sometimes by reason of the insanity of the Army itself.

In one episode, our operating room is under fire, mistakenly, by our own artillery up the line. Hawkeye says, "We're safe as long as they keep aiming at us."

In another episode, a ranking general insisted he wouldn't authorize a bigger plasma refrigerator until we made our compound look pretty. "Look pretty? In the middle of a war?" we said. Yes. That's what the general wanted. So that's what the general got. It was Klinger who was delegated to bring in trees and shrubs, and construct a water fountain in the middle of the compound. Klinger got a group of locals to help him procure the trees and shrubs. And Klinger made the fountain out of a series of interlocking bed pans.

(P.S. The 4077 got the refrigerator before a truck came careening into camp one night and flattened the whole darn fountain. The driver ran it down, but it wasn't really his fault: Who would have expected a water fountain in the middle of our M*A*S*H compound?)

Sometimes, Hawkeye would deal with an insane situation, just by giving an angry speech, one that he didn't deliver in anger, but in more of a half-wounded, half-exasperated tone: "I just don't know why they're shooting at us. All we want to bring them is democracy and white bread, to transplant the American Dream: freedom, achievement, hyperacidity, affluence, flatulence, technology, tension, the inalienable right to an early coronary sitting at your desk while plotting to stab your boss in the back."

Sometimes, Hawkeye could be even more eloquent than that. "Nice war we had. Of course, every war has its cute thing. World War Two had nice songs. The War of Roses had nice flowers. We've got booms, they had blooms. Actually, every war has its 'ooms. You've got doom, gloom, everybody ends in a tomb, the planes go zoom, and they bomb your room."

Sometimes, he would deal with the insanity by a simple one-liner. Col. Potter asks Hawkeye: "You too young to die, Pierce?"

Hawkeye says, "I was hoping to make it to Thursday."

Or by a conversation between Col. Potter and a pilot who had wandered into the 4077 after dropping his bombs in the Korean countryside and ditching his damaged plane:

COL. POTTER (operating on an 8-year-old Korean girl): Somebody dropped a bomb on her building from an airplane.

PILOT: Who did it?

HAWKEYE: He just dropped it. He didn't autograph it.

PILOT: Was it one of theirs or one of ours?

HAWKEYE: What difference does it make?

PILOT: A lot. It makes a lot of difference.

COL. POTTER: Not to her it doesn't.

The pilot blanched and left the OR.

Hawkeye found him sitting forlornly on a bench in the hall. "You brought me in there on purpose, didn't you?" said the pilot.

"Look," said Hawkeye, "you seem like a decent guy, too decent to think this could be anything like a clean war."

"Up there, it is," said the pilot. Then, remembering the 8-year-old girl who may have been struck by one of his bombs, he said, "Was."

One time, Hawkeye and B.J. Hunnicutt were angered by a Col. Kohner, who, a little injured himself, showed up with a few of his wounded men after leading them on a stupid foray behind enemy lines — to pick up some dead American bodies. B.J.

couldn't figure out why it was necessary that a bunch of live Americans had to go in looking for dead Americans so they, too, could become dead Americans.

The colonel didn't get it. Stubbornly, he defended his irrationality by insisting that he felt it was his duty to see that every American soldier gets buried "in an American casket." B.J. and Hawkeye demonstrated what they thought of the colonel upon his departure from the 4077 compound. When the colonel got in his jeep, a chopper dropped a ton of the 4077 garbage right on top of the colonel's head. B.J. and Hawkeye had arranged the drop.

In obvious sympathy with the caper, Col. Potter roared with laughter right along with Hawkeye, B.J. and Klinger — then said, "I didn't see this." But that was part of Col. Potter's job at the 4077 — to overlook some of the peccadilloes and the craziness of Hawkeye, Margaret and the others, because these were good heroic men and women who were getting the job done: saving lives.

Our writers, of course, wanted to keep surprising audiences every week. That, too, is the essence of a TV series. One week, we'd play the entire episode for nothing but laughs. Once, I made book on when a Korean farmer's calf would be born (under the midwifery of Hawkeye and B.J. and Col. Potter). It was pure comedy. But the same episode had me getting very close to Maj. Houlihan when we were stranded on her birthday and she was moved to deliver the monologue that won her an Emmy.

This only proved that our writers were Protean in their ability to switch the feeling of the show, and make each week's story a new kind of surprise. In Greek mythology, Proteus was a wizard who could change form on the instant. One moment, he was an old man, then, suddenly, a tall green tree, then a blinding fire.

Our Proteus, of course, was Larry Gelbart. He won an Emmy in our second season, 1973. But, for my money, he could have, should have, won Emmys every year he was on the show. (He did get nominations, each year, in any event.) His scripts — though they were dealing with the same collection of characters — never seemed to repeat each other, and almost always surprised our ever-growing audiences.

Sometimes, he'd surprise us all by creating a script that simply had the principals each writing a letter home, which ended up being less of your normal drama, more a succession of character vignettes about Hawkeye, Trapper John, Margaret, Frank, Col. Blake, Frank, Radar and myself. Once, Gelbart had a real TV news correspondent named Clete Roberts come over and interview us, ask us how he felt about being in Korea. Klinger said, "You call it a police action back home, right? Over here, it's a war. A police action sounds like we're over here arresting people, handing out parking tickets. War's just killing, that's all." Another time, two other M*A*S*H writers, Ken Levine and David Isaacs, gave audiences a different view of the M*A*S*H unit — as seen, at bedside level, through the eyes of a wounded soldier who had a throat wound that made it impossible for him to speak.

Often enough, there would be no resolution at the end of an episode — often just a sense of wonder that couldn't even be put into words. I remember one episode in which Radar O'Reilly had made friends with one young wounded soldier after he, Radar, had helped save the man's life. But, finally, the man died because his wounds were just too severe. Radar took that very hard. He couldn't understand.

In the show's final scene, the men and women of the 4077 are watching a movie and passing around a helmet full of popcorn. When Col. Potter passes the helmet to Radar, Radar pays absolutely no attention, not because he is watching whatever is up there on the movie screen, but because he is in a state of abstracted anguish over this senseless death. And that's how the episode ends: with a close-up of Radar's wondering face.

If anything, Radar's puzzlement reflected the almost universal feelings of men and women who have to fight a war. They often don't really know what they're doing there. And that may be another answer to the secret of M*A*S*H's success. M*A*S*H, the TV show, didn't have the answers to the mystery. But we tried to reflect the experience of real people who had to live through the puzzlement of it all. As Alan Alda told the people at the 1986 forum in New York, "We had respect for that experience. And we wanted to make sure (in spite of the fact that we were doing comedy) that we didn't trivialize that experience. We always wanted to get down, dig a little deeper, and find out what it must have been like for those people."

24

Celebrity

When Larry Gelbart killed off Col. Henry Blake, the whole nation reacted with the kind of shock they'd have at the sudden death of any public figure. People had been hearing news reports every night during the Vietnam War about 15 men killed, or 1,500, and feeling nothing. Now they were terribly upset over the death of one fictional colonel. The producers got more than 1,000 letters protesting Col. Blake's death. Gelbart hand-wrote more than 300 replies, saying that, well, sometimes people die in war, and, finally, Reynolds had his reply printed, so they could just sign it, and send it off to the people who took the trouble to write us.

The cast was beginning to realize how suddenly visible we had all become. In the industry, TV stars were always considered a notch below movie stars, mainly because we earned far less money. But now we were beginning to see that our ongoing presence in everyone's living room on a regular basis brought us a celebrity beyond belief.

My guess is that each of the M*A*S*H cast had begun to take on a certain extra reality to all our millions of viewers. As written by Gelbart and the other writers, each of us became interesting people in our own right. Together — interacting and reacting to one another — we began to assume the status of real people, people that Mr. and Mrs. North America got to know, almost like members of their own family.

Unfortunately, Mr. and Mrs. North America started treating us all too much like family. Once, in a restaurant in Edmonton, Canada, I was having dinner with my wife when a woman came up to ask me for my autograph. This, of course, is pretty rude behavior — during dinner and all — but I usually oblige. It's quicker to sign, rather than create a scene. But this time, I did not oblige, because the woman asked me to sign her brassiere, the one she was wearing. Her brassiere! That was a new one on me.

But I was suddenly inspired. With a sidelong look at Joy, and a wink at her, I said to the woman, "Sorry, I write bigger than that." Crestfallen, she withdrew, quickly. Which is just what I wanted. Joy, on the other hand, gave me a look of admiration that I will never forget. I was kind of proud, too, of my "perfect squelch." Not bad, not bad at all, on the spur of the moment.

I had thought of myself as just like any guy, going to the factory every day. Now I began to realize what kind of factory I worked in. It was a dream factory. And, in a strange way, those of us who worked in this dream factory became characters in a lot of people's dreams. Once we were in people's dreams, they tended to own us. I have been approached by total strangers who think they know me — intimately. When I don't know them, they can react angrily. "Whaddya mean, you don't know me?" a man told me once in Minneapolis. "I saw every episode of M*A*S*H."

I remember making a personal appearance at a department store in Fairbanks, Alaska, and the security people had to hustle me out of there, to save the store from destruction. When those people saw me, they just rushed me, toppling over displays on the way. Mothers deserted their baby carriages, just because they wanted to touch me. Maybe hug me, who knows? Only a shrink could really say why.

Alan Alda, being the nice guy that he is, tried at first to be nice to strangers who accosted him in public places. He soon learned his lesson. Then he had to teach his wife the same lesson. One night in the first year of the show, he and his wife, Arlene, who was visiting LA (for the Aldas had kept their home in New Jersey) went to a movie at Graumann's Chinese on Hollywood Boulevard. Afterward, they stopped in at C.C. Brown's, a still-famous ice cream parlor known for their hot fudge sundaes, just the two of them. Well, one of the people at the next table asked Alan for his autograph. He shook his head. "I don't wanta do that tonight."

"Oh, Alan," said Arlene, "these people are your fans. You can at least sign your name."

Alan tried to warn Arlene. "You don't know what can happen," he said.

Arlene couldn't believe him. She launched into quite a speech, about the obligations of an actor to the people who make his stardom possible. So, finally, Alan gives in. He signs the guy's autograph. Then he signs a few more, and turns back to Arlene, trying to resume his conversation with her. Suddenly, half the people in the store are gathering around. People are pulling their chairs over to join the Alda party. Now, they are engulfed with people. Arlene looks around, shaking her head in disbelief, and says, "Say, do you people mind? This is a private conversation!"

Alan said, "See? See? Give 'em a finger, they take your hand."

"Now I see what you mean."

After that, on trips to the movies, or to a local shopping mall, Alan would often go out in one disguise or another. His favorite: he went out masquerading as a Frenchman, with a fake mustache, sunglasses and a beret. It helped that Alan speaks French.

I tried disguises, too, but I found it more difficult to disguise my rather more prominent features. What was I going to do? Wear a false nose? Or false eyebrows? And, for me, wearing a dress would draw more attention to me than anything else I could possibly wear, except maybe a gorilla suit.

Once, after a personal appearance in Chicago, I rented a car and drove down to southern Illinois to visit Joy's parents in

Danville, which is, incidentally, the place where a number of stars were born: Gene Hackman, Donald O'Connor, Dick and Jerry Van Dyke, and Bobby Short. Well, I drove through Kankakee, then Joliet, then got to Danville, and checked in at the Holiday Inn, then went off to dinner with Joy's family. After dinner, I made my way back to the Holiday Inn and decided to stop off at that hotel's Take One Bar.

You can imagine what the bar looked like. It was a dim, tacky smoke-filled den, almost deserted. When I walked in, one guy with a cigarette hanging out of his face was telling a long, involved story to a second guy in the bar, to the bartender and to the cocktail waitress. When I appeared in the doorway, this guy stopped in the middle of his story and said to his companions, jerking a thumb in my direction, "Hey, you know who that is? It's that queer on TV." Then he turned to me. "Hey, queer, want a beer?"

Who could resist an invitation like that? Somehow, I managed.

Every one of the M*A*S*H regulars had their own versions of my Take One Bar-treatment in Danville, Illinois. But I couldn't let that bother me. I had to remind myself to remember back not so long ago when hardly anybody knew who I was. Or cared. I decided to enjoy my celebrity and be nice to people who needed to come close.

My celebrity was something — especially since I wasn't making much money. We were in our third season. I was no longer a day player, as I had been in M*A*S*H's first two seasons. Now I was a contract player. But I was only making $2,500 a week — on two 13-week contracts per season, with a guarantee of 10 shows. And I never quite knew whether I'd be around next season, or next week. I honestly thought I was worth more than $50,000 a year, max — to the show, and to Fox. I was now a household name in America. My frocks were setting new trends in fashion.

I jest. But the fact is that I needed more money. You can't be a star and not be treated like a star. You can't dine out at the Automat. You go to Sardi's. You can't go out dressed like a bum. If

you live in LA., you have to drive a nice car. You have to live in a
nice house. At the time, Joy and I were living in our second home,
in Woodland Hills, and still struggling. I was driving an old,
secondhand — excuse me, a pre-owned — Lincoln.

My agent, Lew Deuser, was absolutely no help at all. He had
other clients at Fox. He didn't want to fight for me. He said,
snapping his fingers, "They could write you out of the show just
like that."

Joy and I tried to win over Lew Deuser. What we ended up
doing was like something out of an "I Love Lucy" show, a real
comic plot. We had Lew and his wife over for dinner one night.
Bought an expensive prime rib roast and the best gin, because Lew
liked martinis. Well, we are having a great, funning cocktail hour,
but then Joy flags me from the kitchen. She is really frantic.
"Honey," she says, "I put it in. The oven isn't on."

"Calm down," I said. "You put what in?"

"The roast. The roast is still cold. What are we going to do?
Oh, jeez, I said. Who do we know with a microwave? Yes, Joy's
friend, Beverly Alpert, had one. So, while Joy phoned Beverly, I
made up a fresh pitcher of martinis and freshened everyone's glass,
then slipped out the back door with the roast, hoping Lew
wouldn't miss me for 15 minutes or so.

I was gone at least a half-hour, maybe more, but I came back
with a prime rib roast in a roasting pan on the back seat. "How
well done is it?" whispered Joy as I sneaked in the back door.

"Medium rare."

"I hope," she said, "that Lew likes it medium rare."

By the time dinner was on the table, we had gone through
three pitchers of martinis. So I don't think Lew ever noticed much
about the prime rib. Or even remembered we had prime rib.

But entertaining him didn't seem to help a bit. Lew still
wouldn't go to the Fox management and fight for me. So I made a
few phone calls myself, to the studio's money man, Ron Beckman.
But I wasn't even able to get an appointment to see him.

I consulted a new, good friend of mine, William Holden. (I
was moonlighting at the time on television's first mini-series, The

Blue Knight, which starred Holden. It was an extra job that I
managed to sandwich in, in addition to my Klinger role on
M*A*S*H.) I asked Holden what he thought I should do.

"How much you makin', Jamie?"

I told him. No more than $50,000 a year. At the time, Henry
Winkler was making $25,000 a week, as the Fonz, on "Happy
Days."

Holden said, "That's ridiculous. I know what you're
contributing."

"They could just say, 'Well, if that's what you want, forget
it.'"

"Yeah, they could," said Holden.

"They probably already have a script written: 'Corporal
Klinger Finally Gets His Section Eight.'"

"They probably don't," he said. "Your part helps make the
show work. The show needs you. As long you're not being
unreasonable. As long as you aren't asking for something you don't
deserve...."

I pondered his words, and told Joy that Holden thought I
deserved maybe double what I was making now. And so, with Joy's
support, I summoned up my courage, and decided to go for it, and
use some Klinger-comedy. Nothing else had worked. This was my
last resort, but even so, I knew I was taking a big risk. I could only
do this if I got outside myself and put on the persona of a character
named Maxwell Klinger.

I got a .45 revolver from the prop man, and scurried over
toward the office of Ron Beckman, running from tree to bush to
tree, like some character in a Bugs Bunny cartoon. Finally, I got to
Beckman's ground-floor office, peeked in the window, and saw
that he was alone. Even better, his office door was slightly ajar. So
I went over to the door, kicked it open with my heavy GI boot,
and rushed in with my gun drawn.

Beckman squealed and half-ducked down behind his desk.
"What are you, crazy?"

"Yeah," I said. "Are we gonna make a deal or not?"

He looked at me. He looked at the gun. And I broke up
laughing.

So did he. "Okay, okay," he said. "Come back and see me tomorrow at noon. But put that gun away."

The next day, I came back, bearing a bouquet of roses for him and some expensive cigars. We made our deal. And I got something close to what Holden thought I was worth, but only because I had the guts to demand it — in a very unorthodox way that could have gotten me canned, or even arrested. It was something that Jamie Farr couldn't do. But it was something that Klinger could. Which is probably why I got away with it. I was also lucky that Beckman was such a damn nice guy. He had a sense of humor, and a heart.

If gun play could work for me, it could work for others, too, right? Wrong. A few years later, I heard about another actor in a celebrated TV series who walked into his producer's office to re-negotiate his contract, opened his jacket and put a .38 revolver on the desk. The producer opened his desk drawer, drew out a .357 Magnum, put it on his side of the desk, and said, "What is it that you wanted to see me about?"

Now I had a new contract, making close to $100,000 a year from M*A*S*H, and extra work in things like "The Blue Knight," and some invitations to do dinner theater for Howard Pechet in Edmonton, Alberta, Canada. Life began to get more interesting. Sometimes even bizarre.

In our fourth season, a young woman of 21 started writing me, and eventually came to the studio to meet me — because, as it turned out, she wanted me to adopt her. I was, of course, old enough to be her father, and there didn't seem to be any ideas of romance on this young woman's agenda. But I didn't adopt her. She had never had a real father, I guess, and she thought I would make a good one — someone she could talk to when she needed to, at the very least. I actually gave the matter some serious consideration. It was quite a compliment, being picked out to be someone's father. But I finally told her she could always call me; she didn't need legal adoption to do that.

I don't recall how long after that, but Marvin Davis, the big oil man from Denver, took over Twentieth Century-Fox, and he surprised the cast with bonus checks, out of the blue, for $25,000. This happened about a year after he'd taken over at Fox — long enough for him to see how valuable we were to Fox. And how loved: they had signs up outside Stage 9. POSITIVELY NO ADMITTANCE. AUTHORIZED PERSONNEL ONLY. But no one paid a darn bit of attention to the signs. Everybody was there. Everyone hung out there. Even the guys who produced our M*A*S*H sweatshirts.

Joy and I soon started to learn how to enjoy ourselves as befit our new station in life. We moved farther out in the Valley, to a nicer home in Bell Canyon, where the schools would be better for Jonas and Yvonne. And then, a couple years later, Joy and I and the children jetted all night across the polar route for Paris, the beginning of our first big major vacation trip abroad. Jonas was 10, and Yvonne 7. Now, we figured, they were old enough.

Early in the morning, Paris time, we checked into the famous and very expensive Ritz Hotel and followed the advice of other, more seasoned American travelers who had suggested we sleep on arrival, then get up late in the afternoon, enjoy the evening, and go to bed with the Parisians. That way, we'd avoid jet lag and quickly adjust to a European timetable.

After eight hours sleep, we were hungry. I suggested we go to the hotel dining room. No, the others wanted to venture out into the streets of Paris and choose one or another of Paris' famous restaurants. So we walked. And walked. And walked. My family was right. There were many fine restaurants all around us. So many we couldn't make up our minds. And then the children saw it.

It was that gigantic Erector set, the Eiffel Tower, and a big sign, in English, "Eiffel Tower Restaurant At The Top." This is where the children wanted to eat. I vetoed that. "The place is a tourist trap," I said. "The food is bound to be inferior." They asked for a vote. We took the elevator to the top.

We had no reservations, but that didn't matter to the maitre'd. We were early. The only people in the place were probably American tourists like ourselves. Almost as soon as we were seated and ordering our wine and our colas, word spread that Klinger, the guy on M*A*S*H, the American television star, Jamie Farr, was here. One of the waiters came up and asked for my autograph. But, as I signed my name, he bent close to my ear and whispered, "Monsieur, of all the restaurants in Paris, why did you come here. The food is awful, the wine stinks and the stage show is terrible." I arched my eyebrows and darted my eyes toward the children. He seemed to understand.

And then, a little later, he came back and said, "Let me make you feel better. This is a true story. For years and years, one of France's most celebrated food writers, a man famous for his hatred of the Eiffel Tower's design, came here every Friday evening. We couldn't understand it. It baffled our staff. Finally, I was chosen to ask him why he kept coming here. 'You, of all people, come to eat our awful food and drink our dreadful wine in a place you hate. Why? Why?'

"'Very simple,' he said. 'Because this is the only place in all of Paris where you cannot see the Eiffel Tower!'"

Speaking about the Eiffel Tower, reminds me of Prince Charles, who visited the M*A*S*H set at Fox one day and told us that he and the Queen were faithful M*A*S*H fans. (And a prize to the reader who can figure why the Eiffel Tower reminds me of Prince Charles.) So I presented Prince Charles with one of my favorite tiaras — my gift to the queen. He was a very engaging sort, not at all stuck up. He stayed around to watch us work. And he pretended not to notice when some of the practical jokers who called themselves my friends set out a director's chair with my name on it, misspelled: JAMIE FART. (Of course, I had asked for it by forever introducing myself as Jamie the-T-is-silent-in-Farr.)

When we all lined up for a group picture, Prince Charles found himself standing right in front of Harry Morgan. Morgan, the actor who always knows where the lens is, very gently pushed him aside and said, "Watch it, Prince."

President Gerald Ford also came to visit. After he left the White House and went on the board of Twentieth Century-Fox, Ford and his friend Henry Kissinger (also on the Fox board) visited a number of times. My friends on the crew would tip me off when they saw Ford coming, so I could do some teasing ad libs in the middle of a rehearsal — for Ford's benefit. "And furthermore," I would shout, right in the middle of a bit I was doing, "Ohio State is going to kick the stuffing out of Michigan this season."

Ford, a Michigan alumnus and an All-America guard to boot, would roar in mock anger. And then he would come over and shake my hand, and we would bet $5 on the game. Whenever we see each other now, I remind him that he still owes me $5. "No," he says. "As I recall, I won the last bet. You owe me!"

Of course, it really doesn't matter. The only thing that matters is that I, Jameel Farah from a poor neighborhood in Toledo, can be on such good terms with a man who was the President of the United States. (I am not the only one in my family, however, to be on good terms with the president. In the 1950s, a cousin of mine, Maj. James Jabarra, visited the White House — because he was America's first jet air ace. He shot down 16 MIGs in the Korean War.)

Once, when Henry Kissinger was on the set, we had a baseball pool going. It was a playoff game on October 16, 1981, between the Montreal Expos and the LA Dodgers, and it took all kinds of persuasion to get Kissinger into the pool. All he had to do was fork over a mere $5, but you would have thought we were putting the arm on him for $5,000. "I don't have change," he said, "I only have a ten."

"Oh," somebody said, "we have change for a ten."

So Kissinger forked over his ten, and we gave him change. And guess who won the pool?

25

Other Roles

In M*A*S*H's tenth season, it was clear that Alan Alda was getting burnt out, and we all began to realize that, if this season was to be Alan's last, then M*A*S*H was finished as a series. That meant the rest of us would have to start scrambling, looking for other work. As you will soon see, we would get a bonus season, an eleventh year. But, in the meantime, we had to try to make new deals for ourselves.

My old mentors — people like Red Skelton and Ed Wynn — had encouraged me many years before to work hard and save my money. So, even while I was going strong with M*A*S*H, I had always been on the lookout for other opportunities.

Sometime in the late 1970s, I even tried to go on the road as a standup comic, but I really didn't enjoy it. I remember playing Cherry's Top of the Mall in Niles, Ohio. Turned out this place was owned by the mob. They paid me in hundred dollars bills at the end of the week, and one of the friendlier types at the club whispered, "Don't walk out to the parking lot alone with your cash." What he meant was that some unfriendlier types at the club could have gotten their five or six grand back very quickly.

But, when I wasn't being scared, I mostly bored myself to death. Especially after I started wondering whether I'd already told the audience the joke I was in the middle of, or whether I'd done so in my last appearance. I did have a nice time once at Wellesley College, near Boston; they billed it as "An Evening With Jamie Farr." I was out eight weeks on this particular trip, did some shows in Boston at the Playboy Club, and ended my tour with a stopover in Philadelphia to do the Mike Douglas Show, one of the earliest of the big afternoon talk-and-celebrity shows.

Mike was always happy to see some of the characters from M*A*S*H, and I, for one, enjoyed being on his show. This time, however, I could hardly wait to get home. "One more bit," I told myself, "and you, Jamie, will be back home in Joy's loving arms."

So I did the Douglas Show and headed for the airport.

Sara Vaughan had been on Douglas Show with me that afternoon, the divine Miss Sara, the great and late torch singer who had been entertaining millions of us for years and years. And so, when I got on the jet for LA, it was no surprise for me to find Sara Vaughan on the same plane. We traded some pleasantries on the flight.

But then, four or five hours later, at LAX, she saw me pacing near the curb outside baggage claim. My limo was a no-show. "Child," she said to me, "where do you live?" I told her way out in the West Valley. Well, she lived in the West Valley, too. "You got your bags?" she said. "You get in here." She pointed to her van, where her musicians were loading up her gear and their gear, and she told me to hop in. She wanted to drop me off at my home, on the way to her home in Hidden Hills.

Home. Now that I was so close, after all these weeks, my fantasies became more intense. It was late fall, and in my mind's eye, I could just see Joy, dressed in a gorgeous outfit, drenched in Yves St. Laurent, waiting for me — with, probably, a fire in the fireplace to boot.

Soon we were pulling up in the Farr driveway, and then around to the back of the house outside the kitchen, ablaze with light. Even before I got out of the van, I could see the champagne chilling in a bucket of ice on a counter in the kitchen. And I was not surprised to glance up and see the smoke coming out of our chimney. The home fires (and Joy) were burning, as I had hoped they would be.

Joy came out to greet me, wearing a beautiful outfit and her Rive Gauche, the St. Laurent perfume that I had imagined. It was obvious that she had missed me as much I had missed her, and my arms opened wide to her. Joy came running to me, like in one of those romantic movies, almost as if in slow motion. And then she ran right past me, to greet Sara Vaughan.

"Sara Vaughan?" said Joy. "Sara Vaughan! I can't believe it!"

After Sara and her entourage got back on the road, my romantic fantasies (and my ardor) had cooled considerably — while Joy went on rhapsodizing over this encounter with Miss Sara. "You can't imagine," she said to me. "One of my favorite singers of all time. Sara Vaughan! You just don't know how many of her records I had, how many hours I spent listening to her music! Sara Vaughan!"

Well, now I guess I could imagine. In fact, I did not have to imagine. I could see for myself. And I knew what it felt like — to be dumped by my own wife, for a torch singer!

The next time I was on the Mike Douglas Show, Joy went with me and made an appearance on the show, as well. We made a special trip East for this one, and I can remember dashing for the airport in LA, after taping a Bob Hope Show with Milton Berle. We were both in drag — the skit called for us to show up in the same dress — and the wardrobe people had given me an extra pair of pantyhose for the show. I just tossed them in my bag, went out and did the show, then hopped into my limo for LAX, where I met Joy.

Because Mike Douglas had a tradeout, we stayed at the Ben Franklin Hotel. It is not one of the world's great hotels, mainly because it was built the year Ben Franklin did his standup comedy there. Another comic, David Brenner, said the Ben Franklin was "the only hotel in the world you jumped into to commit suicide." But I wanted Joy to see and experience all the things that I had grown to like in Philadelphia, including the Ben Franklin.

And then, the next afternoon, Joy was all set to go on the show with me — only to discover, just before we were to go on, she had torn her panty hose. "Hey," I said, "I can help you there," as I reached into my travel bag, and handed her my extra pair. (I ask you, what other husband can rescue his wife with emergency underwear?)

I'd been fascinated on previous visits to Philadelphia by all the historic sites — Independence Hall, the birthplace of our nation's Declaration of Independence, and the place that thousands of Americans flock to every year so they can see the Liberty Bell. So I wanted Joy to see these things, too, and we took a cab to Independence Hall, and when we got there I started to show Joy some things on a narrow street called Independence Alley.

"Hey," she said, "I'm really impressed."

"Yeah," I said. "With Independence Alley and the Liberty Bell? All this history?"

"No," she said, "with you?"

"With me?"

"Yeah. You've finally made it. You left the meter running."

I found employment during our summer hiatus in 1982 by signing on with Aaron Spelling, the very successful producer of a number of top-rated TV shows. He wanted me to join an all-star cast with "The Love Boat" on a cruise in the Middle East .

And so, I joined "The Love Boat," a fabulously successful series starring Gavin McLeod, co-produced by Spelling's associate, Douglas Cramer. As you perhaps know, Spelling and Cramer were able to sign on some of the best people in the movie and TV business because they offered not only the most generous salaries in Hollywood, but some unusual perks, too: in this case, luxury cruises (for the stars and their spouses) to some of the world's most fabled places.

This particular "Love Boat" excursion went to the Middle East. We jetted to Athens from Los Angeles, then boarded two ships; the first was the Stella Solaris, the second, the Stella Maris. We headed off to Egypt, and worked our way back to Athens again, then went up to Turkey. That summer, the world's attention was focused on Great Britain's war in the Falklands, but there was still a good deal of tension in the Middle East. There seemed to be armed soldiers everywhere, open enmity between Jews, Arabs and Christians, and much violence.

There were at least five members of the troupe who might run into some trouble in this part of the world. David Hedison and Mike Connors were Armenians, I was Lebanese, and Bernie Kopell and Harvey Korman were Jewish. So, in Turkey, we called the Armenians, David and Mike, "McGonigle and Murphy." In Egypt, we called the Jews, Bernie and Harvey, "Abdullah" and "Salim." In Jerusalem, my friends called me, the Lebanese, "Sol."

We worked hard on the trip, but we also did a lot of hard sightseeing, some of which was recorded for us and preserved on home-videotape by Mercedes Maharis, wife of Bob Maharis, a production assistant on the show. Egypt was a particular fascination for us, a real cradle of ancient civilization. Naturally, we saw the Sphinx, the pyramids, the tombs of the Pharaohs and the Cairo Museum. We loaded up on goods and jewelry that would have cost a good deal more if we had bought them in New York or Beverly Hills. We bought gold jewelry in Tel Aviv and leather goods in Ephesus, and caftans in Jerusalem.

In Jerusalem, we visited one of the most sacred places in Christendom, the Church of the Holy Sepulcher, but I made the mistake of setting out that morning wearing shorts. Rachel, our Sabra guide, noted my attire and said shorts were forbidden in this most sacred shrine, the place where Jesus was buried before He rose from the dead. But, since I was a Christian, she wanted to see if she could get me in anyway. So, when we got to the entrance of the shrine, she called together some of the gals — including Linda Evans, Shirley Jones and Eva Marie Saint — and they made a phalanx around me and smuggled me in, as it were. Well, the ploy got me past the guards and into the church. But, soon after we were inside, an old Arab gentlemen, wearing a heavy winter suit with a vest, a tie and a hat — on a day when the thermometer must have been 100 degrees Fahrenheit — pointed me out to the Israeli police and had me thrown out.

That wasn't all. This man pursued me outside the church, and proceeded to chastise me for my sacrilege. There was a lot of foot traffic here, and a crowd started to gather. I tried to tell him that the God I believed in was not going to get angry at me because my knees were showing. He told me to shut up.

Now this guy didn't know who I was, but some of the people coming by recognized me. "Hey," said these tourists (most of them Americans), "there's Jamie Farr." They started taking pictures. And, in the midst of my discussion with Mr. Rules Committee, I tried to accomodate them by turning every now and then to smile at their cameras, or give someone my autograph, and still continue my conversation with Mr. Rules. He was getting confused — but he was still adamant.

So then I tried speaking to him in Arabic. "I was an altar boy once," I told him. "I'm an actor. I played one of the apostles in 'The Greatest Story Ever Told.'" Whoa! Apostles. That gave me an idea. I had the solution to this problem right under my arm. That very morning, I had purchased an off-white Middle Eastern robe, a linen caftan, just like something St. Jude might have worn. So now, I smiled at the old gentleman, unwrapped my caftan, put it on over my shorts, and proceeded back into the Church of the Holy Sepulcher — much to the old man's confusion.

A couple of days later, outside the Church of the Nativity in Bethlehem, Joy was standing next to an older man when a prosperous-looking gentleman approached him and offered to purchase Joy. The older man said, "Oh, she's not my daughter." Then he turned to Joy and told her the man was making a quite generous offer for her. "Thirty sheep, a dozen goats and three camels."

"Really?" Joy said. "Three camels, huh?" She called me over. "How'd you like three camels?"

"Three camels?"

"And a dozen goats and thirty sheep." She inclined her head slightly toward the generous Arab who had taken a shine to her.

"It's only his first offer. Maybe you can get him to go a little higher."

I told Joy that, for her, I wouldn't consider anything less than a hundred camels. She was pleased. She was pleased to know what a California girl was really worth. In camels.

I wanted to see Lebanon. The closest I came was a hilltop in Haifa where Rachel, the Sabra, a native Jew, not a transplant, told me I could see Lebanon in the distance. Some of our group, including Mike Connors, made it to the gambling tables at Rhodes. At the airport in Istanbul, uniformed men with dogs searched our luggage, looking for drugs. (They all wanted to search the person of Linda Evans.) We'd been warned, of course, so there were no embarrassing incidents, no scenario like the one in a movie called "Midnight Express" where some Americans were imprisoned and brutalized in a Turkish prison for being so stupid as to be carrying some grass.

In fact, considering the size of cast and crew and all the logistics of moving us around the Middle East for more than two months, we had only one major disaster. In Ishmir, Turkey, one member of our cast, Fred Grandy, could have died. (Fred played the purser on "The Love Boat," a character named Gopher; he was a Harvard grad, and a man of many parts; he has since gone on to become a member of Congress from Iowa, and in 1994, he lost a primary campaign for governor in Iowa.) Well, we were returning to our boat from this party in Ishmir, and everyone was carrying these balloons, given out as party favors.

Grandy, Ted Lange, Lauren Tewes, and Lauren's boyfriend Paolo were climbing into their car, and Mercedes and Bob Maharis and I were headed for a bus, not far away. But as soon as this foursome got in the car, there was a big explosion. I thought it was a car bomb. I knocked Bob and Mercedes to the ground, and I hit the ground, too. I thought it might have been a terrorist attack. What was I to think? We were in the Middle East, where anything could happen.

As it turned out, it wasn't a bomb that exploded, it was those party balloons. They weren't filled with helium, but with

271

hydrogen, a gas so dangerous and volatile that it is hardly ever used to fill balloons with anymore. Except in Turkey. Apparently, somebody in that car lit a cigarette, and a spark ignited one of the balloons. So it might as well have been a bomb. A good thing that the windows were open. Otherwise, everyone inside might have been incinerated. Instead, they were only singed. Except for Fred Grandy.

Fred was seriously hurt. He went into shock and had to be sped away in an ambulance. He sustained major burns over much of his upper body, and needed skin grafts to repair the damage, especially to his hands and arms.

Even though he was still suffering from his burns, Fred Grandy appeared in the rest of his scenes wearing flesh-colored rubber gloves. He went on with the show.

26

The Last M*A*S*H

On Feb. 28, 1983, we aired our last episode of M*A*S*H. It was called "Goodbye, Farewell and Amen," and it drew the largest audience ever to watch a single television program in the U.S. Many Americans gathered for M*A*S*H parties, so they could laugh — and weep — together.

Many felt sad, because they had grown used to Hawkeye and B.J. and Col. Potter, to Majors Houlihan and Winchester, to Father Mulcahy and Corporal Maxwell Klinger — who had given up on wearing Carmen Miranda outfits and masquering as Lady Godiva, but was still trying, by hook or crook to get out of Korea and back to Toledo. And now they knew it was goodbye.

They hadn't counted on the re-runs — although one editorial cartoonist, Sayers of *The Milwaukee Journal*, was a seer. He had a man kneeling before a priest in the confessional, saying with some anguish, "Tell me, Father, is there life after M*A*S*H?" — and the priest replying, "Yes, my son, there is eternal re-run."

But many of the nation's editorial cartoonists gave simple expression to a kind of national grief at the demise of a series that had engaged their hearts and minds for eleven years. Power of the *Jackson Sun* drew a shot of our p.a.'s familiar loudspeaker, blaring forth the familiar announcement: ATTENTION ALL PERSONNEL: INCOMING WOUNDED. But, in this case, "the incoming wounded" was a cutout of the entire continental U.S., emblazoned with a broken heart, airborne by three helicopters, heading toward the M*A*S*H 4077. Several cartoonists played with the idea that, after M*A*S*H, there'd be nothing more to watch on television. Stayskal of *The Chicago Tribune* had a couple sitting in from the TV trying to figure what to watch: "M*A*S*H Revisited," "The Editing of M*A*S*H," "Alda on M*A*S*H," "M*A*S*H Bloopers" or "M*A*S*H Plays the Harlem Globetrotters."

Though it is true that M*A*S*H re-runs play now in no less than 54 countries, few get a chance, today, to see the finale, "Goodbye, Farewell and Amen." It's not in most video stores, and for now at least, it's pretty much out of circulation. So, I'd like to tell readers (especially those who weren't watching much TV in 1983) a little bit about that last show.

There was a point, toward the end of our tenth season, when we thought there wouldn't be an eleventh at all. Alan Alda said he was coming close to burning out on M*A*S*H, and it wasn't too hard to see why. He had taken on greater responsibilities on the show, writing and directing and overseeing more and more of the scripts, and he had every right to plead exhaustion. (He was also besieged by a good many other lucrative offers to do other things). But the rest of the cast put some pressure on him. We all wanted to go on, and we said as much to Alan. He blew up. "Don't try to coerce me!" he shouted.

But he turned out to be the ultimate good guy. I think he just sat down and thought about us, and put his own wishes aside for another year. He'd been making far more than we were, and he had participation in the profits for years to come. But, in light of the show's success, the rest of us had been underpaid. Now, he

knew that if we could do one more season, we would all be in a
position to negotiate new, one-year contracts with Fox, contracts
that would give us a chance to finally earn something closer to
what we were worth — to the studio and to CBS. And so, when
Alan said yes, he'd do one more full season, we were in the money.
Each of the principals were now slated to earn something like
$30,000 a week. I don't remember the exact figure. But were all to
get the same. All except Bill Christopher.

The rest of us thought that was unfair. The Father Mulcahy
character was important, an integral part of our ensemble. With
moral support from the rest, Farrell and I went to management and
insisted Bill get the same pay we did. They gave it to him.

So it was settled then. We'd shoot 15 half-hour episodes and
a two-and-a-half hour special, which would take many weeks to
shoot.

That final two-and-a-half-hour special was written by a whole
team of M*A*S*H writers:Alan Alda, Burt Metcalfe, John
Rappaport, Thad Mumford, Dan Wilcox, David Pollock, Elias
Davis and Karen Hall, and it was directed by Alan Alda himself,
who, once he decided on an eleventh season, had really thrown
himself into it.

Alda's own personal feeling of exhaustion may have had
something to do with the first plot point of the film: Capt.
Hawkeye Pierce had finally cracked under the strain of a war that
had gone on too long. As a matter of historic fact, the fighting in
Korea grew more fierce as the end drew near. Some of the most
savage acts of the war were committed while the final peace
negotiations were going on in Panmunjon.

It was logical, then, that in our script, one more tiny savage
act take place inside an Army bus, filled with members of the
4077, coming back from a Fourth of July outing at the beach. On
the way back to the 4077, the bus had stopped to pick up some
Korean refugees. About a half mile up the road, the bus stopped
again, to pick up some wounded GIs. "We gotta get this bus into
the bushes," said one of the GIs. "There's an enemy patrol coming
down the road. Everyone get quiet. Nobody make a sound until
they've passed us."

So they hid the bus, and everyone hunkered down inside it, to wait in terror. In the back of the bus, a baby in its mother's arms began to cry. Twice, Hawkeye came to the back of the bus and told the mother to quiet her baby. Next time he checked, he found she had smothered the kid. That did it for Hawkeye. He went over the edge. When their bus finally made it safely back to the 4077, Hawkeye was sent to a psychiatric ward near Seoul.

"Dear Dad," he wrote, "Sorry I haven't written you for a while, but I've been on R&R at this wonderful resort — the Seoul Old Soldiers Never Die They Just Giggle Academy. We're planning on having a bridge tournament here as soon as we can find someone with a full deck."

With the help of our visiting psychiatrist, Dr. Sidney Freedman, Hawkeye made a tentative recovery and returned to the 4077, only to find more than the usual chaos there. B.J. Hunnicut had already gone home, and, to Hawkeye's disgust, hadn't even left a note to say goodbye. Enemy artillery fire was raining down on his compatriots. Father Mulcahy, thinking nothing of his own safety, ran from cover to unlock some vulnerable prisoners of war, and was knocked senseless by a bomb blast. (He lost the hearing in one ear. But he wouldn't think of telling anyone about it, because, if the authorities learned of his disability, they would have shipped him out. He couldn't have that. What would happen to the children in the nearby orphanage, for whom he had grown increasingly responsible?)

As for Klinger, well, Klinger had fallen in love with a beautiful Korean girl, Soon-Lee, and now he was as distraught as she was over the disappearance of her parents in war-torn Korea. His compulsive personality had taken a new turn. Now he couldn't rest until he found Soon-Lee's parents. He even stole a jeep and went off looking for them. Soon-Lee was sure he could find them because she had described them so well, "short, with dark hair" — in a land where everyone was short and had dark hair.

Maj. Winchester took under his tutelage five Korean POWs — musicians not soldiers — and they learned to play a fairly acceptable version of Mozart's Quintet for Clarinet and Strings before they were sent away on a truck for re-patriation. But a bomb hits their truck on the way and kills all but one of them, who is borne back to the 4077 with part of his chest blown away. For Winchester, it is the last senseless act of a senseless war. "He wasn't even a soldier. He was a musician," says Winchester, and he goes off and smashes his recording of Mozart's Quintet for Clarinet and Strings.

Finally, peace is declared. Everyone prepares, at last, to leave Korea. All except Klinger. He has asked the lovely Soon-Lee to marry him and she has said yes. But she cannot leave Korea until she finds her parents. And so, neither can he. It is a second, major plot point in the last M*A*S*H, and it must have come as a surprise to many of the 125 million fans who were watching on that winter's night. The one man who spent eleven TV seasons trying to get out of Korea is the only one who stays, and it is for the love of the lovely Soon-Lee.

They marry, of course, and at the ceremony performed by Father Mulcahy in the middle of the compound, Soon-Lee wears one of Klinger's white gowns. "John Francis Patrick Mulcahy," says the priest as he gives them his blessing. "Remember that name if you name any children after me." Klinger and Soon-Lee go off in the only transportation available, an ox cart with a "Just Married" sign trailing a string of Klinger's old high heels.

There are other conciliations. B.J. is yanked back from his assignment home and returned to the 4077, where he can now give Hawkeye a proper goodbye. Maj. Winchester, who had been feuding with Maj. Houlihan for years when he wasn't simply remote and unapproachable and aloof, gives her a gift, a copy of Elizabeth Barrett Browning's Sonnets from the Portuguese, then kisses her hand. Hawkeye and B.J. give Col. Potter something they'd never ever given him before, a proper and very respectful military salute. And Hawkeye give Maj. Houlihan a goodbye kiss. (The kiss lasted 34.8 seconds on film, and since commercial time on this show cost $900,000 a minute, a feature writer figured out this kiss was "worth" $522,000.)

That's pretty much the story line of the last M*A*S*H. Shooting it — well, that's another story. We were only half finished with it when, on Oct. 11, 1982, one of those giant LA brush fires swept toward our location in Malibu Canyon. The Los Angeles County Fire Department wanted us out of there, but under orders from the studio's production supervisor, Mark Evans, we stayed until late that Friday night, finished shooting that week's scenes and then got out.

At home, I was awakened by a phone call from a dear friend, Frankie Avalon, the singer. He wanted to know if we were all right. "What do you mean, 'All right?'" I said.

"Well," he said, "the fire has jumped the Ventura Freeway, and it looks, as far I can tell from the TV, that it's headed your way."

He was right. I looked east and south and saw it was coming our way. We have these big brush fires just about every five years or so in LA, and this was one of the biggest I'd ever seen. I woke the family, and we hooked up a John Deere water pump to our swimming pool, so we could douse everything on and around the house. Then we watched (and videotaped) the blaze that was racing toward our home.

We weren't sure we could have survived this one without help. But we got that help from firefighters of both LA and Ventura County who came and built a backfire that met the oncoming fire-front. (I always like to think that the fire chief chose to make a stand right in front of our house because his daughter was staying with us that night.) Now we could see two raging fires racing toward each other, and we stood, fascinated, and watched the collision — resulting in a huge fireball that exploded 75 feet into the air, and then subsided into silence.

Meanwhile, back at Malibu Canyon, site of our M*A*S*H compound, pretty much everything was gone. Our big tin hospital building had melted and lay in little puddles on the ground. In fact, the fire was so intense that it even melted our Jeeps and our tanks. By staying late that Friday night, we had taken a terrible risk.

The surrounding hills were covered with smoldering ash. Rather cleverly, I thought, Alda and Metcalfe incorporated the fire into the plot of the last M*A*S*H. The fires of war were swooping down on the 4077. (The producers got actual footage of the real fires that appeared in our final cut.) So we had to evacuate. We really did: we found a new location at Lake Sherwood, a sylvan community only a few miles northwest of Malibu Canyon, and, all of a sudden, the headquarters of the 4077 is near a pond populated with the ducks of Sherwood.

As an actor on the set, Alan was as much an anarchist as any of us. He sang a different tune, however, when he was directing. G.W. Bailey, the gravel-voiced actor who played our transportation sergeant on the show, Sgt. Rizzo, remembers a moment in those last days when Alan was struggling to get a difficult shot before the sun disappeared behind a bank of oncoming clouds. Then the food wagon appeared and lunch was called. Alan, the Great Humanitarian, sank back in his director's chair, cursing and pounding his fist. "I'm losing the light, and these bastards have to eat?"

As we neared the end of our production days at M*A*S*H, we grew increasingly sentimental. "Goodbye, Farewell and Amen," though the last show, wasn't the last show we shot. We finished "Goodbye" in the October, then went on to do the remainder of the 15 shows scheduled for our last season. In one of them, we were to bury a time capsule filled with memorabilia of our days in the 4077. Loretta had most of the lines in a final scene. But she started to break down each time she got to the line, "And I'm sure each of us hopes that when someone opens this in a hundred years, he or she will know this land was occupied by good, decent —" And then she would cry.

She was not thinking, of course, about Hawkeye, but Alan Alda, not about Col. Potter, but Harry Morgan, not about Klinger, but about me. I, too, was getting awfully sentimental in those last days. Anybody come up to me to say goodbye and my eyes would start to fill up with tears and I'd say, "Come on. Don't do this to me."

It didn't help any when, during the last week of shooting, the press started crowding into Stage 9 to watch us work, do interviews, and try to find the story angles that would meet what they sensed was a public need to know what was happening to us as we wound up our work on something the whole nation had come to love — and that would soon be no more. We were rather overwhelmed by this sudden flood of press attention. On the last day of shooting, with 400 press people on the set, we found it hard to concentrate. Alan said he felt like he was on stage playing to an empty house — "with the entire audience watching from the wings."

When Burt Metcalfe yelled his final "Cut" and the final shot was over, there was such a crush of people pushing in and around us — and a storm of flashing strobes, microphones and video lenses — that we were unable to get to most of the people we wanted to say goodbye to.

Good thing that, some days before this chaotic moment, we, the M*A*S*H principals decided to bury our own time capsule. I said to the group, "If we can do it in the script, why can't we do it for real?" The others agreed, and everyone came up with a memento or two that might help explain to someone who unearthed our time capsule in the 21st century what we were all about. We secured a small, watertight metal box and collected some mementos of M*A*S*H. We found a couple of scripts, and some little dolls representing each of the principals that had been used in a previous episode, and wrote a note to the person who, we imagined, might unearth this piece of history a hundred years hence.

Late one night, after a long day's shoot, we sneaked off to a likely spot on the lot with our little treasure chest and buried our box by flashlight. (Our special effects man, Jay King, was kind enough to dig the hole for us; we swore him to secrecy.)

Imagine our surprise, a few months later, when we heard that a construction crew, excavating for a new building, had dug up our buried treasure. Alan Alda got the word by telephone. "What do you want me to do with this?" said the foreman of the crew that dug it up.

"It's yours," said Alda. That was the stipulation in our note of conveyance, one we had placed on top of the box. Finders keepers.

"I mean," he said, "where do you want it?"

"No," said Alan. "You don't understand. We don't want it. It's yours to keep. It's a piece of history."

But telling him it was a piece of history didn't much help his understanding. As far as we know, this guy tossed our history in his company's dumpster.

On the night when the whole nation was watching "Goodbye, Farewell and Amen," we, the M*A*S*H principals, would have our own quiet goodbye. We went to a private screening room at Fox with our families, saw "Goodbye, Farewell and Amen" the same time that people were watching it on the East Coast, then we all went to dinner together while everyone on the West Coast was watching the show. It was the first of what would turn out to be many dinners together for the M*A*S*H alumni, and we allowed ourselves to reminisce about many of the good times — no great times — we had together. We've remained good friends, all of us. I don't think that I will ever have any better ones.

Part of our closeness comes from knowing that we, as artists of a sort, created something good together, something that none of us would have been able to do alone.

And it was nice to get some confirmation of that from "the boss." The next day, March 1, 1983, Alan got a telegram from William S. Paley, the CEO at CBS — his congratulations on the final episode, which he called "a triumphant and poignantly fitting conclusion to a series which has done honor to the history of television." He used a lot of the nice words: "national outpouring of enthusiasm and affection...touched the hearts of your audience... new dimensions to the art of television...proud network...thanks and very best wishes...."

And then we stopped going in to the studio every day.

27

Beyond M*A*S*H

So, then, what did I say when my friends started asking me, "Whaddya doin' these days, Jamie?"

The truth is that, beyond M*A*S*H, I just kept on doing what I'd been doing before M*A*S*H and during M*A*S*H — working my head off — trying to get other TV and movie assignments, acting on the legitimate stage, appearing on television game shows, doing commercials.

In the early 1980s, I landed parts in the Cannonball movies — "Cannonball Run," and "Cannonball II." The Cannonball movies were fun because they got me back in touch with some old friends. I'd known Burt Reynolds since before the time he made his appearance as a centerfold in *Cosmopolitan*. He was a big *macher* then, at the top of his game, and I was in my third season of M*A*S*H, and one night, we were both booked on the Merv Griffin Show. This was going to be my first appearance on a national talk show, so I had gone out and bought a new suit, and was waiting anxiously in the Green Room, waiting my turn, while Burt was regaling Griffin and a national audience with some wonderful stories.

But then, an unexpected guest arrived, an old friend of Burt's named Lee Majors, the star of TV's "Six Million Dollar Man." So Merv put Majors on the show, and there was no time left for me. I didn't get to go on at all. In my new suit.

When Reynolds realized what had had happened, he came running down to the Green Room and told me he would make Merv promise to give me another shot, and Merv did. And from then on, Reynolds became a friend, as well. He tried a number of times to get me and Joy to join him on private jet flights to Florida, where he owned a pro football team. Our kids were very young then, and it wasn't that easy to jet off to Florida with Burt, just like that. But Burt kept calling and leaving messages on our answering machine. "Hey," he teased, "I don't know why I'm leaving messages for you. I shouldn't have to do this. I'm a star. I'm Burt Reynolds."

Well now, in 1981, Reynolds made his first Cannonball picture. These features will never be listed in anyone's list of the top 100 movies ever made. They were happy, quirky, race-across-the-country-on-a-bet stories, featuring Burt Reynolds and a bunch of his friends. But they were a heckuva lot of fun to make, even though our locations, like the one in Georgia where we did much of "Cannonball Run," was fairly sweltering in a series of 100-degree days and humid nights.

Every evening, we would get together to watch the dailies. The producers always had a lot of fine food for us, and we'd just sit around and tell jokes all night long and completely forget about the humidity. Dean Martin, Shirley MacLaine and Dom DeLuise were on location with us there in "Cannonball II," and that gave me a chance to get closer to these show business legends.

Dean Martin was a charismatic kind of guy. He didn't have to do anything but make an appearance, and people would crack up laughing. I'd seen him in the stage in Las Vegas and marveled how he could hold an audience. He'd start many a song. But he'd never finish one of them. Always stop to tell a joke, or just stand there and giggle, or have another sip of his J&B scotch right there on stage. Here in Decatur, Georgia, I began to see Dean Martin's charm close up. He always had stories to tell, and, because of the way he told them, they were always funny.

Dean had a friend, for instance, who regularly ran the 100-yard dash in 6.2 seconds.

"What a minute, Dean. The world record is 9.2."

"My friend knows a short cut."

On "Cannonball II," we were also on location in Tucson, and one day, everybody was in a tizzy, because the great Frank Sinatra was coming to the set. Since I had the day off anyway, I had made plans to play some golf, sorry that I'd miss Frank. That day, however, somebody broke into my car and stole my shoulder bag — including my Miraculous Medal, one that I had gotten from my grandmother. It had no great value — except sentimental value. But the thieves didn't know that, and when they tried to pawn the medal, the cops were able to nab them. And I got my medal back.

Telly Savalas was in "Cannonball II." And I joked with him about the theft that night. "I don't stick around to meet Frank Sinatra. So he sends somebody to see me. And steal my medal."

Telly reminded me of the guys in my old neighborhood. He talked like they did. He ate like they did. One night, he insisted I join him and his brother, Gus, to go out for some Greek food. Telly had a long, white Lincoln limousine, with everything in it — bar, TV, stereo, ice machine, everything but a bowling alley — and he insisted on driving it. He never allowed anyone else to drive it. No chauffeur for him. He put me and Gus in the back and drove us to his favorite Greek restaurant in Tucson.

That dinner reminded me of all the times I had eaten at the home of my Toledo friend, Gregory Morris, whose mom made a delicious *avgo lemono*, literally egg-lemon soup, but really more like a fine chicken broth, with rice in it, no meat, and a delicious touch of lemon. Not knowing *avgo lemono*, I hesitated. "Eat, eat," said his mom. "Eat, eat." Okay, already, I followed orders. I ate.

Now, here I was being served the same *avgo lemono*, urged on by Telly Savalas and Gus in the same tones: "Eat, eat."

"You ever had Domestika wine?" said Telly. "Drink. Drink."

I returned his hospitality by lending him an audio tape I had, some great Greek music. But he never returned the tape. That became a running gag between us for years. He's snap his fingers every time he'd see me. "Jamie! Damn! I still haven't gotten that tape back to you, have I?" No. And you know something? He never did. Alas, he never will. Who loves ya, Baby? We love ya, Baby.

Even when I was working steadily on M*A*S*H, I had found working in regional theater a good way to augment my modest stipends from Fox. During our summer breaks, I had been doing Howard Pechet's Stage West dinner theaters in Canada for years before others from the M*A*S*H cast finally realized these were very nice assignments. When, after M*A*S*H, some of them finally took summer residence at these theaters, they were amazed to see my face plastered all over the lobbies. My M*A*S*H colleagues could see, like the famous Kilroy of World War II, I had already been there. Even today, M*A*S*H principals find it is rather easy to get theater jobs on the summer circuit in the East, and in regional theater, including Canada, the year round. The reason is simple: impresarios find that we sell a lot of tickets.

At this point, you may have noticed something about me. I'm a guy who could only make it in this difficult business by being totally professional, suppressing outbursts of ego, being a good team player, learning my lines and sticking to the script. According to my life script, I said good things about people when I liked them. When I didn't like them, I usually said nothing. Who was I to criticize? I always took the position that everybody was doing the best they could with the talents that had been given them.

As a result, people continued to hire me, and I continued to work, wherever and whenever I could do so, with dignity. Sometimes, even without dignity. As for example, when I began showing up rather regularly on a number of different game shows.

I was invited, for instance, to be among the first celebrity panelists on a game show produced by a wild man named Chuck Barris, a show that has become more than a legend in America. It was called "The Gong Show," a kind of cross between the "Ted Mack's Amateur Hour" and Arthur Godfrey's "Talent Scouts." I'd first heard of it before it even went on the air. Barris was offering it for syndication at a television executives' convention in San Francisco, and everyone in the convention hotel was talking about it, and many were buying it, because it was just so obviously wacky.

It was wacky because it was apparent to everyone that Barris wasn't so much interested in talent as he was in "no talent." He had made the extraordinary discovery that there was no limit to the dumb things that people would do to get themselves noticed. Especially if their act, or trick, or whatever, would get them on television.

Next thing I knew, NBC had bought "The Gong Show" for daytime, and I was asked to be one of a group of three guest panelists. The format was a simple one: People would get up and do their act, and then one or another of the panelists would gong them — the TV equivalent of vaudeville's hook — and then try to explain why they weren't deemed good enough to continue.

We did the first five shows one Saturday at the NBC Studios in Burbank. The band wore straw hats and striped jackets. John Barbour, the host, did his manful best to act like a cross between Ted Mack and Arthur Godfrey. The first three panelists on the show — Joanne Worley (of NBC's "Laugh In," Jack Cassidy (the husband of Shirley Jones and the father of David Cassidy) and I — we quickly realized that what we were being asked to do was going to get very boring. There were only so many way to hit a gong. At one point, Joanne Worley blindfolded me and spun me around, and like a kid playing Pin The Tail On The Donkey, I was supposed to find the gong.

After those first five shows (which would be presented one-a-day in an upcoming week), Chuck Barris took me aside and asked me what I thought about the show. "Chuck," I said, "in its current format, this show is going nowhere. How long can the panelists suggest to these people that they consider taking lessons? Or that they should consider going into another line of work? This isn't very much fun."

Barris said, "Well, what are we gonna do?"

Since this was a kind of a put-on of the old talent show idea, I suggested we go even further with the put-on. I suggested we enclose this very undignified display of non-talent in a very dignified package. Have the orchestra dress in tuxedos. Have the panelists come out in tuxedos and ball gowns, and play opposite what we were presenting. We could milk some laughs by giving our supposedly judicious consideration to the efforts of a guy wearing a tutu who stood on his head while playing Stravinsky's "Fire Dance" on the violin. It wasn't a serious act. But treating it as if it were serious — well, that might create some extra laughs.

Then, too, if our celebrity panelists were allowed to play over- dignified, then they could expect more laughs when they suddenly put on a lampshade. Barris bought my thinking. The next week, the orchestra was togged in tuxes, and the very distinguished panelists were doing some very undistinguished things. At the beginning, we were bidden to follow all the rules set by the Standards and Practices Division of NBC. But, little by little, we began to ignore the rules. Eventually, the only rule was that we never gonged a person, but only the act. Otherwise, the rule was "anything goes." Jaye P. Morgan, the singer, started trying to take down the top of her gown, and I took to wrestling with her on camera, trying to stop her. (Once, when I wasn't there, she actually did expose herself and NBC had a fit.)

None of this meant that our contestants (or their loved ones who invariably accompanied them to the show) would necessarily like what we were doing. After the shows (we always did a whole week's worth of shows in one day), a disgruntled dad would often be waiting for me in the parking lot with a baseball bat in his hand and fire in his eye. I was never struck by a bat, but, for a while there, we needed police escorts to our cars. When I was under escort, I found people could at least make me the target of some

288

interesting curses. I remember one: "May a diseased yak, sir, find it a delight to sit on your face!"

I found that a good many people who never watched M*A*S*H were fans of "The Gong Show." Once, a group of Japanese tourists visited Stage 9 at Fox; they did not recognize any of the others in the cast, but were soon exclaiming over me, and pointing their 35mm Minoltas at me. "Oooo, Jah-mee Fall, Jah-mee Fall, Gong Show, Gong Show." Then there were always the shopkeepers, garage mechanics, hatcheck girls and occasional bartenders who wanted to audition for a spot on the show. Once, in the men's room of a well-known restaurant in Beverly Hills, a man turned from his spot in front of a urinal to face me, and said, "Jamie Farr! 'The Gong Show!' Whaddya think of this?"

I stopped him. "I'm on 'The Gong Show,'" I said. "Not the Dong Show." Maybe he got the wrong idea after he saw one girl on the show with enormous breasts who sang, "Memories" — only she pronounced it "mammaries."

Imagine the audition stories Barris can tell. Hopeful contestants coming up to him in the airport, doing a tap dance, or asking him to pick a card. On a flight from New York to LA, a dignified businessman kneels down next to Barris's aisle seat and does his lizard imitation — capping his performance by licking Chuck's cheek with his tongue. At a Rangers' hockey game in Madison Square Garden, a woman slithers down the aisle to his seat, and sings "Hello, Dolly," standing on her head. Her tipsy friend does an instrumental version of "Dixie." He has no instruments: he does it by thwacking his arm pit.

I did "The Gong Show" for several years. Over the years, the next Judy Garland never came forward. But Paul Reubens came back again and again, playing different characters, until he finally settled on Pee Wee Herman. One day, Chuck caught one of the stage hands, a janitor named Gene Patton, dancing with his broom — not moving his feet at all, just shaking his behind, backed by a Count Basie number playing on his radio. So Chuck put him on the show, shuffling with his broom to the tune of "One O'clock Jump." He became Gene, Gene, the Dancing Machine, and an overnight national sensation.

Chuck Barris took over the job of host himself. He was terrific. He let us get away with anything. During one break, Jaye P. Morgan, Arte Johnson (from NBC's "Laugh In") and I decided we'd had enough of Barris. So we borrowed some rope and some tape from the stage crew and, with the cameras rolling on the next show, captured Barris and bound and gagged him. The director liked that. During the next acts, he kept cutting away to Barris, struggling to rid himself of his bonds. And then Arte Johnson decided to tie up both Jaye P. Morgan and myself, so that, by the end of the show, Arte was totally in charge (and totally mad).

During this period of my life, I'd do other game shows. We always did five shows on a single day, usually on a Saturday. Then they'd run them Monday through Friday. So, for each show, we were supposed to wear a different outfit. Unless we were always wearing tuxedos, we could have been burdened by five different suits on a single Saturday. Vincent Price solved that by always wearing a blazer, with five different ties.

Many is the Saturday that I'd go and do five shows for something like "Hollywood Squares," then head for the parking lot — only to be asked by Barris, or some other producer, if I could fill in on another show for a guest panelist who didn't show. So then I'd go back in, to do another five shows for one or another of the other shows. One weekend, Saturday and Sunday, I did four different game shows, and knocked down $6,000 doing 20 shows back to back.

Barris once had eight different game or variety shows going at the same time, including "The Dating Game." No wonder they called him "The Game Show King." I saw a graffito once in a Hollywood men's room: STOP ME, BEFORE I CREATE AGAIN. It was signed, "Chuck Barris."

Chuck might be still doing game shows today except, if you can believe his account, he went too far by booking a sister act on "The Gong Show," called The Popsicle Twins. The twins were two pretty teen-agers, one 16, one 17, cute, sexy blondes, with blue-eyes, freckles, and ripe bodies that were hardly contained in the skimpy halter tops and short-shorts they wore in the show.

The girls skipped out to center stage, sat down, crossed their legs yoga fashion, and to the music of "I'm In The Mood For Love," sucked off orange popsicles.

Barris said the twins made television history, principally because a U.S. senator's wife tried to get "The Gong Show" banned from the airways. Frowned on mightily by NBC, Barris soon quit the TV business, retired to the French Riviera and wrote two autobiographies, *Confessions of a Dangerous Mind*, and *The Game Show King*.

I was on "$25,000 Pyramid" and "Super Password" a good many times. An all-time favorite "Super Password" show happened on the watch of host Bert Convy. I was in a bonus round that had escalated to an all time high of $50,000. My partner was a black woman who had won her way into this bonus round with me. We were both pretty keyed up. After all, a $50,000 prize on this show was very rare.

So now we begin. Behind her, I could see a list of 10 words. Behind me, she could see a series of letters. My job: to feed her 10 rapid-fire clues that would trigger in her the right 10 words, all in 60 seconds. If the first word was "daughter," I might say, "Son?" If the second word was "car," I might say, "Cadillac." If the third word was "salt," I might say, "pepper?"

So, I look up and I see the first word on our list is "deer." She sees, behind me, the letter "D." Now I could have said, "Animal." But if I wanted to be more specific, I might have said, "Antelope?" Instead, quick-like, I say, "Doe." I was thinking of that song in "The Sound of Music," do, a doe, a female deer.

But she comes back, just as quick, with, "Knob."

I blink. "Doe...knob?" Well, aside from the fact that "knob" doesn't begin with a "d," I didn't say "door." I said "doe." But she heard "door." I couldn't go on. I just started to laugh so hard that Convy had to restrain me. The audience was dying. The only one who didn't know what was happening was the contestant. But Convy and I had to compose ourselves, and just try to go on. Needless to say, we didn't win the $50,000. But the producers really loved that show and talked about it for years. It provided more laughs than if we had sailed through it without a hitch. They should have given us the $50,000 on the side.

On a game show, the uninhibited surprises always provided the biggest laughs. Here's the kind of exchange Barris liked to present on national TV:

HOST: What will your husband say is his least favorite condiment on his wiener?

WIFE #1. Mustard.

WIFE #2. Ketchup.

WIFE #3. Ketchup.

WIFE #4. Ben Gay.

Once, Monte Hall had a show called "Split Second" that was going off the air. At the break in the middle of the last show, he asked his announcer, Jay Stewart, if they had any extra prize money, he'd like to see if he could hand it over to a little lady who had been a longtime regular in the audience, always sitting in the same front row seat. "We've got about four hundred dollars," said Stewart.

"Okay," said Hall. "When we come out of commercial, I'll take the microphone over to her and I'll ask her a very very simple question, like, 'Who was the first man?' And she'll say, 'Adam,' and we'll give her the four hundred."

So, they come out of the commercial, and there's the usual applause, applause, applause from the audience. Then Monte Hall saunters down to the front row and says, "As you know, this is our last show, and we have four hundred dollars left. Madame, what is your name?"

"Sadie."

"Sadie," he says, "for four hundred dollars, who was the first man?"

"For a *thousand* dollars," she says, "I wouldn't tell ya."

You may wonder why I even bothered with the game shows. Hadn't I become rich on the M*A*S*H re-runs? Let me tell you about the re-runs. The only people who made money (and are still making money) off the re-runs of M*A*S*H are Alan Alda, Larry Gelbart and Twentieth Century-Fox. My guess is that Fox has made something on the order of a billion dollars on the syndication of M*A*S*H.

Gene Reynolds made zilch. Reynolds, the executive producer of television's M*A*S*H from the very beginning, the guy who hired Gelbart, got no participation in the show because, as Reynolds now recalls, Fox simply reneged on a promise to give him a percentage. Soon after that, after five seasons on M*A*S*H, Reynolds left to produce another hit on CBS, "Lou Grant," starring Ed Asner.

As for the rest of the M*A*S*H cast, we got (and still get) a mere pittance from the re-runs — maybe a little more than $10,000 a year, total, from all the U.S. re-runs and maybe an extra $3,000 from the rest of the world. There are times when I have opened my mail and found residual checks (from one of my other shows, not M*A*S*H) for as little as three cents. Don't get me wrong. Every little bit of income helps, because it has allowed us to keep our health insurance current, which, as you all know, is no small benefit.

Sure, we like to see ourselves in re-runs for one reason: it keeps our names alive, in the hinterlands. But not in Hollywood. That was one of the career problems that all the regulars had to face, and try to conquer. Identification with the M*A*S*H characters could just absolutely ruin many chances for other TV and movie roles, especially in a business where actors and actresses win fame and fortune by getting type cast — and then playing and re-playing that type for the rest of their acting lives.

Gary Burghoff is a great actor. He didn't have to keep playing a simple little company clerk from Iowa, for the rest of his life. I didn't have to keep playing a wacko who would do anything to get out of the Army. But some of the decision makers in network television seemed to have tunnel vision, and they were not very likely to give us anything that went counter to their stereotype. Hey, we're in a business of "let's pretend." But when some casting director fails to give us a chance, they're not letting us play let's pretend. They've terminated our lives, based on the last thing we did.

It's also something of a myth to think that commercial work keeps starving actors alive until they get lucky. Starving actors usually get paid minimum Guild scale for the shoot, plus ten percent. They always get residuals, but they are never of any consequence. The only real money goes to actors and actresses who can land jobs as spokespersons for a product, and those only happen, typically, when they're hot — in other words, at precisely that point in their lives when they don't need the work.

But, sometimes, there are wonderful surprises.

Several years after M*A*S*H's last show in 1983, one of Joy's psychic friends told Joy that the M*A*S*H principals would be getting together again soon, and they'd be doing something that would make them a lot of money. "C'mon," I said, "get outta here. What could it be? We're not gonna do a M*A*S*H movie. We're not going to do a retrospective."

Not too long after that, I got a call from my agent, telling me IBM was putting together a big sales pitch for their personal computers. And they wanted all the M*A*S*H principals to be a part of a multimedia campaign — TV, radio, magazines, everything. We all signed identical, high-six-figure contracts. But that's because we were still hot.

I was a spokesman once for Mars bars. The Mars company also made Milky Way and Snickers, but its ad agency told me Mars didn't have to worry about marketing them. They seemed to sell themselves. But Mars bars weren't doing too well. The solution was to give the Mars bar a signature, more of an identity. The plan was to do that through a spokesperson with an identity. And so the ad agency picked me. The whole campaign was: "You've done something good today. Reward yourself." I did some great spots. And I helped move Mars up from number 15 to number 12, which represented millions of dollars in extra sales. If something ain't broke, you don't fix it. But ad agencies are always trying to pick off other agencies' clients by promising to do better. Eventually, somebody picked off the agency that hired me on the Mars account, and the new agency was then obliged to fix something that wasn't broken. It dumped me. But then, I soon became the spokesman for After Six tuxedos, and I was again in the money. I turned a nice piece of change on After Six. Burt Reynolds once made $500,000 a year promoting Florida orange juice. Susan Sullivan makes six figures a year as a spokesperson for Tylenol. For several years, I earned this kind of money for my work on behalf of IBM, Mars and After Six.

In sum, I made millions of dollars on my commercials. I probably made more money over the years on my commercials than I ever did on all 11 seasons of M*A*S*H. Funny thing is, I never felt any different after I started getting this big money. I have a business manager, Sid Pazoff, who, for years, has given me an allowance — a few hundred dollars a week — and I never see the big money, because Sid has it funnelled into my investments.

This reminds me of a story about Jack Klugman, an actor who has proven he can do superb comedy and drama in any medium. When Jack was starring in television's "Odd Couple" with Tony Randall, and making top dollars, he was suddenly overtaken by a feeling of sadness every payday. On those days, Jack would see most of the others in the cast getting their checks, and feeling like working folks feel almost everywhere. You know how it is on pay day. Pay day gives you a sense of pride, satisfaction, even at times a certain exhilaration. It's nice to know your work counts.

Now, Klugman was getting none of these good feelings, because he, too, had a business manager handling everything. He never saw his money. Finally, he couldn't stand it. He called his business manager and the studio and demanded that his pay be delivered to him next week in a briefcase, in cold cash. Well, he got what he wanted. Next payday, a uniformed guard appeared on the set at lunchtime with a very large briefcase and presented it to Mr. Klugman.

Jack opened the case. His eyes lit up and his heart warmed at the sight of nothing but $100 bills in $5,000 packets. "So this," he said, "hefting the packets and thumbing the bills, "this is what it's all about!"

"Okay," he told the guard. "Take it back and have it sent to my business guy. I've seen it. I've touched it. Now I know it's real."

28

The Sweeter Life

At the beginning of this book, I told you that I never wanted to go back to Toledo. I also told you that I had made a promise to myself that I'd never go back unless I could go back in triumph. That day came in 1977, when I went back to my home town for the 25th anniversary reunion of my graduating class and wound up being honored with a Jamie Farr Day And A Half. In most places, it is customary to give a star, usually a sports star, a special day. But, in the case of Jamie Farr, Toledo wanted to do something extra special. They gave me A Day And A Half.

During that Day And A Half in Toledo, I donated two commercials for Blue Cross at Mercy Hospital, where I was born, and I helped dedicate the Performing Arts Center at Scott High School. There was a cartoon in *The Toledo Blade*, putting me forward for mayor. The real mayor didn't seem to mind. He gave me the key to the city. Since Toledo was then known as the glass capital of the world, it was a glass key. At the time, I told Columnist Seymour Rothman of *The Toledo Blade* that my fame hadn't changed me much. "I still buy gasoline at the self-service pump. Good credits are great. But good credit is better."

Toledo loved me, of course, for putting Toledo on the map, at least as far as America's television viewers were concerned. I had helped make the Mud Hens famous. I had made Packo's hot dogs an international household name. Why shouldn't the city fathers give me a key to the city? Why shouldn't the people of Toledo nominate me for mayor, if only in jest?

Of course, I in turn tried to give something back to Toledo. That's the way it is with friendships, including the most important friendship of all, the friendships we have with our husbands and wives: there's never an end to the giving, back and forth. The love of friendship is like alternating current. It only lights up a light bulb — or a city — if it goes back and forth.

Speaking of Toledo makes me think, again, of Danny Thomas, whose footsteps I tried to follow for much of my life. (After Danny showed up driving a Lincoln into north Toledo when I was still at Woodward High, I had a lifelong preference for Lincolns, even if they were old, formerly owned Lincolns.) Trouble was, I couldn't get Danny to pay much attention to me. I had heard him speak at more than one community dinner, heard him tell everyone how we should help our own. But, never experiencing any of that help in my own case, I couldn't help think it was all empty rhetoric. He had raised my spirits, only to let me down.

He had his own production company, a real comedy factory that was turning out three and four comedy series every season, including "The Danny Thomas Show." Once, he was casting about for someone to play the part of his nephew on that show. The part was made to order for me, the kid from his own neighborhood in north Toledo. Instead, Danny gave it to an actor named Don Penny. I could never get him to notice me.

But then, one night at a fancy New Year's Party at Marvin Davis' home in Rancho Mirage, Danny Thomas came up to the table where Joy and I were sitting with Bud Grant, then the president of CBS, and said, "Jameel, I'm proud of you. You have gotten where you are without any help from me."

His words made me very sad. There was so much he could have done for me. But I said nothing to him, other than, "Thank you, thank you, Danny." Nor did I say anything to Joy. But she read my mind.

Afer he left the table, Joy said, "Well, that was nice of him. But I wanted to ask him, 'Why did you make this man suffer so much? You could have helped. But you didn't.'" Joy knew: All my life, Danny Thomas had been a model for me, and, all my life, I grieved because he never seemed to notice me.

Until the very end. Then, not long before he died, Danny was being honored at the Friar's Club with a Lifetime Achieve-ment Award, and who do you think he invited to sit right behind him on the three-tiered dais? Me, Jamie Farr, the kid named Jameel who had resurrected his "Extravaganza," years after he had left Woodward High.

As grudging as Danny seemed for all those years, finally, he recognized me. For an actor and an entertainer, I think recognition is the ultimate turn-on, especially from those whose work you have long admired. There are more important things in life, of course, and you should never try to build your happiness on the opinion of others. In the entertainment business, however, the opinion of others can often be the difference. As Bob Hope has said, "One day you're drinking the wine and the next day you're crushing the grapes." And so, in my business, you don't turn your back on fame when she walks in the door. You learn to enjoy fame when you have it, and make it work for you, and for your family.

In 1981, a company called TvQ, which is in the business of rating celebrities who appear on television, had me high on its list of "the most famous and well-liked people in the world." In 1981, Alan Alda was number one on the TvQ. But I was number 10, tied with George Burns and Clint Eastwood. I'd be less than frank if I told you I didn't enjoy that TvQ rating. Today, more than ten years after M*A*S*H's farewell, I still enjoy the hellos I get on the streets of New York, at Heathrow Airport in London, or when I am stopped for a red light in Beverly Hills. I still enjoy the dozens of letters I get every week, and I am still flattered by the invitations that pour in, asking me to make personal appearances around the country, generally on behalf of some charity or other.

During my middle years with M*A*S*H, I was introduced to the celebrity circuit by Marvin Davis, the Denver oil man who had bought Twentieth Century-Fox. He invited the M*A*S*H principals to attend his Carousel Ball in Denver. Others in the cast didn't seem that keen on going. But I wanted to go, and I did go. I enjoyed being picked up in the limo that Marvin Davis had sent to my home, and flying me to Colorado for the ball on one of his private jets. (This first year, Joy didn't attend the ball; neither did any of the others in the M*A*S*H cast.) I remember my first trip on his Gulfstream II. Inside the cabin, it looked more like a living room than an airplane.

As I boarded, I noted who the others were: Hal Linden was on the plane, with his wife, Fran; Lucy Arnaz and her husband, Larry Luckinbill; and the great lady herself, Lucille Ball. Gregory Peck and his wife, Veronica, were in the middle of the plane. And toward the rear, Cary Grant and his wife, Barbara. Wow! I thought, what a cast list!

We had an elegant lunch on the plane, the stewards poured some libations, and soon we were in Denver. Marvin Davis was waiting, along with a fleet of limos. "Well, Jamie," he said, "how was the flight?"

I frowned at him and said, "Don't you ever do this to me again."

He seemed alarmed. "Wasn't it a good trip?"

"It was great," I said. "But you know who was aboard." I ticked off their names.

"So?"

I said, "Do you realize that if that plane had crashed, I would have gotten last billing?"

Proceeds for this glittering, black-tie affair went to the Barbara Davis Juvenile Diabetes Foundation. One of the Davis daughters had diabetes, and this was what had spurred the Davises to raise funds for this cause. At this Carousel Ball, I recall that Merv Griffin served as master of ceremonies, and that Frank Sinatra, Diana Ross, and Kenny Rogers entertained.

Barbara Davis was Marvin Davis' wife, a lovely, unpretentious woman, who once allowed one of our ADs, a tense young woman, to throw her and her party right off Stage 9 without a protest. This on our M*A*S*H set, mind you, where the rules were never enforced. For once, this AD decided to enforce them — and with a woman who was the wife of the man who owned the studio. The AD didn't even know who Marvin Davis was.

The Carousel Ball showed me how "the other half" lived. Well, I thought, I could learn to like this. And I had a frank admiration for the people who could bring off a party like this one. It was, in essence, a big fund-raiser for a good cause. The Carousel Ball generated millions of dollars each year for the Foundation. Marvin and Barbara Davis realized that, for all their money, they could not make their daughter's diabetes disappear. That took research, and research cost millions. And Marvin Davis not only helped raise it. He contributed himself. I was on the dais the night he reached into his own pocket (figuratively speaking) and tossed in an additional $10 million for the foundation.

I persuaded Joy to go with me to the next year's Carousel Ball. Joy and I kept attending the Carousel Ball each year, parties that left us with some fond memories — and some more great stories to tell. I have already told you about Joy's meeting with Henry Kissinger — her friend, whom she insisted on calling Henry.

Let me tell you another. At one of those balls, Joy and I sat on the dais with Mr. and Mrs. Frank Sinatra, Mr. and Mrs. Cary Grant, Mr. Arnold Schwarzenegger, Mr. Donald Sutherland, Mr. and Mrs. James Stewart, Mr. Merv Griffin, Mr. Art Buchwald, Mr. and Mrs. Gerald Ford — well, you get the idea.

After dinner, Alan Hirshfield, then the studio head at Twentieth Century-Fox, approached the dais and presented me and Arnold Schwarzenegger, who was sitting at the other end of the head table, not far from Donald Sutherland and Cary Grant, with long Punch Cuban cigars to smoke with our coffee. Arnold and I, both of us cigar lovers, were in cigar heaven. These were the best cigars in the universe. We smiled, saluted each other with our Punch Cubans as if they were batons, then simultaneously crimped the ends and lit up.

As I puffed away in ecstasy, Donald Sutherland got up and approached my chair. I thought, what a nice gesture! Mr. Sutherland probably watches M*A*S*H and enjoys my character and performance so much that he wants to tell me.

"Jamie," he said, "would you mind putting out your cigar? Mr. Cary Grant and I have terrible allergies and the smoke is really annoying."

I pretended that I was pleased with his effrontery, but I said, "Look, this is a very expensive cigar, very rare. I couldn't just put it out. That would ruin it. But with your permission, I won't puff on it, just let it die out in the ash tray and that way I'll be able to enjoy it later in my room."

Sutherland said that would be all right. He started to return to his seat.

But I stopped him. "Donald, may I ask you something? Arnold Schwarzenegger is sitting between you and Cary Grant and he is smoking the same cigar I have here. He still is. Why didn't you ask him to put out his cigar?"

He hesitated. "Well. Uh. Jamie, if I had wanted to do that, I would have done it with a note. And signed it 'The Phantom.'"

The next morning, we flew back to LA, on Mr. Davis' private Gulfstream II with an all-star cast of the world's most elegant people — including Robert Wagner and Jill St. John, Donald Sutherland and Joan Collins and her husband. It had been a glitzy affair, one marked by the opulence, most notably, of the women who were there. Joy was in a kind of revery, recalling how Mrs. Davis had been bedizened with two matching necklaces, one with diamonds and rubies and the other with emeralds. Large diamonds and rubies. Large emeralds. And how Candy Spelling had been wearing, a 40-carat diamond ring. Joy said, "You could play the

World Series on that diamond." Mrs. Davis called it "cute." By the time we were touching down at LAX, Joy was just about overdosed on rich and famous. She was very quiet.

"Is there anything wrong?" I asked.

She smiled and said, "I feel as if I've eaten too much of my favorite candy. And now I'm sick."

But she had a solution. After the chauffeur had put our things in the trunk, he opened the car door for us. Joy turned to him and said, "Quick, drive us through a ghetto."

This was a lady, mind you, who had waited 13 years for her engagement ring. I had never been able to afford one. Now I could. So I went out and bought her a 1.5-carat emerald and diamond ring, and when I told Loretta Swit what I had done, Loretta helped celebrate the occasion by doing a small painting of some daisies, and an inscription.

I decided to make the presentation at a family dinner at the Calabasas Inn. As Joy and I and the kids were waiting for our appetizers, the maitre d' (according to my earlier instructions) came up with a silver-domed tray and said to Joy, "Madame, we thought you'd like this." He removed the cover with a flourish, and there lay Joy's engagement ring. At that moment, I slipped Loretta's painting right next to the tray, an artistic celebration of my sentiments: Loretta's daisies and the words, YOU ARE THE JOY OF MY LIFE.

We told the curious waiters this was an engagement ring. And they said they thought I was a pretty decent guy, making an honest woman out of the lady who had already borne these two kids.

After we stopped shooting M*A*S*H, for the first time in my life, I had a little time, time to take it easy, time to get active in a sport that I had always looked upon from afar. I thought I'd try golf. I got started by buying a set of starter clubs, Wilson GE 1200s, and I walked out and dumped them in the back of my Jeep Cherokee. (They were making the Jeep in Toledo then, maybe still are, and the Jeep people in Toledo were only too happy to make one special for me.)

So now, Jonas and I are looking around for a driving range where I can give my new clubs a try. We drive over to the closest golf course to our home, the Calabasas Country Club, and stop near the 18th tee. By chance, two friends of mine, Frankie Avalon, the singer, and Louis Gallo, a producer, are preparing to tee off.

"Hey," I shout, "where can I find a driving range?"

They told me that Calabasas had a nice range. But it was for members only. Did I want to be a member? Well, sure. At this point, I wasn't the kid from Toledo who worried, first, what a thing cost. As a matter of fact, however, I got a helluva bargain. They sent me up the club's office, to see if there were any openings. And after they finished their round, they popped in to vouch for me, and I got a membership on the spot, for a mere $3,000, and I went happily off, with Jonas, and we hit a few buckets of balls.

I thought that was pretty cool. Now I could afford to pay $3,000 for an afternoon on a driving range. Joking aside, I got a heckuva bargain. Memberships in Calabasas today cost $35,000, if you can get one. I don't have an equity membership, so I can't sell mine for $35,000. But if I choose to leave the club, I will get $2,000 back. For an effective investment of $1,000, then, I have a membership in a very fine club.

The Calabasas Country Club has a great course, designed by Robert Trent Jones Jr. It's on a site that used to be the Warner Ranch, and each of the holes are named after a classic movie that was filmed there, at least in part. The fourth hole: "Giant." The seventh hole: "Show Boat." The fourteenth hole: "The Good Earth." The seventeenth hole: "Stalag 17." But I'd hardly call it snobbish, or even exclusive.

There are country clubs that are so exclusive that they won't consider memberships for actors. Or, at least, there were clubs like that at one time. The Los Angeles Country Club was one of them. When Randolph Scott put in an application there, the board turned him down. He said, "Actor? I've got dozens of movies to prove I'm not."

Affluent Jews in Los Angeles who couldn't get in the LACC went to the West Side and built their own country club, Hillcrest, just for Jews. They picked out a good piece of land. Oil was soon discovered there, and the wells are still producing — which means that it's the only country club in the land where the original members don't pay dues, but get dividends instead.

The Hillcrest board let in one token Christian — Danny Thomas. Which prompted some wag to say, "If they were going to let in a Christian, why didn't they let in a Christian who looks like a Christian?" True enough: Danny Thomas, Lebanese-born, could have passed for a Jew anywhere.

It wasn't long before I started playing in one celebrity tournament after another, and eventually ended up promoting a charity tournament of my own, the Jamie Farr Ladies Professional Golf Association Toledo Golf Classic, played every summer at the Highland Meadows Country Club in nearby Sylvania, Ohio.

We had our tenth annual tournament in July 1994, and, by every measure, our ten years have been a big success. Don Michel, a local McDonald's operator and one of my best schoolhood chums, helped us get started by underwriting our first two tourneys. Great thing about Michel. His father, a shoe repairman, was so poor that he'd travel to local farms and repair harnesses to barter for the family's food. Now Don owns a dozen McDonald's, and keeps supporting our tourney most generously. So far, we've raised roughly $1 million for various children's charities in the Toledo area, and we've been able to raise our purse every year.

I also give credit to Frankie Avalon, the singer, and Tommy Dreesen, the standup comic, for donating their talent at our banquets. They gave us the prestige and the notoriety we needed to make our success at the beginning.

In '94, our contestants competed for a purse of $500,000. One of them, Kim Williams, a tall, LPGA veteran, got a good deal of press attention by playing in our tourney with a bullet lodged in her neck. The week before, going into a drugstore in Niles, Ohio, she felt a sudden pain the left side of her neck. It felt like she'd been hit with a baseball. It was a bullet from a 9-mm semiautomatic handgun that had been fired from a mile away. It burrowed under her right collarbone and came to rest just above the top rib on her right side, close to her esophagus.

The doctors decided not to remove it, at least for the time being, for fear they might do more harm than good. So Kim played in our tourney, with the sensation of a bullet against her throat every time she swallowed. On her first round, she played her best golf of the year (she shot a three-under-par 68) and she ended up with 10th-prize money, and two-under-par for the entire tournament. I told her she was lucky she didn't end up six-under. Ground, that is.

The Jamie Farr LPGA Toledo Classic was not my idea. It came from a local golf enthusiast named Judd Silverman. He knew the LPGA was looking for another city, and he said, "Why not Toledo?" And if Toledo, then why not get Jamie Farr to put his name on it and help promote it? As Judd explained it to me, "You're proud of Toledo. And Toledo is proud of you."

I gave the matter some thought, and finally said I'd do it — on one condition: that I didn't want anything out of it. As far as I was concerned, this was a charity thing all the way. And with that principle firmly established, I could feel free to invite a half-dozen of my friends every year to come to the tournament and participate in our big dinner show the night before the pro-am. This past July, we had 2,000 attending that affair, with Scott Record, an impressionist and comedian, and the Temptations providing the entertainment.

Judd's claim to fame (I jest) dates back to the time in 1988 when he caddied for Craig Stadler in the Andy Williams San Diego Open at Torrey Pines. Seems that he made the mistake of handing a towel to Stadler when he hit a drive off the 16th tee that landed under some low-lying pine trees. Stadler had to get down on one knee to punch his ball out from under, and he took the towel and put it under his knee, so as not to get pine sap all over his pants — an unnecessary move, since Stadler was a craggy type who couldn't care less about his appearance.

No one noticed the towel business at the time, but NBC made it a highlight on their next day's telecast, and viewers around the country started phoning in and saying that using a towel in these circumstances amounted to "building a stance" — which was against the rules. It was an obscure rule, but they were right.

If Stadler had noted this when he signed his card the day before, he would have taken a two-stroke penalty. Once he signed his card without doing that, however, the judges had to disqualify him. They took away his second place money, which came to $40,000. I guess he could have bought quite a few pairs of pants with that.

I am very thankful for my good fortune. I express my thanks by trying to give back something of myself to the people out there who have helped make me what I am. In May of 1981, for example, I served as the honorary chairman and master of ceremonies of a celebration commemorating the 100th anniversary of the Red Cross. It was held in the Hall of the Daughters of the American Revolution in Washington, D.C.

President Reagan and Vice President Bush had been scheduled to attend this event, so I made it an occasion to give them mementos of M*A*S*H. They were beautiful blue nylon jackets, with the M*A*S*H logo and a red cross on the back, good for jogging, or warming up before a game of tennis, or playing golf in a drizzle, or whatever. One of the jackets had the letters PRES emblazoned on the front, and the other said, VICE PRES.

When I got to the hall, I learned that Vice President Bush was coming, but that President Reagan couldn't be in attendance. He had an emergency meeting with Helmut Schmidt, the chancellor of West Germany, who was in Washington on a state visit. Even so, the security at the DAR Hall was very tight. In March, there'd been a recent assassination attempt on President Reagan, so the Secret Service people were really on the alert. They had metal detectors scanning everyone as they entered the building. They had dogs sniffing for traces of firearms or gunpowder. And they had large badges for all the VIPs, with different colors of badges for different levels of VIP to help the Secret Service know who belonged where in this gathering.

As the event's emcee, of course, I was given entree to a special room filled with the most important dignitaries, and I only gave the Secret Service a little pause when I showed up with my gifts for Mr. Reagan and Mr. Bush. "These are jackets," I said. The agent with the metal detector could plainly see that; I knew better than to bring these gifts from me and the M*A*S*H troupe done up in any kind of wrapping. "One is for President Reagan, and the other for Vice President Bush. I just want to know if it's okay for me to present them to the vice president this evening?"

The agent-in-charge was summoned, and though he didn't seem too thrilled with the idea, he said, "Okay. But you have to make it quick. When he shows up, just get over there, give him the jackets and get out of there."

"Okay," I said. "Yes sir!" So when the vice president appears, I walk over, introduce myself, present the jackets and start to move off. But George Bush has other ideas. He wants to talk to me, and he won't let me go. Now, remembering my promise to the Secret Service, I am nervous. I nod and I do not exchange any small talk with Mr. Bush, and I start to move off again. He follows me. He isn't finished. He wants to talk some more about M*A*S*H. It is pretty much of a one-way conversation. He's telling me what he loves about M*A*S*H, and I'm nodding and saying, "Thank you, Mr. Vice President. Uh huh. Thank you, Mr. Bush."

Now, all this time, I can see the agent-in-charge standing behind Mr. Bush is getting furious because I am not doing what he told me to do. And I am getting nervous, too. So I move away a third time. Now it appears I am stiffing the vice president of the United States. And he won't be stiffed. He's following me. And the Secret Service guy is going nuts. Now he's waving me away and mouthing the words (yeah, I can read these lips), "Get away from him!"

In this situation, however, getting away is not possible. Finally, I said, "Excuse me a moment, Mr. Vice President." Then I turned to the Secret Service man and said, "Don't tell me! Tell him!"

When it was time for the program to begin, we all took our places in the auditorium, or on the stage. I took over the podium and, as emcee, started to make everyone feel welcome. I had told, maybe, two jokes.

And then, the sound of a gun reverberated through the hall. A hush fell over the crowd and everyone froze.

I thought, "My god are they shooting at me?" I checked to see if there were any holes in my jacket. Or in me. And then I said, "Gee, I haven't been on that long to be that bad."

Well, that piece of improvisation broke the tension. Everyone roared. It broke up the house. And we went on to have a nice celebration

But what about that gunshot? Where had it come from? And why? Someone later explained that one of the musicians in the Marine Band had dropped his hammer on the xylophone, and on a particular key of the xylophone, right next to a live mike. To everyone in the room, except that man with the xylophone, it sounded just like a shot.

Sometime after that, maybe in 1987 or so, I was in Washington again, to serve as an honorary chairman of a U.S. Savings Bond drive, and this time Joy was with me. Vice President Bush heard we were there, and he sent word that he'd like to see us in his office.

"Joy," I said, "this is great. I'll take you to the White House and then we'll go over to see Mr. Bush." He greeted us, spent 45 minutes with us, and then he had a photographer come in and take our picture with him.

"You running for president?" I asked him.

"Ah, I don't know," he said.

"Well, Mr. Bush," I said, "I'm not much into politics. But if I can ever help you...."

Cut to 1988. I'm driving along Sherman Way in Canoga Park, California, heading to my barber's, and the phone rings in my car. I couldn't imagine who it was. The only people who had the number of my car phone were Joy and my agent, and I wasn't expecting any calls from either of them.

It was the White House. The vice president's office was calling. They wondered if I'd mind flying to Bowling Green, Ohio, this very night — they already had a reservation for me on a commercial jet — to appear the next morning with Mr. Reagan, who was going to kick off Mr. Bush's campaign in Ohio.

"Well, uh," I said. "Okay." And then I thought, "How does the White House know the unlisted number of my car phone? Or know that I was in my car at this moment? I knew they hadn't talked to Joy. She was out of town. I didn't ask. I didn't want to know. I still don't know.

I went on to Bowling Green. I found myself on the platform with Bob Feller, the Hall of Fame pitcher of the Cleveland Indians, Bernie Kosar, then the quarterback with the Cleveland Browns, and a number of other luminaries. After the rally, I hopped another plane, and hurried home. The phone was ringing when I walked in the door. It was the White House again. They wanted to know if I'd get on the plane again — that very night — and fly to Toledo so I could join Vice President at a campaign appearance on the campus of the University of Toledo.

"No," I said, laughing at the absurdity of it all. I was just there in Ohio. If they'd asked me to go to Toledo when I was in Bowling Green, I would have stayed in Ohio an extra day. But now here I was, back in California, holding down the fort for Joy. I couldn't get on another plane and go right back again.

But I was happy to do some more political rallies for Mr. Bush in 1988. I remember going to one in Sacramento with Charlton Heston, and to something called "The Rally in the Valley" — the San Fernando Valley, that is — led by Chuck Norris. Joy and I went to another campaign function (probably a fund-raiser) at Bob Hope's home in Toluca Lake. And then I was the co-chair of another Bush rally in West Covina, along with Joan Rivers, Foster Brooks, Barbara Eden, Don DeFore, Robert Stack and Cesar Romero.

I did not spend all my time with Republicans. I have a beautiful carved silver belt buckle, a very prized memento of a program I did at the invitation of President Carter in 1980 for a special show at the Kennedy Center in Washington. It was in honor of the Americans who qualified for the Olympic Games in Moscow — but didn't get to go because the U.S. withdrew at the eleventh hour in protest over the Soviet invasion of Afghanistan..

I did a ten-minute monologue, standup comedy, at the Kennedy Center. Afterward, we had a real All-American backyard picnic at the White House — hot dogs, hamburgers, ice cream and apple pie — and I met President and Mrs. Carter and had my picture taken with them. I was given the same silver belt buckle given to the members of the U.S. Olympic Team, the kids who qualified for the trip to Russia, but never went to Russia.

Right at the end of the 1988 campaign, the Bush people asked me to make one more appearance with the candidate, this time in San Diego, on the eve of election day in November. They had a whole slew of Hollywood celebrities there, two rows of celebrities, and I ended up in the second row, right behind President Reagan. "Hey," I said, "this is pretty good. Kid from Toledo, sitting right behind the president of the United States!" I was sitting tall, proud as can be.

I suddenly remembered the 1981 assassination attempt on the president, and I asked myself if this was really the place to be. Then I noted that President Reagan himself seemed really — well, solid, more husky than I'd remembered him. But, of course, I soon realized that he was swathed in bullet-proof garments under his suit. And I wasn't.

Now I wasn't sitting so tall. Jeez, if somebody decides to take a shot at President Reagan.... I could get it. What was I doing here? You remember the movie, "The Incredible Shrinking Man?" Well, that was me. As the speeches wore on, I kept getting smaller and smaller. If you had taken a picture of the two rows of people on that platform, you wouldn't have seen me. You would have seen an empty seat behind the president. I was the man who wasn't there.

29

People to Love

I could go on and on about directors I have worked with. My first two Hollywood directors — Richard Brooks and Vincente Minelli — couldn't have been more of a contrast. Brooks was this tough ex-Marine who always seemed to be wearing the same shirt, drank gallons of teaming coffee every day out of a big mug and stomped around the set in heavy boots, shouting at us. Minelli wore matching outfits, pressed shirt and pants, maybe orange one day and powder blue the next, he sipped demitasse coffee, flitted about the set like a dancer and never talked to us. One guy was sandpaper, and the other one was satin.

I had three favorite directors when I was on M*A*S*H. One of them was Hy Averback, who had my nose, once, but had it fixed. Vic Damone and Dean Martin both had noses like mine, but they had theirs bobbed. Milton Berle says he never had his nose fixed, but at Sardi's they have two Berle portraits hanging on their hallowed walls; in one of them he has my nose, in the other, his current nose. I think I am the only guy left in Hollywood with my nose.

Charles S. Dubin was another favorite director of mine on the M*A*S*H set. He used to wear an old crumpled hat during his more than 50 M*A*S*H's, and often brought one of his dogs to the set. He was a bright, lovable man who had the temperament of Job. Today, 75 years young, he's still very active. He's doing a film documentary on a world-famed piano teacher Karl Ulrich Schnabel, son of the great concert pianist, Artur Schnabel. He's also taping the Bella Lewitsky Dance Company for the Jerome Robbins Dance Archives, and like many of us, he has a couple movie scripts making the rounds. This past August, he married the love of his life, Mary Lou Chayes.

And Burt Metcalfe, of course. He belongs on this short list of my favorite directors. He not only directed. He was in charge of M*A*S*H for its last six years, and he ran the company like he was a combination of King Solomon and C.B. DeMille.

I'm reminded of a story about DeMille, the man who practically invented the Biblical epic with one blockbuster after another. But marshaling his huge casts tended to make Mr. D. think he could walk on water, and to hear some of the old-timers talk about him, I am not sure that he didn't. He strode his sets like a Colossus. And, when he felt like sitting down, he just sat down, knowing full well that one of his assistants, the man who followed him around with a folding director's chair, would be there to slip the seat under his buns as he started to bend his knees. He never looked to see if the chair was there. He always knew it would be. And it was.

DeMille was a tyrant on his sets, a general who took a real zest in moving his cameras and his cast of thousands by the power of his voice — amplified by a huge megaphone, or, later in his career, by a battery-run bullhorn, or, if possible, a gigantic p.a. system. On "The Ten Commandments," the story goes, DeMille took all morning to set up a tremendous shot — more than a thousand extras and at least four strategically placed cameras.

Then he was ready. He called for silence. And then, just before his call for action, from his coign of vantage on a special platform, he spied one woman who had turned and started talking to another extra.

"You there!" he boomed. "That's right! You! I asked for silence. And you continued to talk. Now, what you have to say must be more important than what I'm doing here. So I want you to share with all of us what it is that you were saying." He and the entire cast and crew waited while one of DeMille's minions rushed over to her with a live microphone connected to the loudspeakers surrounding the set. "That's right," he continued. "Speak right into the mike. Tell us. Tell us all. Or I'll make certain you never work here again."

The extra was frightened. So frightened that she knew she dare not tell DeMille, this great, godlike figure, anything other than the unvarnished truth. She cleared her throat. And then she spoke: "I was just wondering when the bald-headed bastard with the microphone was going to call lunch."

Silence. No one laughed. No one dared. More than a thousand waited to see what their leader would do.

After a moment or so, DeMille leaned into his mike and said, "Lunch."

I had many occasions to study directors at work. These directors were all different, all had different ways of getting the most out of a script, and out of an actor. I once had the pleasure of watching Elia Kazan, a man who had directed the Broadway plays of greats like Thornton Wilder, Tennessee Williams, Robert Anderson, Archibald MacLeish, and William Inge. He won two Academy awards, as director of "On the Waterfront" and "Gentleman's Agreement." He also directed "Viva Zapata" and "East of Eden." And now I was there to see him direct "A Face in the Crowd," from a screenplay by Budd Schulberg, starring Andy Griffith, Lee Remick, Walter Matthau and Patricia Neal.

With these actors, Kazan was the kind of man who preferred to listen first, then act, after he had collected all the information he could. Kazan seemed to work overtime, polling his actors and actresses, to find out what they thought, how they saw the role, and what they thought they could bring to it. "Hmmm," he would say to Patricia Neal. "You really think so? Hmmm. Well, let's try that. Or, what do you think if maybe we do it this way?" You see, in the end, his actors all ended up doing everything he wanted. But, often enough, he didn't know what he wanted until he talked to his stars — for whom he had nothing but regard. Consequently, they had a lot of respect for him. The result: first-class work.

Other directors had other styles. Mervyn LeRoy, who had directed me in "No Time for Sergeants," tended to talk in riddles, making us all guess what he had in mind. Peter Ustinov has a better memory than I do about LeRoy, who directed Peter in "Quo Vadis." Peter, as you recall, played the part of Nero. But when he sought some guidance from LeRoy, some tip on how he might interpret the role, LeRoy said, cryptically, "Nero? Sonuvabitch." That was all.

As they say in film, let us dissolve to the balcony scene in "Quo Vadis" where Nero and some Roman senators were supposed to watch Rome go down in flames. It was a hot day, very hot. To add to the heat, braziers were burning all around the balcony. LeRoy was shouting orders from a crane, and Peter was miserable, little rivers of sweat pouring down his face from a stinking laurel wreath made of inferior metal. Peter's lungs began heaving, and his nostrils grew black with the dust from the braziers. The assistant director cried to the mob of extras, "Attenzione!" Ready?

No. Just then, LeRoy cried, "Let me down. Let me down, will you?" He disappeared. And then Peter felt the balcony begin to shake. LeRoy was climbing it. In due course, as Peter tells it, "his head appeared over the battlements, a cigar gripped in his teeth, his eyes confident and understanding, like those of a manager telling a half-dead boxer that he's leading on points." He bid Peter come closer. "Don't forget," he said, waving his cigar at the burning city, "you're responsible for all this."

Then there are directors like Robert Altman, who, at age 72, after doing his 32nd movie, "Short Cuts," told Harry Smith of CBS "Sunday Morning," "I never tell my actors how to play the scene. I ask them how they think it ought to be played. Then I just get out of the way and let them play it. It works better that way."

Maybe this is why Altman — the director who did the full-length feature movie for Fox called M*A*S*H — is so successful at getting some of the biggest names in Hollywood to play mere bit parts in movies like "Nashville" and "The Player" and "Short Cuts." Altman respects everyone around him in this, the most collaborative of the arts. And so everyone around him respects him. It is easier to respect a man who is humble.

But, in Hollywood, humility often gets you nowhere. What works best in Hollywood is bluff. As Albert S. Ruddy, the producer of the Burt Reynolds "Cannonball" movies, and later a successful producer at Paramount, has proven more than once. He tells this story on himself.

One day, at Paramount, Al got a phone call from Charles Bluhdorn, the head of Paramount's parent company, Gulf & Western. Mr. Bluhdorn was quite excited about a recent acquisition. He'd just bought the rights to Mario Puzo's best-selling novel, *The Godfather*. Now he wanted Ruddy's thoughts on the project.

Without a beat, Ruddy told Bluhdorn how the film should be done: Great characters in this book. With the right development, this could mean Oscars for some of the actors and actresses. Need some big name stars and some unknowns, but all of them had to be brilliant actors and actresses. No shooting on a sound stage. Everything on location. Big budget, of course. Top director. Get the author to help write the screenplay, with the help of a seasoned scriptwriter.

Bluhdorn said these were his feelings, too. And since Ruddy felt this way, he should be the one to produce "The Godfather." Then he hung up.

Al Ruddy turned to his secretary. "Say," he said, "Would you make a quick run to the bookstore? I need a copy of a book called *The Godfather*. I want to read it right away."

Speaking of great directors, I cannot help thinking about a good many of them who are still alive and well and living in

Hollywood — and unemployed. The sorry fact is that there's an illegitimate form of discrimination at work on the entertainment business today. It's called ageism. Like racism or sexism, it works against people simply because of what they are, not what they can do. In this case, they are in the cold because they are old.

Doesn't seem to matter how much talent a man has. If he's old, forget him. Kill him (slowly) if he's old. This ageism is most indefensible when it works against writers and directors (whose looks don't matter, and whose talents can only get better, like wine, with age).

There's one story, oft told by members of the Writers Guild, about Fred Zinnemann, an Oscar-winning director, on his way to see one of these young whippersnappers, who happened to be production chief of a major studio at 29, though he had no credits whatsoever. Zinnemann was one of the most respected men in Hollywood, a man who'd done pictures like "High Noon," one of the greatest Westerns ever made, and two films that won him Oscars, "From Here to Eternity" and "A Man For All Seasons." But when he walks into this young man's office, the kid says, "Well, Mr. Zinnemann, I'm unfamiliar with your work. Tell me your credits."

Zinnemann was almost speechless. But not quite. He said, "You first."

Then there was Andrew Duggan, a veteran who did some nice guest shots for us on M*A*S*H, walking into the office of a young producer, who was reading the morning paper, with his mocassined feet up on his desk, wearing no socks. Duggan enters. The producer looks over the top of his paper and comes out with the same question. "Tell me, Duggan! What have you done lately?"

"Nothing," said Duggan. "It smelled like this when I walked in."

On my occasional visits to the retirement community of the Motion Picture and Television Fund in Woodland Hills, I have had the pleasure of hearing other stories about great old directors. I heard one from the actor, William Campbell, about a rough

318

diamond of a director named Raoul Walsh. Walsh was a two-fisted, ex-Marine with an eye patch, who had done a lot of movie work with John Ford, one of those directors beloved of his actors for his loyalty to them. If he liked an actor, he tended to keep hiring him.

One of Walsh's favorite extras was a craggy-faced guy whom everyone called "Cheyenne Billy." Walsh put him in everything. And so, when Cheyenne Billy died in Hollywood, Walsh threw an old-fashioned Irish wake for him. At the party, someone said it was a pity that Cheyenne Billy had no friends or family to mourn his passing. Someone else suggested they send him back to Wyoming. "Great idea!" said Walsh, who proceeded to have Billy boxed up and sent back to a funeral home in Cheyenne for proper burial.

Imagine Walsh's surprise when he got a check for $1,000 from the authorities in Wyoming, along with a WANTED POSTER. Seems that they'd been looking for Cheyenne Billy for years. The poster said authorities had long been offering a $1,000 reward for the delivery of Cheyenne Billy — "Dead or Alive."

With a smile and a sigh, Walsh pocketed the dough, and said, "I guess that pays for the wake."

Speaking of wakes reminds me of another story, related to me by A.C. Lyles, a fixture around Hollywood for many years, a man who started in the mail room at Paramount Pictures and worked his way up to producer. He was driving along Melrose Avenue one day and an old vintage car ahead of him caught his eye. He pulled alongside the car to get a closer look, noticed a tiny woman at the wheel, and a distinguished gentleman in the back seat smoking a cigarette in a long holder. Then he saw a plaque on the side of the car: PROPERTY OF FRANCIS X. BUSHMAN.

In his office at Paramount, Lyles thought about that car. Maybe he could buy it from Mr. Bushman. He wondered how he could find Bushman. He was sure this silent screen star (he had done the first film version of "Ben Hur") had retired long ago. But no. Lyles secretary found him right away. He still had representation, and Bushman's agent was happy to hand on F.X.'s home phone number to a Paramount producer.

"No," Mr. Bushman told Lyles in a very deep and very youthful-sounding voice, "I'm not interested in selling my Buick. But tell me more about yourself, Mr. Lyles. What are you producing these days?"

Lyles said it was a Western.

"A Western? You know, Mr. Lyles, in all my years in film, I have never been in a Western. I wonder if you have a part for me. I understand. It doesn't have to be a large part."

As a matter of fact, Lyles did have the part of a sheriff. "But it's only four or five lines."

"There are no small parts, sir. I would be delighted to play the sheriff."

So Lyles sent him the script, and over the next few weeks, Bushman was on the phone to Lyles, reading his interpretation of the lines for Lyles' approval. Each time he phoned, Lyles said he sounded wonderful. One morning, Lyles read a story in Variety. F.X. Bushman was coming out of retirement to star in a Western for Paramount. Lyles got phone calls from all over the world, asking for verification of the story. And, of course, he got a call from Bushman and more line readings. Neither of them mentioned the news story in Variety.

Just a few days before Bushman was scheduled to step before the cameras at Paramount, Lyles got a phone call. It was from Mrs. Bushman, the tiny woman he had seen driving the big, vintage Buick. "Well, A.C.," she said. "We've lost him."

"What do you mean? He was out and couldn't find his way back?"

"No, I mean we've really lost him. He died this morning. I'm making arrangements now. I'm wondering. Would you be one of the pallbearers? I know Francis would want that."

Lyles was there at the funeral home with the other pallbearers when Mrs. Bushman announced that the eulogy would be delivered by one of her husband's oldest and closest friends, Paramount Pictures Producer A.C. Lyles.

Lyles was surprised. But he'd done some research on Bushman when the Variety story had appeared, so he was prepared. Calmly, he walked to the side of the casket and delivered a eulogy on the spot, on Francis X. Bushman, a man he had seen only once in a moving car, and had talked to on the telephone a few times. Lyles gave the performance of his career. Today, A.C. Lyles is not on the lookout for vintage cars. He says you never know who might be riding in one. Besides, he's not producing Westerns any more. Nor eulogies either.

30

Triumph on Broadway

I had not exactly been a stranger to the legitimate stage. During M*A*S*H's eleven years, I had sought, and found work in dinner theaters all across the land — and, sometimes most successfully, in Canada. But I never got very close to working on Broadway itself, except in fantasy.

Once, in 1992, I was up for a job in the road company of Neil Simon's "Rumors. I was doing a play in Toronto at the time, and I had to zip down to New York on my one day off to try out for the role of Lenny Ganz, a role done in the Broadway company by Ron Leibman.

Try outs were on the stage of the Martin Beck, and I couldn't believe all the actors who had come in for this part. The director, Gene Saks (not to be confused with Jerry Zaks) seemed ready to be bored when I took the stage. He was sitting down in the middle of the theater, almost daring me to entertain him when I started reading my big scene. But I had seen the show, I'd gotten the script for "Rumors," and I'd stayed up late the night before working on it. I was really prepared. When I was finished with my reading, he rushed to the stage. "Fabulous!" he said. "As far as I'm concerned, the part is yours." Moments later, the show's casting director told me, "This is the best cold reading I've ever heard anybody give, anywhere."

Later, I went over to B. Smith's for lunch with my agent, David Kalodner, from APA, the Agency for the Performing Arts. He was stunned to see all the people on the street who stopped me to say hello. And then, inside the restaurant, he almost fell off his chair when Sidney Poitier walked in, spied me, and rushed over with a hearty "Jameel!" and embraced me like a long-lost brother.

My tryout in New York for "Rumors" was simply a prelude to my meeting Neil Simon himself, and selling him. I did that, too, even though he happened to be on an extended visit to LA at the time. To see Simon, I had to jet all the way to LA from Toronto a week later, on my next day off. Simon, too, loved my presentation. And, just like that, he said, "You've got the job."

Then he said he was curious. "You came all the way from Toronto for this reading?" he said.

I nodded.

"And you have to fly back tonight on the red-eye?"

"Uh huh."

He said, "Jamie, I couldn't do anything like that."

"Mr. Simon," I said. "You don't have to."

Reminds me of the time that Ralph Bellamy came up to me at one of Harry Morgan's parties. "How are you, m'boy?" He always called me "m'boy." He said he'd seen me on some game shows and said, in frank admiration, "I couldn't do that." I didn't tell him that he didn't have to. But I could have.

Anyway, Neil Simon laughed. And he offered me the job. It wasn't Broadway. It was just a road company offer. But it was with Neil Simon, and I could have flown back to Toronto just by flapping my arms. As it turned out, I found I couldn't take on the burden. Simon turned around and licensed "Rumors" to the Pace

Theater Owners, another national company. But he had retained the rights to Los Angeles for himself. So, if I went ahead with the Pace group, I would have been bound to 48 weeks on the road without a chance to play Los Angeles, an important showcase, because so much hiring is done there for movies and television. And I'd be bound to a no-cut contract besides. A no-cut contract isn't what it sounds like. It means I can't cut them. If I get a better offer elsewhere, even a TV series or a feature movie, I can't take it. I am stuck. But they can cut me. So, for these reasons, this part in "Rumors" didn't sound so much like a career move for me. It became a job. I didn't take it.

But then, a few months later, when I heard Jerry Zaks was casting a Broadway revival of "Guys and Dolls," I insisted on auditioning for the part of Nathan Detroit. As you know, this piece of musical theater, with words and music by Frank Loesser, is an adaptation of the story by Damon Runyon about a gambler who falls in love with a Salvation Army worker. Without exaggeration, it is one of the classics of the American musical theater. It first opened on Broadway in November 1950, and that original run did 1,200 performances in New York and London. And then, in 1955, it became a hit movie, with Marlon Brando, Jean Simmons, Frank Sinatra and Vivian Blaine. In the past 40 years, it's been done by every repertory company and college theater group in the land.

I did the audition in Los Angeles, and I had Detroit down pat. Detroit was made famous by Frank Sinatra, and my take on the role couldn't help but follow his. The slick operator, Runyonesque rhythm, pin-striped suit, and all. (I even took a pair of dice to the audition, which I used as a prop in my number, and kept throwing 7s.)

My agent had asked that I do an audition, and the casting people turned me down. They did so, because they'd already decided to "cast young." But I didn't know that, so I insisted on an audition. I think they finally let me do it because I was a friend of Jerry Zaks, the director. He wanted to be nice to me, because I had been nice to him 20 years before, when he was a day player on M*A*S*H, and I was on contract, but never too stuck on myself not to talk to day players.

325

Zaks didn't pursue an acting career. Instead, he became a highly regarded director on the legitimate stage. Twice before, he had called and offered me jobs in other productions. The first time, he wanted me to consider playing the gangster role in a road company of "Anything Goes" with Leslie Uggams. But I had to turn him down. I couldn't afford to go on the road for the salary this show had budgeted for my role.

Sometime later, Zaks called me a second time — to do the lead in a road company doing Ken Ludwig's "Lend Me a Tenor." At the time, I was already in the throes of playing the part of Ali Hakim in a road company production of "Oklahoma," 16 weeks on the road with John Davidson. We'd already started playing Atlanta, and then Zaks offered me a better deal. Now that was very attractive, and I had an "Oklahoma" contract that said I could leave at any time. But then I found out that my leaving could put the entire company in jeopardy. I didn't want to put all the kids on the show out of work. So I stuck with "Oklahoma" and said no, once more, to Jerry Zaks, explaining to him that I would have been as loyal to him, if the situation were reversed.

I had figured that the third time with Zaks — this audition for this 1992 Broadway revival of "Guys and Dolls" — would be the charm. I was wrong. Zaks and his casting director had already decided on Nathan Lane for the role of Nathan Detroit. I was close, but I got no cigar. And I began to think that this was as close as I would ever get to appearing on Broadway. I went back to improving my golf game.

Meanwhile, on Broadway, the revival of "Guys and Dolls" was a great success. Nathan Lane and Josie deGuzman, Faith Prince and Peter Gallagher had their opening, they were declared worthy in that all-important great review from The New York Times, and then all they had to do was keep showing up eight times a week. Of course, they did much more than that, and they started this production off to becoming the longest-running Broadway revival on record.

All of which redounded to my benefit. In the spring of 1994, much to my delight and my surprise, after "Guys and Dolls" had

had a successful, almost-two-year run, and after Lane had moved on, Jerry Zaks and the show's backers realized the show still had a lot of life in it. After Lane left the show, and others brought in to replace him, Zaks was casting about for another Nathan Detroit. Then he remembered my reading of two years before. I had insisted on that audition two years before, I was aggressive, and so Jerry saw me and liked me. I had proved myself then, and he remembered. He brought me to the Great White Way, and all of a sudden, I was making my Broadway debut, after more than 40 years in show business.

It was fitting, I think, that I'd make that debut in "Guys and Dolls." This show was the first piece of legitimate Broadway theater I'd ever seen. (I saw a road show company version in Toledo in 1951 with Allan Jones, the father of the pop singer Jack Jones.) The role of Nathan Detroit was a part I always wanted to play. And I had grown up in Toledo with Runyonesque characters like Harry the Horse and Nicely Nicely Johnson. In fact, I could have borrowed the famous brown, pin-striped suit of my Toledo classmate, Mike Prephan. It would have been perfect.

All things considered, then, I had imagined that I was ready to step right into "Guys and Dolls." But I had just been playing the kind of mind game that actors play whenever they're up for a role. Without even realizing it, we actors tend to pile up all the reasons why we are "perfect for the role" — any role. But suddenly it wasn't a mind game any more. It was real. And the reality of making my Broadway debut more than 40 years after I'd started my acting career was a shock to me. It wasn't going to be all that darned easy.

I only had two weeks to rehearse, and I didn't even get the kind of rehearsal time that the principals had gotten when they first mounted the show. I had done some rehearsals alone with the stage manager. The dance captain put me through my floor routines. I had a few casual rehearsals with the understudies. I had one partial rehearsal with the full cast, and then, on the afternoon of the Tueday night I opened, I went through my only full dress rehearsal.

And then I was on, and I was as scared as any 17-year-old ingenue might be in the same setting. This was important. The Nathan Detroit character was the driving force of the show, and for that reason, it wasn't just a matter of knowing my lines, or being confident in knowing the right stage blocking for my numbers. I had to bring an extra intensity to the part to keep the show moving. Did I have what it took to do that?

I also had three musical numbers that worried me, most particularly a duet, "Sue Me," that I did with Jennifer Allen, Nathan's girl friend. I am not a singer, yet there I was, sweating almost alone on the stage — with Miss Allen, the orchestra and the conductor — hoping I could at least be on pitch. I was also part of a big, raucous rock-rap number, "Sit Down, You're Rockin' the Boat," full of complex dance movements. I not only had to get my part right, I had to be in synch with the rest of the cast. I simply couldn't make any mistakes. Any misstep at all would be all-too-obvious, and would throw off everyone else besides.

What to do? Well, as usual, I thought I'd give St. Jude, the patron saint of hopeless causes, another shot. He'd helped me before. He could help me again. And then I talked to my wife. On the phone from LA, Joy pointed out very calmly, "Look, Jamie, you're there for one reason: people like you. The people who hired you. The people who bought tickets to see you."

She also pointed out that everyone has two guardian angels sitting on their shoulders. When I was out there on the stage, I should remember mine.

In all the hubbub of the Tuesday rehearsals, I forgot about my angels. But, once out there in front of the footlights that night, I had a sense that my old friend, Joe Matarano, also known as Joe Corey, was there with me. He was technically dead now; but alive as a presence to me. If he could help me get my first agent, he could help me now, help get me through the intense challenge of my first opening.

And then, when the orchestra struck the first chords of "If I Were A Bell," I felt another presence, as well. It was my first girl friend, Janice Falce, also deceased. It was as if I could sense her spirit hovering over the stage. "If I Were A Bell" was Janice's favorite song. She sang it all the time when were dating. Now, right here on the stage of the Martin Beck, I could hear Janice:

Ask me now that we're cozy and clinging
Well, sir, all I can say is,
If I were a bell I'd be ringing.

I got goose pimples. I felt she was there.

With St. Jude's help, and the presence of my two guardian angels, how could I go wrong? I didn't go wrong. Clive Barnes, the long time theater critic for *The New York Post*, said I helped return the show to its roots, to Sam Levene's "foxy, shifty charm in the role." And everyone — even Mrs. Frank Loesser — said I made a darn good Nathan Detroit.

What a kick it has been for me, becoming something of a star on Broadway. Back at the Pasadena Playhouse, I had dreamed of appearing on Broadway. Little by little, the dream faded — only to burst into reality in the 60th year of my life. I have tried to make the most of it in my usual way — by working hard and being nice to the people around me.

They say I'm an example to the kids in "Guys and Dolls." I don't know about that. I do know that when I arrived, they were somewhat guarded. They'd seen me in M*A*S*H, but they didn't know what they could expect from me on the Broadway stage. I could have been one of the great horrors. But I soon earned their respect and friendship, and I think I did that because I wasn't stuffy or snobbish. They found they could have a lot of fun with me, and soon many of them became great friends — the kind of friends you make only in a stage production.

The stage isn't like making a movie or a TV show. There, you can always re-shoot. On stage, somebody goofs a line, others are there to cover for him. The other night, one of the dancer's beaded costumes started to come apart early in the show. Soon, it was raining beads all over the stage. For the rest of the night, we were on the lookout for those beads, kicking them out of the way, hoping no one would do a dance step on one of the beads and go sprawling.

Doing eight shows a week is like an Army campaign, and we feel we're all in this together, me and the principals who replaced the original stars. As I write this, Martin Vidnovic is playing Sky Masterson, Kim Crosby is playing Sister Sarah and Jennifer Allen is playing Adelaide. They deserve a lot of credit for keeping this show going. Clive Barnes said our production is the best revival of "Guys and Dolls" ever, "with the sole brilliant exception of Richard Eyre's London staging for Britain's National Theater in 1982." Maybe that's why we're playing to near-full audiences. And why they say we have a good chance of breaking the record set during the original run in the 1950s.

I think that in the theater, you come damn close to life on a pro team like the New York Knicks, or the San Francisco 49ers, or the Los Angeles Dodgers. Old pros play hurt. In the theater, you learn that, no matter what, the play must go on.

Early on in "Guys and Dolls," I twisted my back during a dance number. Some New York stages aren't flat; they're canted down toward the audience, and, if you're not used to them, they can be tricky. But I only missed two performances. Holidays don't matter. Injuries don't matter. Exhaustion like you can't imagine doesn't matter. The curtain goes up, and you've got to be there, in shape, giving it everything you've got.

I've come to love New York, too. It may be hard to believe, I know, because Manhattan can be a very rude place. But, New Yorkers are easy marks for anyone who shows up in town with some kind of credits to his name. No matter where I go in Manhattan, people do a quick double take. Then they smile and point at me and say, "Hey, I know you!" Shopkeepers hail me. I get phones installed in record time and TV sets delivered on the instant. New York cops come by the stage door and wait for me so they can have their picture taken with me. Just the other day, a gentleman followed along beside me as I walked up Seventh Avenue toward the Martin Beck. "I didn't know you could sing," he said, "I caught your show on Sunday. You're a great singer."

I do not know about that. Sometimes, I do a version of the Randolph Scott line: "Sing? Of course I can't sing. I do eight performances a week to prove it." In essence, I sing one tuneful song in the whole show, "Sue Me," but I have fun with it, and people seem to enjoy it.

I know that teen-agers are showing up for the show in packs. They come in on buses from all over the East. They see the show and they love it. Some of them have come backstage afterward to meet me, and tell me how different "Guys and Dolls" is from the big Andrew Lloyd Webber extravaganzas they also see. Different, but just as entertaining.

New York is a place where you run into people. It has restaurants like Sardi's, moreover, where people go to see and be seen. Sardi's typifies the warmth of this town, and I am not just saying that because Sardi's has my caricature up on its hallowed walls, alongside all the Broadway greats, past and present. Who in the business can ever drop into New York and not visit Sardi's?

Which reminds me of a story. It seems that Howard Pechet (rhymes with "Becket"), my friend from Canada who had owned all the Stage West dinner theaters in Canada, was dining there one evening, after a play, with Arthur Hiller, the director of such well-known movies as "The Out of Towners," "Love Story," "Plaza Suite" and "Man of La Mancha." Howard was there with his wife, Henriette. Arthur was there with his wife, Gwen.

Now Hiller is Howard Pechet's uncle, and there was no doubt in his mind that Hiller was justly more famous than he. But, on this night at Sardi's, Howard was getting somewhat morose when, it seemed, everybody who walked in the front door came over to pay homage to Arthur Hiller. Sally Struthers came over. James Coco came over. Rita Moreno came over. They all paid their respects to Hiller. No one seemed to notice Howard at all.

Finally, Howard had had enough. He said to his uncle, "Arthur, I am somebody, too. Somebody will come in soon and recognize me."

"You wanna bet?" said Hiller.

"Sure," said Howard. "I'll bet. I'll bet you $100 that the next famous person to walk into Sardi's will know me, not you."

"You're on," said Hiller.

So now we cut to Jamie Farr and his wife, Joy, approaching Sardi's' front door. They open the door. They enter the restaurant. They look around. Sardi's is the kind of place where you always look around. And Jamie spies — Howard Pechet.

"Howard!" I cry. And I go over and hug his wife. "Henriette!" By now this man at the table with Howard, whom I do not recognize, is handing over a $100 bill to my friend, Howard Pechet.

Not long ago, I got a letter from an elderly couple who had seen "Guys and Dolls" on their New York honeymoon, and they were coming to see it again, on their second honeymoon. I wrote them back, and told them I would help them get house seats. They jumped at the chance, then came back to my dressing room and had their picture taken with me.

As you can see, I am not a snob. I do not think I am better than others. Some people operate on the assumption that success and fame take them up above everyone else. I never believed that. I just deal with people openly and honestly, try to find out who they are, get interested in them. Often enough, I find that they have fascinating stories to tell me about their lives.

I just hope they realize, after see me on stage, and after we meet, that I am not Corporal Maxwell Klinger. I am Jamie Farr. Now that I have finally made it to Broadway, in a role that is a million miles removed from Klinger, I think I am proving to myself, as well as to the audiences, what every real actor wants to go on proving all his life — that, if he is an actor, he is versatile enough to do anything.

Which reminds me of a story about the reporter who saw a man on the street one day. "Excuse me, sir, but you have an interesting face. What do you do?"

The man had a thick Yiddish accent. "I'm a heck-tah."

"What? I don't understand."

"I'm a heck-tah. You know, I heckt."

"Excuse me?"

"I do plays."

"Oh, an actor! What kind of plays do you do?"

"Shakespeare."

Now, the reporter thought to himself, this is getting interesting. "Let me hear you do a little Shakespeare."

In a deep Oxford accent, sounding every bit as polished as Sir Laurence Olivier, the man said, "To be, or not to be, that is the question. Whether 'tis nobler in the hearts of men —"

The reporter said, "That's incredible. How do you do that?"

The man shrugged. "Det's heckting."

31

Rx: Laughter

To this day, on my travels, I always carry an iron and an ironing board. Red Skelton used to do that. He'd always be ironing something backstage. Joy laughs at this. But my mother taught me how to iron. I have never forgotten how. Don't want to, either. It is good not to forget the things your mother teaches you. Average, normal parents ought to be able to spank their kids, reprimand them, chastise them, give them all kinds of advice, go shopping with them, introduce them to friends who can help them in their careers — without being charged with child abuse.

I used to get spankings. I used to dust the legs of the household furniture. That didn't start me off robbing convenience stores. I didn't say, "My mother gave me a dust cloth, that's why I'm a criminal." There's got be some gray matter up there. Your mother is a human being. She had her good days and her bad days. Yeah, in a normal home, you're going to find that a good mother will sometimes give you a spanking. But you don't say, "My mother gave me a spanking and that is why I burned down this building."

I do my own ironing on the road because I have never forgotten who I am. Danny Thomas, my *landsman* — there I go again, using a Yiddish word — helped me once by telling me a story to remind me. (Don't laugh. A good story is one of the nicest things that anyone can give me. It makes me richer, and it doesn't lessen the giver's own account.) This is a story that has always helped me keep things in perspective.

Seems that Danny put his money down at a box office window, took his tickets, grabbed his change and dropped a dime on the sidewalk. He started to reach down for it. Then he realized there were a lot of people behind him, and he was sure they all saw him drop the dime. He straightened up. "Hey, wait a minute," he told himself, "I am Danny Thomas. I'm one of the world's top comedians. I've made millions. I'm not bending down to pick up that dime." He started to walk away.

Then he stopped himself. "Hey, in reality," he said, "I am Amos Jacobs of Toledo, Ohio, and Amos Jacobs knows how hard it is to earn a dime." He took a step back and he picked up the dime.

I have tried never to forget that I am, in reality, Jameel Farah of Toledo, Ohio. I always stoop to pick up the dime.

But if all I had to work for was dimes, or, even millions of dimes, I doubt that I'd have persevered through all life's hard knocks. The only thing that has really sustained me, after all is said and done, is the thought that I have helped a great, great many people get through the ordinary hard times experienced by everyone on this planet — by making them laugh.

In November 1975, when MASH was hitting its peak, a book called The Name Above the Title, appeared on the bestseller list. It was Frank Capra's own life story, and I was thrilled because I not only enjoyed Capra's movies as a young man, I think they helped form my character. So I wrote Mr. Capra a fan letter. He was living in La Quinta, near Palm Springs, at the time. And I could hardly believe the note he sent me in reply:

"Dear Jamie, Your note almost made me bawl. I'm a sucker for any sincere Joe who makes a happy comment about my films or my book. I liked your line, 'Part of my desire to enter show business was due to your warm, funny works of art.' Man, that's the alpha and the omega. That makes up for all the blood and sweat and the years with Harry Cohn. Thank you, Jamie, thank you for a refill of faith in God and man and in fine young actors. Best of luck and warmest regards. Frank Capra."

It wasn't very long after I got this note from Capra that I opened my paper one morning — I have been a longtime reader of *The Daily News*, a Valley newspaper now owned by Jack Kent Cooke — to read one of my favorite columnists, Dennis McCarthy. Imagine my chagrin when I found that his column putting the knock on the Hollywood Walk of Fame was about me. McCarthy noted that Jamie Farr, Billy Dee Williams and Melissa Gilbert had just been given stars on the Walk of Fame. McCarthy wrote, "The last three Walk-of-Famers couldn't light up a closet, much less a sidewalk. Gable, Wayne and Garbo have to be thinking about moving out of the neighborhood. Even Ronald Reagan's star has to be asking, 'Jamie Who?'"

Needless to say, I was angry. I wanted to phone him or write a scathing letter to the editor, and say that, if I hadn't lighted up many closets, I had lighted up many faces. But my p.r. people at Rogers & Cowan advised against it. "Never get in an argument with anybody who buys ink by the barrel," they said.

Well, now that I have bought a barrel of ink to publish this book, I'd like to say this: I liked Dennis McCarthy's columns. Many of them told me he was a man who liked people. He had a real nice, as they say, human touch. But, on this one, he just didn't do his homework. The Walk of Fame is not the center court at Graumann's Chinese Theater (now called Mann's Chinese), a place reserved for Hollywood's immortals. It is a promotion by the Hollywood Chamber of Commerce to put some glitter on the sidewalks of Hollywood. And the people whose names go on those sidewalks are all people who have made a contribution to the business and to the community. Not everyone recognizes some of the names because some of the names have made contributions in some very special areas of the industry.

You know Yakima Canutt? Probably not. But he was John Wayne's stuntman, one of the finest stuntmen in the history of Hollywood. And he has a star on the Walk of Fame. You know Eddie Anderson? Probably not. But he has a star, too, because, if you had your head in a radio during the 1930s and 1940s, you laughed at him and with him every Sunday night. He was Jack Benny's chauffeur — called Rochester — and he helped make broadcast history.

So, in fact, did I. And you know what? Unlike Eddie Anderson, whose famous bits on Jack Benny's radio program are now unavailable anywhere outside the Museum of Broadcasting, I am still making history, and will continue to do so as long as people watch TV. I call this "The Pam Factor."

Let me explain. I got on a plane the other day and found myself the object of much attention by a most beautiful flight attendant in her early 20s, whose name happened to be Pam. "Oh, Jamie," she said. "I grew up with you. I've been watching you on M*A*S*H since I was ten years old. I still watch M*A*S*H. It's on every night at midnight in New York, and every night at 11:30 in LA. In fact, on Sunday nights in LA, I can see two M*A*S*H re-runs, from 11 p.m. until midnight."

That, my friends, is the power of television. People may decry its power when it presents material of obvious bad taste. But they cannot deny its power to lift up people's hearts, to make them laugh or feel for others. Which is what I thought my friends and I at M*A*S*H were doing all along.

I guess I shouldn't be so hard on Dennis McCarthy. As a columnist, he has to provoke people, try to make them think, entertain them. I must have sympathy for him because I, too, have unwittingly tread on people's toes with some of my jokes. Once, on the Joan Rivers Show, Miss Rivers was making all kinds of cracks about Jewish princesses. (It's one of her shticks.) And then she turned to me and asked, "Is your wife Jewish?"

I said, "No, she wears a cloth coat."

Well. (As Jack Benny would say.) You cannot imagine all the protest letters I got from Jewish women, who said I had no right to imply that only Jews wear fur coats. I wasn't implying anything of the sort. I was just making a joke — in the spirit of the proceedings that I was a part of, the Joan Rivers Show. But you can't make jokes like that today. And I think it's a shame.

The whole history of comedy in this country — starting with vaudeville — is full of ethnic and racial stereotypes. Jews, above all people, have enriched America with humor that is often done at their own expense.

But now I wonder, in this era when we are all supposed to be "politically correct," whether I can even tell a joke like this one, one that I told at a West Covina, California, rally for George Bush in 1992: My son Jonas, as you know, folks, is an American Arab. And, like me, he grew to love sports. And so, in junior high school, he began to take up sports, one by one. He took up hockey. But then, when he found he wasn't all that good in hockey, he came home and said, "Dad, were there ever any great Lebanese hockey players?" No, son, I said. There were not.

A couple months later, he came home and said, "Dad, were there any great Lebanese basketball players?" No, son, I said. There were not.

A couple months later, he came home and said, "Dad, were there any great Lebanese baseball players?" No, son, I said. There were not. Now, I could see how crestfallen he was. He loved sports so much, and he hadn't done all that well in hockey, or basketball or baseball. I could almost read his mind. What was he going to do?

I hugged him and said, "Son, why don't you do what the Jews do? Own the team!"

But wouldn't you know? I got an angry letter from a dentist in West Covina. He said I was stereotyping Jews. Well, yeah, I guess I was. But I wasn't doing it in an unfriendly way. Think about it. What did my story add up to? It said that Jews were smart, savvy people. And that I could only hope that my own son would grow up to be smart and savvy, too.

Just Farr Fun

Backstage recently at the Martin Beck Theater in New York, where I am playing in "Guys and Dolls," I got a note from a young lady who had seen the play on a visit to New York. She said her name was Erin, and she was from Cedar Rapids, Iowa, and she told me she wanted to be an actress when she grew up. My heart went out to her. (For one thing, my mother was born in Cedar Rapids, Iowa.) And so, I wrote her back. "May your dreams come true!" I meant it. What kind of a world will we live in if we do not encourage our children to dream? No, we can't all be Albert Einsteins, or Michael Jordans or Barbra Streisands. But we can all aspire to be somebody. I aspired. And, within my limitations (who isn't limited?), I did become somebody.

I did not become John Gielgud. But I did become Jamie Farr, and as I walk down Broadway these days and wave back to the hundreds of people who recognize me on the street, I can say that it is not bad to be Jamie Farr. I think back to that September day in 1952 when I showed up at the Pasadena Playhouse, full of anxiety because I was just Jameel Farah, a poor kid from Toledo, and all these other young people were so much above me. They had far more talent than I. They were better singers and dancers, were far better looking, had better smiles, better legs than I. (And some of them were girls!) Many of them came from wealthy families. Yet none of them has gone as far as I did in the entertainment business.

Yes, I am in the entertainment business. That's how people should judge me. It's how I judge myself. Did I entertain people tonight? That's the only question I ever dare ask myself. When I ask myself who I am, I have an unequivocal answer. I am an entertainer. I take a measure of pride in this. I am not vaunting myself. I am playing a small role in my world. But it is an important role because I am, in essence, making people laugh — at the world and at themselves — and thereby helping them to have faith, and hope, in themselves. If I and my partners in comedy weren't doing that, then the grimness of this world would simply overwhelm.

Once, when I was doing a play in Edmonton, Alberta, in Canada, I got a request from a local prison. Would I mind terribly

340

visiting the men there? The warden phoned me and told me the men had been watching M*A*S*H in their recreation rooms, and since I was in the neighborhood, as it were, they sure would appreciate a visit from Klinger. I said I would, if I could show one of my recent movies, "Cannonball Run." (Maybe I had remembered what Burt said of this picture: "It's the kind of movie they show in prisons and airplanes because nobody can leave.")

Well, naturally, the warden agreed, and I got the studio to lend me a copy of "Cannonball Run." I took it along with me, and after some introductory remarks, I had the prison projectionist start the picture. I enjoyed it — again. But I found myself not paying as much attention to the movie as I was to the audience, fairly hooting over the antics of Burt Reynolds and the bunch. I was suddenly overcome with a sense that I had seen this prison scene somewhere before.

Of course. I'd seen the same idea developed by Preston Sturges in a classic movie called "Sullivan's Travels." John L. Sullivan (played by Joel McCrea) is a movie director named after the famous boxer who has achieved fame as a man of comedy. But he's tired of that. He wants to do something more important, something that reflects the despair of society's outcasts. His research among the underclass, however, literally knocks him out. He wakes up, all unwilling, and unaware of who he is, as a convict in a Georgia chain gang.

One night, however, prison guards take the cons off to see a movie at the local black Baptist church. It is a Mickey Mouse cartoon and Sullivan really enjoys it. No, not the movie. He is absolutely delighted to watch the faces of the convicts, and of the poor Baptist congregation, laughing their sides off at this pure comedy.

You can begin to see a glimmer of a light going on inside Sullivan's brain. The light becomes brighter when, back in prison, he unties a package wrapped with an old newspaper, one with a headline announcing the death of John L. Sullivan in an LA railroad yard. Now, he knows who he is — in more ways than one.

He goes to the warden and confesses to the murder of John L. Sullivan. And when this picture of the Georgia convict, his picture, makes the front page, his friends in Hollywood realize what's happened and bring him back in Hollywood, where he now knows he doesn't want to make "more important pictures." People need laughter. And he knows comedy. Why would he want to do anything else?

After the house lights came up in that prison auditorium in Edmonton, which had been rocking with laughter all the evening, I realized that I was John L. Sullivan — what Red Skelton once called me, "a doctor of comedy." (I didn't exactly have my doctorate then, but, in time, I'd earn one.)

And so, I say simply that I'm an entertainer. I may not be a great actor. I may not be a tragedian. I'm certainly not a stand-up comic. I am not a good-looking guy. (I am not a bad-looking guy, either.) I only know one thing. I give people something they need. They need laughter. So I give them comedy. They love it. And they love me. Why would I want to do anything else?"

Epilogue

So, now I return to where I began — with me having dinner at a Chinese restaurant in Tokyo, pondering the question posed by the Japanese lady who had once been in the consular service of her country.

"What is your greatest treasure, Jamie?"

Mentally, I made a few tentative guesses, but finally confessed that I didn't really know. I was only 25. What does any young man, or woman, know at 25?

She said, "Your memories, Jamie. Your memories. They belong only to you. And they're the only things you take with you when you die."

Postscript to St. Jude

Dear St. Jude,

Danny Thomas has already built you a hospital. Now, as I promised you, I am continuing to encourage people to ask for your help when they need it. A lot of us have hopeless cases. A lot of us *are* hopeless cases. But, with your help, and our faith, things will work out. Printing your prayer here — this much I can do.

Jamie Farr

Prayer to St. Jude

Most holy apostle St. Jude, faithful servant and friend of Jesus, the name of the traitor who delivered your beloved Master into the hands of His enemies has caused you to be forgotten by many, but the Church honors and invokes you universally, as the patron of hopeless cases, of things despaired of. Pray for me who am so miserable; make use I implore you, of that particular privilege accorded to you, to bring visible and speedy help where help is almost despaired of. Come to my assistance in this great need that I may receive the consolations and help of heaven in all my necessities, tribulations, and sufferings, particularly — [here make your request] — and that I may bless God with you and all the elect forever. I promise you, O blessed St. Jude, to be ever mindful of this great favor, and I will never cease to honor you as my special and powerful patron and to gratefully encourage devotion to you, Amen.